TURN YOUR RADIO ON!

The Broadcast Career
of a Lifetime

Lee Alan

KWP Publishing

Published by KWP Publishing

Copyright © 2004 by KWP Publishing

First Edition: August 2004

10 9 8 7 6 5 4 3 2 1

ISBN: 0-9760130-0-2

All rights reserved under International and Pan-American Copyright Conventions. No part of this work covered by the copyright heron may be reproduced or used in any form or by any means - graphics, electronic, or mechanical, including photocopying, recording, taping or information storage and retrieval systems - without the written permission of the copyright owner.

Manufactured and distributed in the United States of America by:

Allied Printing Company, Inc.
Allied Distribution Center
22438 Woodward Avenue
Ferndale, MI 48220
Telephone: 800-791-7234

For more information about Lee Alan:
www.detroitradiolegends.com

Disclaimer
Except when specifically mentioning the label for which singers and artists recorded, mention and use of the word "Motown" throughout this book is intended as a general reference to the city of Detroit as an abbreviation for the words "Motor Town"; meaning Detroit, Michigan.

DEDICATIONS:

To Mom and Dad, My Two Biggest Fans - Now, In Heaven.

Bernadine Clara Reicheld   Allan Leighton Reicheld

*For Nancy - My wife, who encouraged me to write –
and just tell the truth.*

For my daughter Dawne who lived this story with me,
never knew the truth and never asked.

Bill – Lee - Sara.

To my son Bill, his wife Lisa and Grandchildren Jake, Shane, & Allie
My son Lee - My Daughter Sara
And to Jennifer and Laura, my granddaughters, whom I love and miss terribly.

To my Stepson Kenneth Daw who helped immeasurably with this book.

My Step Daughter Dayna and Grandsons Daniel and Max

And to my sister Karen

. . . .with my love

ACKNOWLEDGEMENTS

First and foremost I want to acknowledge the listeners who still seem to remember the good times we had together on the radio. My relationship with them was always very personal and one of mutual love and respect.

I could never fully express my gratitude to the small core of selfless, loyal friends who helped and supported me during the three-year period prior to the publication of this book. It was the most difficult period of my personal and professional life. When I was down and had nothing to offer them, money, jobs, or prestige, they were there to help, comfort and protect. I shall forever be humbled and in awe of their individual sacrifices in the name of friendship and love, all the while expecting nothing in return.

Writing this was more work, more exhilarating, and more painful than I ever imagined. The memories of my colleagues, and friends came rushing back. As you read these pages you'll get to know them. Many are no longer with us. Without these dear people there never would have been a career, a story to tell, or a book to write. At their request some of them shall remain nameless. I want to acknowledge some of the others here and in no particular order.

John F. Pival, Del Shannon, Stevie Wonder, Ernie Durham, Florence Ballard, Don Large, H. Douglas Kole, Fred Wolf, Paul Winter, Joel Sebastian, Don Zee, Chuck Fritz, Ed Hardy, Mickey Shorr, Don McLeod, Rita Bell, Conrad Patrick, Porter Borne, Joe Vaughn, Bob Hardt, Tom MacIntyre, Joe Placido, Marvin Gaye, Mary Wells, Jack Wilson, John Dew, Dick Kernan, Jim Hampton, Dick Osgood, Bob Finder, Fern Robinson, Hal Neal, Elvis Presley, Jerry Lewis, Chuck Berry, Mohammed Ali, Bob Baker, Dick Rackovan, Augie Espri, Jim Rockwell, Robin Seymor, Fred Knorr, Nellie Knorr, Dave Diles, Rita

Bell, Leon McNew, Pat Murphy, Danny Taylor, Steve Lundy, Fred Weiss, Joey Reynolds, J.P. McCarthy, Al Dinoble, Milton DeLoach, Jim Christy, Van Patrick, John Gilbert, Tom Clay, Jim Rockwell, Larry Fisher, Martha Reeves, Marie Fotion, Smokey Robinson, Berry Gordy Jr., Louie Dumont, Bob Koch, Pat Riggert, Frank Gaal, Clark Reid, Byron Macgregor, Charlie Park, Oakland County (Michigan) Sheriff Michael J. Bouchard, Fabian Forte, Johnny Randall, Ann Margaret, Connie Francis, Brenda Lee, Frankie Valli, Barney Ales, Ann Huchison Sawalha, Brace Beemer, Dave Klemm, John Lennon, Paul McCartney, John Chickering, Ringo Starr, George Harrison, Dick Rakovan, Jimmy James, Michael Dwyer, Marie Foshen, Sharon Adams, Jack Scott, Dr. Harry Broomfield, Pastor Doug Schmidt, Pastor Cliff Lambert, Paul Dudek, Dick Femmel, Patti Robertson, Fred Foy, Joe Gentile, Ralph Binge, Johnny Ginger, Bill Hengstebeck, Don Davenport, David Staudt, Chuck Livingston, Harry Martin, Specs Howard, Larry O'Brien, Bud Reynolds, Pete Strand, Fran Striker, Jack Tierney, John Todd, Tom Waber, Robert E. Lee, and possibly hundreds more.

I only hope you'll enjoy the stories they made possible in the pages that follow.

Happy Memories………..Lee Alan

 # The Horn Remembers...

Mister Sinatra .... Page 38

Elvis Presley .... Page 44

Connie Francis .... Page 62

Crazy Guggenheim .... Page 68

Mohammed Ali .... Page 78

Del Shannon .... Page 86

Fabian .... Page 102

Ann Margaret .... Page 110

Dwight Eisenhower .... Page 122

Lyndon Johnson .... Page 126

Jerry Lewis .... Page 136

Florence Ballard & the Supremes .... Page 156

Table of Contents

Introduction
Preface
Chapter 1: THEN 1
Chapter 2: WALLED LAKE CASINO 5
Chapter 3: BEGININGS 7
Chapter 4: RADIO DAYS 15
Chapter 5: ACT ONE 17
Chapter 6: WJLB 31
Chapter 7: BACK IN ACTION 39
Chapter 8: A NEW KIND OF RADIO 45
Chapter 9: RIGGED QUIZ SHOWS & PAYOLA 49
Chapter 10: BIG MOUTH 53
Chapter 11: HEADLINES 59
Chapter 12: FIRED! 63
Chapter 13: FUROR 65
Chapter 14: MICKEY 69
Chapter 15: WKMH RADIO 79
Chapter 16: THE HORN 81
Chapter 17: LEGEND 87
Chapter 18: JACKIE AND BERRY 89
Chapter 19: GORDY 95
Chapter 20: SOCK HOPS & TEEN DANCES 97
Chapter 21: MICHAEL 103
Chapter 22: MOREY'S 111
Chapter 23: TROUBLE 115
Chapter 24: THE JOURNEY BEGINS 123
Chapter 25: THE CALL THAT CHANGED MY LIFE 127
Chapter 26: THE MEETING 131
Chapter 27: DAY ONE 137
Chapter 28: THE INNER SANCTUM .141
Chapter 29: 5 - 4 - 3 - 2 - 1 147
Chapter 30: TUESDAY 157
Chapter 31: CHANGE 161
Chapter 32: THE FAMILY FEUD 165
Chapter 33: CLUB 182 171
Chapter 34: WYXIE RANTS AND RAVES 175
Chapter 35: THE PHONE CALL 181
Chapter 36: ANOTHER CALL 187
Chapter 37: CHECKMATE 191
Chapter 38: TELEVISION 197

Chapter 39:	MONSTER	203
Chapter 40:	RADIO NIGHTMARE	207
Chapter 41:	SANGOO...	213
Chapter 42:	CLUB 1270	217
Chapter 43:	CHUCK BERRY	221
Chapter 44:	REELIN' AND ROCKIN	225
Chapter 45:	THE BLIND GENIUS	231
Chapter 46:	SET ME FREE	243
Chapter 47:	CHICAGO CALLING	247
Chapter 48:	CHUCK AGAIN	255
Chapter 49:	THE KEENER REVOLUTION	261
Chapter 50:	BEATLE MANIA	265
Chapter 51:	A TRIP TO MIAMI	269
Chapter 52:	STORY UNTOLD	283
Chapter 53:	CHANGE...	291
Chapter 54:	BEGINNING OF THE END	295
Chapter 55:	PATTI & DAWNE	299
Chapter 56:	MILTON	301
Chapter 57:	INVESTIGATION	307
Chapter 58:	BACK FROM THE DEAD	311
Chapter 59:	REACTION	317
Chapter 60:	DOWNFALL	323
Chapter 61:	JOEY	327
Chapter 62:	HOME	331
Chapter 63:	BEGINNING AGAIN	333
Chapter 64:	COOKIN'	335
Chapter 65:	1966 - BATTLE FOR RATINGS	339
Chapter 66:	AGAIN	343
Chapter 67:	DEAD AGAIN	347
Chapter 68:	ADVERTISING...	351
Chapter 69:	THE FM REVOLUTION	353
Chapter 70:	THE AGENCY	359
Chapter 71:	SUSPICION	367
Chapter 72:	ADVERTISING	371
Chapter 73:	THE AMERICANS	385
Chapter 74:	BACK IN THE 60s - AGAIN	391
Chapter 75:	CRIMESTOPPERS	395
Chapter 76:	CASINO - THE FINAL DEATH	405
EPILOGUE		419
MY FRIENDS & COLLEGUES NOW IN HEAVEN		431
WHERE ARE THEY NOW...		435

Introduction

FOR SOME THE DECADE OF THE SIXTIES MEANT TRAGEDY. Assassinations – War. Sacrifices made for freedom. Death on battlefields in far off countries with strange names. Draft card burnings. Questions of international purpose. The struggle for equality and dignity.

For others, the sixties were wondrous years. Beginnings. Firsts. Humankind would take its first steps into space. There was a musical invasion from England and a new kind of music was born on the back streets of Detroit. The Detroit Sound. The Motown Sound.

For everyone this was the decade that changed everything…forever. The early sixties were simple, innocent, and full of promise for the future. Then in 1963, Camelot was shattered. In an instant an assassin's bullet sent a shockwave that touched off a chain of events that made the sixties unlike any decade before or since. And that was only the beginning. By the end of the decade we had changed many more times. The innocence was gone.

Lee Alan has been called one of the nation's *"Human Oldies, But Goodies"*. The radio personality with a meteoric rise and high

INTRODUCTION

double-digit ratings in the early and mid sixties. Even now Lee is mentioned nearly every day on radio. Callers to programs and present day personalities remember Lee. They still talk about him and his "Fine toned Horn". Crazy, serious, personal, friendly, wild, understanding, fun. Lee was all of those.

When Lee Alan first met Berry Gordy Jr., the founder of Motown Records, they were both young men trying to succeed in the entertainment business. It was early in 1960. Lee was on the air at WKMH radio in Dearborn, Michigan, a suburb of Detroit. Berry was a frequent visitor to the station. Lee would often visit Berry's office and studio in the old houses on West Grand Boulevard near downtown Detroit that would later be known as Hitsville USA. There was always a new record. The Motown dynasty was in its infancy and Lee Alan was there.

Today; Motown as we knew it is gone. But the old houses and studio are still there. Literally, a museum. A silent witness to another time. Lee Alan made his lasting impression on the decade while at WXYZ radio and television then both owned and operated by ABC. The radio station had a long list of original thinkers and historic firsts, not the least of which, decades earlier, was The Lone Ranger, The Green Hornet, and Challenge of the Yukon. All radio programs that originated from WXYZ in the thirties, forties, and fifties. They were the original Motown Sound. "The Detroit Sound" of an earlier day.

To many, Lee Alan is the personification of the sixties. Lee went into his own business late in the decade, but didn't leave the airwaves entirely until 1971. After that, except for occasional guest appearances on radio and television, and some New Years Eves specials in the 1980s, he never looked back. At least that's what he wanted everyone to think.

Today, Lee Alan is back on the air in Motown and around the world on the Internet sharing his stories and sounding the same as

INTRODUCTION

he did when the world first took notice.

And so it begins. The memories. The good times. The drama. The trauma. The successes. The failures. The personal and professional tragedies written word for word by Lee Alan. So,

TURN YOUR RADIO ON . . . This is his story.

PREFACE

IT TOOK ALMOST 20 YEARS FOR ME TO WRITE THIS FIRST SENTENCE.

I've told these stories so many times that now when I start telling them, my friends finish them for me with no further prompting. After hearing them for the third or fourth time they all say: "Lee, you should write a book". They've been saying that for years. I always told them I never kept a diary and I couldn't remember enough for a book.

I was wrong.

My life, my loves, successes, failures, career, and opinions may not be interesting to anyone but me, but for my own reasons I'm writing it all down. Even just thinking about doing this was painful. I can't imagine what feelings and emotions the following pages will drag me through. Sort of like a baseball player reliving the days when he could throw the ball 95 miles an hour, or belt it clean out of the park. Days remembered, but only as cameos. Fleeting glimpses in fading memory. Words, actions, thoughts, and events recalled. Some regretted, but impossible to change or reverse.

Recently, after learning that I was writing this book, someone

PREFACE

whom I love deeply wrote to me and put it this way:

I am pleased to hear you are writing. They say when you write about your own life, that you have to pull out all the stops and face the realities that sometimes make us laugh, sometimes cry, make us angry, desperate, empty, but it also gives us a new understanding of who and what we are now.

Maybe that is why it is so hard to write at all, you have to face who you are now, and if you like who you see then it was all worth it, if not then you have to live with the truth and I have known people that weren't strong enough to live with who they have become or the destructive path they have left behind them. Just make sure you want to face it all, and all at once because that is where it is going to lead you, to the real truth. The truth can't always set you free, it can scare you to death.

And so I stand at a door that can only be opened with my own mind. I seek the truth, whatever it reveals, wherever it leads, and with excitement and some fear I will come face to face with myself. Then and now.

Life is about the choices we make.

I have made some good ones and some terrible ones.

They're all here.

I will reach back in time and tell it all. All that I remember. I have done very little research. Nearly everything is from memory. I will not bore you with statistics, dates, or details that really are just page fillers.

I had to start somewhere though so one day not long ago I got in my car and drove to the small town of Walled Lake, Michigan. In the 60s it was the site of the largest weekly show and dance in the country. I was part of it. It was my idea. If I was ever going to get started writing this book a visit to Walled Lake could start my brain and my memory in the right direction. That's what I thought.

I was right.

Chapter 1
THEN

I HADN'T BEEN OUT HERE IN NEARLY 40 YEARS. The lake is beautiful. Back then I never noticed. I came here did my shows and left. Never stood here like this before. I came to see if being here would raise some of the old memories of what happened on this spot.

It's a park now. Sort of.

Grass, trees, a bike path where the road was, sounds of the lake. No benches to sit on. No swings or monkey bars for the kids. No one else here but me. Just a pretty thirteen-acre plot of ground directly on the shores of Walled Lake. No sign or clue of what took place here.

The laughter and applause of hundreds of thousands of people have long escaped into space. They say once a sound is made it never dies. Like a recording, it stays in some other dimension. Travels somewhere out there forever.

All I can hear now is a quiet lapping of little waves rustled up by a soft breeze. I can still hear those sounds though. There is only one person in the universe who knows how I feel right now. Inside. Being here again. Alone by the lake. Memories rushing back like little one act plays. All so vivid. And the people. They're all alive, well, and young again. I loved them, truly loved them, all of them.

No pictures here either. I can still see them though. People dancing, laughing, talking, enjoying. And the entertainers. I feel their presence. They came here, played here, sang here. I sense them still here. Tommy Dorsey, Count Basie, Glenn Miller, Frank Sinatra, Louis Armstrong, Lionel Hampton, Little Stevie Wonder, Fabian, The Supremes, and Dionne Warwick, Chuck Berry, The Rolling Stones, hundreds of others.

They made music here. They played a part in memories for thousands of people who flocked to see them. All here in little Walled Lake, Michigan. All of their signatures were on a secret wall back stage. There's no historic plaque here, not one word telling what this was. No clue to what happened here for nearly 40 years. There's nothing to tell how what stood on his site actually made a town, made it famous, and probably saved it. Trees, grass and the lake. That's all. Only silence bearing no witness to other days.

The roads are all changed now too and it's hard to tell where everything was. The only building left is a small bar and restaurant on Novi Road. A few minutes ago I wandered in there. It's just a small, pleasant, neighborhood place. A dozen people were scattered at the tables, two at the bar. I sat down, ordered a coke. On the wall was an old aerial photo. I could see Walled Lake Amusement Park in it, and even this little bar. But where was the dance hall? Where was Walled Lake Casino? I remember it being right across the street.

Walled Lake Casino, one of the most famous dance halls in America was right here, but it didn't show in the picture.

The overweight lady with a welcome smile behind the bar looked to be about 45 or 50 years old. I asked her where on this picture was Walled Lake Casino. She said she didn't know anything about it. Said she was too young. She asked the others. No one knew.

I went outside. A man there smoking a cigarette knew about the area but wasn't sure where the dance hall was either. "You know why they call this Walled Lake?", he asked. "I'm a pilot. If you fly over the lake you can see an actual wall under the water comin' out from the shore over there. Indians built it. Walled Lake", he said. "Know why they never built anything more on them 13 acres? They's Indians buried there. Sacred ground."

Another man walked up and started talking to him. I asked him the same question. Where was the Walled Lake Casino dance hall? He smiled and pointed directly to the left and beyond the present road. He knew.

Wallace, nice looking with deep lines in his face, is a local guy and grew up right across the street. "I been here a while", he said. He knew all about it and finally recognized me. "Lee Alan. I want to look at you real close. Are you Lee Alan? I listened to you on the radio all the time back then", he said with a big smile on his face. That's when I realized that the lines in his face were from smiling. Typical of the people here.

"It was great out here in those days.", he said. "I remember when Chuck Berry was here, Stevie Wonder, Fabian. Couldn't get in the place. You could hear the music for miles. And the roller coaster in the park over there. Way up in the air so high I swear some nights you couldn't see the top of it. But you could hear it. Click, click, click." He said. "When the clicking stopped we knew in only another second the screamin' would start. Clicks on the way up, screams on the way down. Always the same". That coaster was the first thing everybody saw when they came into town.

We talked for a while. I asked him: "What if we could recreate those days, do it again just for a weekend or two, rebuild the Amusement Park and bring all those entertainers back to the site of that old Dance hall, the same ones and maybe some from today's music. Would people come?"

He just squinted, looked at me, smiled that big grinning smile, made all those wrinkles again and said: "Yeah, they would." And then, "Well, I gotta go in and get a beer now. Oh by the way, that stuff about them Indians buried over there. Bunch of bunk!"

We shook hands. He looked in my eyes and smiled again like we were old friends as if to say we had something in common from those days and was glad I came back here. Wallace disappeared into the bar.

I walked across the street through the park.

So here I am standing alone on the shores of Walled Lake because I want to write it all down now. Preserve some of it. And because I have a wild idea that maybe I could bring it all back just once. One or two weekends. One time. Thousands of people, scores of entertainers, the old amusement park too. Echoes of the past alive again, along with me, trying to recapture other days and years spent in this microcosm that the whole country once knew as Walled Lake Casino.

Chapter 2
WALLED LAKE CASINO

It died a violent, painful, agonizing, horrible death. The fire was only part of what killed it though. Nothing could have saved Walled Lake Casino that night. Christmas night 1965. I wasn't there. I left a few months earlier in controversy and disgust.

I heard about it the next morning. "Hey Lee", Tom McIntyre, my long time friend said as he headed for the newsroom. "Hear about the Casino? Burned down last night." I was on the air at WXYZ in Detroit. Tom was about to let the world know what happened out there in his newscast. His voice was strong and distinctive. When he talked, everyone listened. He told the world all about it on the radio.

You'd think after all those years and nights I spent broadcasting and performing on that stage I would have raced out there to see it. I didn't though. Strange, never even thought of it until just now as I am writing this nearly 40 years later.

It took seven fire departments and they still couldn't save it. Seventy wouldn't have made a difference. The fire raged for hours. They said the flames, paying little attention to the bitter cold that winter's night leaped so high in the air you couldn't see the tops of them. Fire so intense, it could've heated the whole town of Walled Lake. Probably did.

It happened at 2AM after everybody had left. Everybody then was practically nobody. No crowds of any size were coming anymore. The chemistry was gone.

I wondered if that was what they call a convenient fire. Before he went for his beer I asked Wallace what he thought. "Convenient fire?, he said. Then he just looked up at me and smiled. The smile told me what he thought.

I've seen pictures taken in the morning light. A heap of black rubble. Walled lake Casino was gone and with it thousands of stories of thrilling nights, personal love discovered and lost, future wives meeting future husbands, entertainment moments never captured, pictures never taken, indelible memories. Just gone.

Memories reside in the brain as flashing pictures. I can see them now. I can hear them. So what follows are some of my memories of the 60s. Hundreds of pages and pictures. The music, the sounds, entertainers from all over the world, the people, who they were, what they did, and where they all gathered every week to meet, to dance, to live, to love and make memories. Indelible memories never to be forgotten.

Chapter 3
BEGINNINGS

TO ME IT WAS BORING. Going To Walled Lake Casino. If you want the truth I don't really remember how I even know about it. I was a kid then. In the 40s I mean. I wasn't even old enough to be called a kid. I do remember that place though.

Walled Lake Casino. Guess my parents took me there. And I didn't see any kids there. Well, there were kids across the street, but wait...

At that time Walled Lake was way outside of Detroit. I mean way outside. A real "are we there yet dad "journey. Walled Lake Casino was not a gambling Casino, at least not that I could ever see. Now that I think of it I don't have the faintest idea why it was ever named that way. Some of the old articles talk about some sort of gambling, but nothing clear. It was a place to go and dance, that's all. A big building that would hold thousands of people. Across the street was an amusement park. Walled Lake Amusement park, what else?

The pictures in my mind are of old people slow dancing and big bands on the stage playing loud music that I wasn't interested in. Thousands of old people 18 to 40 years old at least, every one of them. That's old right? And these were real big bands too. Some of them had 25 to 40 musicians. Every one had a band leader out front with a baton in his hand swinging it wildly back and forth in time with the music. Or was the music in time with the baton?

They had singers too. Called them band singers. They sat in chairs off to the side smiling and clapping their hands to the rhythm the band made until it was their turn. They'd get up, do their song and just sit back down. Some of them were good I guess, but not very exciting. The bands all looked like Lawrence Welk to me. I don't remember but one of them might even have been Lawrence Welk for all I know. Lawrence Welk played there many times, even maintained a residence in the area. Ah one and ah two and ah….

Big names came there. Benny Goodman, Gene Krupa, Artie Shaw, Harry James, Dozens more. There was a large circuit of these big band dance halls and they all made the rounds. Walled Lake was definitely one of the prime spots on their dance card. They all wanted to play the Casino.

Walled Lake Casino was a gigantic building. The Lake was about 700 acres. The dance floor was 110 by 140 feet. It had a very high domed ceiling and a huge revolving ball hanging from the highest point in the center of the room. The ball was covered with tiny mirrors. There were small spotlights aimed at the ball. As it revolved there were hundreds of little pinpoint lights that reflected from the mirrors. Lights were moving everywhere, on the floor, the walls, and the people. It made for a very cool and yes, romantic atmosphere. There was a hardwood floor and ringing the dance area were tables where you could sit out or wait to be asked to dance. At one end of the Casino there was a stage the entire width of the building. There was a theater curtain behind which acts could set up before going on. The curtain would part and there they were. Behind the back wall was a passageway that allowed performers to go from one side to the other without being seen by the audience.

Walking back there was like a trip into the past. There on the wall were the names of everyone who had ever performed at Walled Lake Casino. Hundreds of autographs the famous and the forgotten.

At the opposite end of the building was another stage, much smaller and raised about 15 feet off the floor. Getting to it meant climbing a circle stairway. When one band would finish on the main stage the next one would start on this one. Continuous music. That was one use for it. Many years later I found another use for it that some people talk about even to this day.

Sustained by the popularity of the big bands Walled lake Casino was jammed whenever it was open. So was the amusement park across the street and the town of Walled Lake. It was a very big deal then. It was what Walled Lake was known for. Wasn't anything to me then. I was too young. But for those old folks it was big time!. I was more into radio.

Radio was another world. I could sit by the radio and get lost in the programs. Yes they were programs. Whole stories. Nobody ever heard of disc jockeys in those days. DJs were at least ten years away. Radio was wonderful. It was filled with adventure, comedy, drama, heroes, and suspense. I would listen and imagine. The action, voices, and places were real to me. So real that there were pictures in my mind. I could see them all. Superman could fly. Not the television Superman, MY Superman, Grand Central Station was real; the creaking door of the Inner Sanctum was a hundred feet tall and filled with cobwebs. The Shadow was invisible…but I knew he was really Lamont Cranston and I could see him.

Programs with names like The Green Hornet, Challenge of the Yukon, Blondie, Gunsmoke, Mr. Keen, Tracer of Lost Persons, Fred Allen with his Allen's Alley. Anyone remember Senator Claghorn when he's say: That's the South Son, I say..I say The South!!"

There was even one called the Lux Radio Theater. Lux was

the name of a soap. In those days the sponsor controlled everything so the sponsor's name was part of the program's name. The Lux program recreated movies on the radio. That's how powerful radio was. A movie on the radio with the original actors, can you believe it?. Every week there they were. Actors like Humphrey Bogart, Bacall, Clark Gable, Spencer Tracey, Gregory Peck, Peter Lorre, Rita Hayworth, all acting their movie roles on the radio. What pictures that made. Didn't need the movie.

Jack Benny. Now there was a wonderful and unique character. I know very little about his career. Only what I heard on the radio along with millions of others. On his program Jack Benny had an entire cast of players each with their own personalities and each connected to Jack in some way.

On the program was Benny's real life better half Mary Livingston whom he met at Macey's department store. Don Wilson a rotund big voiced announcer, Phil Harris, Jack's bandleader on the show was portrayed as a very hip guy whose band members were always hitting the sauce. Jack's valet was known only as Rochester a very funny and smart addition to the show. Mel Blanc, the voice of Bugs Bunny and other comic characters was a continuing part of the cast. Mel played many parts and had a thousand voices. He was even the voice of Jack's car, an old Maxwell that would rarely start. Dennis Day played the part of a young, shy, Irish kid with a wonderful tenor singing voice.

I hear that Jack Benny was one of the nicest and most generous of people and also that he was a fine and accomplished violinist. However, on his program he was portrayed as the world's biggest tightwad. I guess cheap is the word. So cheap that he not only saved every cent, but stored all his money in a giant vault deep beneath his house in Beverly Hills, California. Also, on the program he was known as a guy who thought he was a good violin player and told everyone that his violin sound was perfect, but when he picked up the instrument to play, everyone knew it sounded like fingernails on a chalkboard.

About every third show Jack would go down into the vault to visit his money. We would hear him walking down endless stairs, each step echoing as he descended. There was a moat to get across that was filled with man-eating crocodiles, gates that creaked open, locks unlocking, chains clanking, and finally the big door to the vault. There was always a password and if I remember, inside there was a guard who always had a question. Like: "Mr. Benny, how is Mr. Lincoln? Did he ever get over that problem in the theater?". Or something like that. Benny would then survey his holdings and then make a withdrawal of maybe 25 cents and leave.

There is a very famous scene that describes Jack Benny's radio reputation. Benny is walking along a city street. You can hear the footsteps and traffic noises when suddenly a voice says "Alright hands up." Jack says: "What?" The other voice says: "This is a stickup. Your money or your life." There is a very long pause. Maybe 5 or 10 seconds. Do you realize how long that is? Go ahead; time 10 seconds on your watch. It's a long time to have silence on the radio. All you can hear is the traffic going by. Then the stickup man says "Didn't you hear me? I said your money or your life...." Another silence. Finally Benny replies:
"I'm thinking....I'm thinking."

My favorite program was The Lone Ranger. Mom didn't want me to listen to The Lone Ranger though. Too much "blood and guts" she would say. There were others on her no no list, but whenever I could I listened anyway.

The Lone Ranger was created and broadcast in Detroit. So was The Green Hornet and Challenge of the Yukon. You might remember that one if I told you it was all about Sergeant Preston of the Canadian Mounted Police and his husky dog King. I can still hear him. "On King...On you husky...."! I had a perfect picture of all of them in my mind. They were absolutely real, bigger than life, stronger than anyone, and invincible.

One night my mom and dad took my sister and I out to dinner at a restaurant they frequented. A lot of Detroit movers and shakers went there. I think the owner was involved with the mob. He later moved to Vegas and was a pit boss at the Sahara Casino. His restaurant in Detroit was always jammed and this night was no exception. I can clearly remember my dad saying to me that The Lone Ranger just walked in. Did I want to meet him he asked? And then pushing through the crowd with me in tow my dad stopped at a table near the back of the restaurant. One of the men stood up and my dad introduced me.

I was devastated. I was hoping it wasn't a joke. My dad was always a nice man and very kind to me so I knew it wasn't. The reason? The man's name was Earl Graser. He was the actor who played The Lone Ranger on the radio and he was short and fat!

The Lone Ranger…short and fat. My little world crashed that night.

The program originated from WXYZ radio. Earl Graser played the part on the air but he never appeared anywhere in person as The Lone Ranger. Personal appearances were done by the program's deep voiced announcer, Brace Beemer. The actor who played Tonto never appeared in person as Tonto either. His name was John Todd. He was not an Indian. He was an older man, Caucasian, a Shakespearean actor, and a professor at Wayne University in Detroit. He looked nothing like the Lone Ranger's faithful companion. I never met him. In a way that's a good thing. To me he was Tonto.

Beemer was tall, slim, good looking and the perfect Lone Ranger. Graser was only the voice. Not long after that there was another terrible night. Earl Graser was killed in a car crash. His voice was stilled. Funny though, I heard about it but never believed that the Lone Ranger was dead or would ever die.

In spite of Mom's orders I found a way to listen to the next program after the crash. In it the Lone Ranger was wounded and couldn't speak. It seemed like weeks before he recovered and we began to hear his voice again. Slowly with each succeeding program the voice emerged deeper, stronger, more resonant than ever.

This only confirmed my belief that the Lone Ranger was immortal. It was true that Earl Graser died in that crash, but the Lone Ranger didn't. The new voice introduced to the radio audience ever so slowly was that of the announcer, Brace Beemer. He not only sounded like the Lone Ranger, but he looked like him. Dressed like him, owned an actual ranch in Oxford, Michigan just outside of Detroit and had horses there. One of them was a white stallion. The stallion's name was Silver. Until his death in 1964 Brace Beemer not only played the part on the radio….. he *was* the Lone Ranger. He believed his part. That was the year I finally came face to face with my boyhood hero. Just before he died. More about that later. Brace Beemer was dead, but to this day the Lone Ranger lives.

World War II ended. The Korean Police Action started and never ended. Somewhere along the way the big bands started to fade. Music changed. The late 40s brought us pictures with sound. Radio changed too. One by one all those wonderful radio programs stopped, including the last broadcast of my Lone Ranger in 1953.

The living room now had television. It was black and white but it was there. Imagination was not needed. The pictures were decided for us in advance and provided for us. They said radio was dying too. The middle 50s brought different sounds that were popular with young people. In New York Alan Freed called it Rock 'N Roll. In Chicago they followed suit, and in Los Angeles, San Francisco, Detroit, all of them no longer on the network. Each city by itself influenced it's own area. Bill Haley and the Comets exploded on the music scene with Rock Around The Clock. In Memphis Sam Phillips gave a chance to young Elvis Presley who would soon change music forever. And then, Jerry Lee Lewis. RockaBilly.

There were others, hundreds of others, and all at once. A flood of recorded music from every corner of the country.

What followed killed the big bands. Killed them dead!

All over America big band dance halls were faltering. Television was here. Music was different. Radio drama and comedy programs ended. Stations were using hosts on the radio to play recorded music instead. Disc Jockeys played the new music. Young audiences were listening to what the DJs said and what they played. Not the old music.

People stopped coming to the dance halls. The bands stopped playing. Dance halls and clubs all over America were downsizing or closing.

In 1960 Walled Lake Casino closed. The lights were out. Temporarily.

Chapter 4
RADIO DAYS

THEY WERE ALL WRONG ABOUT RADIO. Television didn't kill it. Just changed it. It became more local. More personal. Radio tried to commit suicide a few times. Still tries. Every day. The people who control radio programming today are smart executives who survey everything and know all the right things to say and play. Problem is not one in ten know as much about radio and its beginnings as you have read in just the last few pages.

I think Ronald Reagan said it best: "If we don't know who we were, we won't know who we are." Ironic, coming from him isn't it. Sadly, as a victim of Alzheimer's President Reagan proved his own point. He couldn't remember who he was.

Doctors study the origins of medicine, attorneys the history of law, and so on. I believe that most of today's radio people would have a tough time with a simple 20-question quiz about their own industry. I recently visited the Museum Of Broadcast Communications in Chicago's Cultural Center. Every radio person in America should make that trip. There they were, the radio minds that brought us from the beginning to today. There in the Radio Hall of Fame they live forever. All their stories, sounds, pictures, and history. Go there. You will come away enlightened, in awe, and with a hunger to know even more. Just as I did.

Radio hasn't succeeded in self destructing yet, but one sure thing in life is change. Radio will continue to change. Radio as we know it today will kill itself. Give it a little more time. But I'm getting ahead of this story.

Chapter 5
ACT ONE

I WAS BORN A VERY UGLY KID ON THE BANKS OF THE MISSISSIPPI RIVER in Jane Lamb Hospital in Clinton, Iowa across from Fulton, Illinois. Tom Sawyer country. My mother had a tough time with me on that cold day. The doctor had to use forceps to save my life and hers. I was not a pretty sight. Still have the scars to prove it. Some will say I'm still not a pretty sight and who am I to argue? That was only the beginning of the trouble I would be for her.

I am an amateur genealogist and have over 35,000 names recorded in my family tree. Nothing spectacular there really. My Iowa grandmother's family has some folks who helped George Washington cross the Delaware, a state Supreme Court Judge and her father Captain John Claussen, 16th Iowa Infantry who fought at Shiloh, Corinth, and was wounded and imprisoned at the infamous Andersonville prison.

My Iowa grandfather was the most influential person in my young life. His name was Harry B. Keeler. I put his name here just because I think he deserves to have his name in a book. He and my grandmother had twins, fraternal twins. My mother and her twin brother Buddy. Buddy died suddenly of heart complications at the age of 15. I don't remember my grandparents ever talking about it. I think they grieved the rest of their life but never showed it. They lost a son.

Harry Keeler was a Juvenile Probation Officer in the District Court, ran once for Sheriff of Clinton County, Iowa and was a smiling, jovial, courteous, always laughing man who smoked too much, drank one beer a month when my grandmother would let him, drove a 1937 Buick, and made $4,000 a year. Total.

He had a CABIN on the Mississippi River not far from Comanche, Iowa near Clinton. It was not a cottage. It was a CABIN. He and my grandmother spent every weekend there in the summer. When my sister Karen and I were there on vacation, we did too. There was running water inside but the bathroom was a "Two Holer" at least 50 yards from the CABIN.

Anyone who knew Harry B. Keeler loved him. He told the same jokes to the same people every day and laughed at them louder than anyone else. Told them as if he'd never told them before. When we laughed he thought we were laughing at the jokes when we were really laughing at him…laughing.

He had a flat boat with a small outboard engine and a little dock on Swan Slough, a swift moving tributary of the Mississippi. Swan Slough, Ha! I always wondered who named it. Swan Slough was muddier than the main river. Put your hand down in that water even an inch and it was gone!

Grandpa Harry would sit in that boat for hours with a fishing pole rigged with a hook with a night crawler, a lead weight and a large bobber waiting for a bite. When he'd pull up the line to check it there'd be a muddy gel clinging to the line. It was like filthy Jello. He would hold the line between his two fingers stripping the line of the pollution and under his breath you could hear him say: "Damn Glucose Factory." That's what it was, and the river was polluted with what they dumped in it. Harry Keeler always told me someday he wished he could go to: "one of those blue water lakes you've got up north." How he wanted to go there and just go fishing.

There were railroad tracks in back of the CABIN. Grandmother Keeler (Grandma Ann) was a real trooper and would often take us on adventures with her on foot. There we'd be, walking down the tracks with fishing rods, small tackle boxes, cans of live night crawlers that we caught at night in the schoolyard near their house in Clinton before our weekend trips, and big straw hats to protect from the sun.

This was Tom Sawyer country and I thought I was him!

For miles along the tracks there were muddy backwaters. We'd stop, sit on the bank and throw our lines in. Once in a while we'd catch something. Mostly Bullheads; like little catfish. Maybe a Carp now and then. We'd pick up pickers on our pants. Every time we did she'd tell us that's how those pickers gave somebody the idea for Velcro. We'd talk. Ask questions. She was our Grandmother and our pal.

We also got jiggers. Little no-see-ums that would get in our clothing and under our skin. They'd bite us all weekend. Everyone would be scratching.

Back we would go to the Cabin. Many times on Saturday nights other family members would come for games of Gin Rummy. I can still hear them telling their stories, talking about their lives, and over all of it was his laughter. Grandpa Harry telling the same jokes as last week and laughing louder with each one. Sometimes when he would get a little risqué Grandma Ann would try to stop him:

I remember one of them he told at least a dozen times a week:

In a Southern accent and with a high voice Grandpa Harry would say:

Grandpa Harry: "Yes, I hear you knocking on my door, but Sorry, I can't open it right now. I'm in bed with ARTHUR ITUS

(Arthritis)............

Grandma Ann: (Loudly Interrupting. she knew what was coming) HARRY!! HARRY!!

Grandpa Harry: (continuing anyway...) And I don't even know the Gentleman!!!

And then uproarious laughter from HIM!

My father was born in Dutton, Ontario Canada the oldest of three children. His brother and sister both died before they were 21 years of age. Elmer, after a bout with Rheumatic Fever only at 13 and Laura in childbirth at 19. Grandfather Reichheld was somewhat of a celebrity in the small town of only about 4,000 people. He was Dutton's only blacksmith as well as the Massy Harris Farm Implement dealer. With his small showroom and shop in the center of town, almost everyone saw him everyday shoeing horses, doing marvelous things with his forge, anvil, and hammer and whenever a farmer broke down in the field he was the only one they could call.

Every summer for many years Mom and Dad would drive us the 100 miles or so from Detroit to Dutton where we stayed for at least part of our school vacation. I loved to go "uptown" to the "shop" and watch him swing that hammer to a glowing piece of metal on the anvil and watch it slowly take shape. And like a country doctor, when the call came from some farmer whose thrasher or binder was broken down in the field, Grandpa Reichheld would grab parts, tools, and me, jump in his 1937 Ford Coupe, drive miles to the scene of the problem and perform farm implement surgery.

Once when I was about fourteen he had a call to repair a farmer's machine that was stalled in a cornfield. Grandpa Reichheld was under the machine. I was close by just sitting there in the hot sun watching. He peeked out.

"Here. Catch"

He threw me the keys to the car and said:

"Go ahead. Let's see if you can drive that thing. You know

how to work the clutch?"

I had never driven a car in my life. But that's the day I learned. By myself. Manual shift and all.

Ha! Good thing those corn stalks weren't other cars or people.

Another time when I was maybe 9 or 10 years old I was hanging around in his shop playing with the tools, sitting in the seat of a new tractor he had on display in his little showroom, and just fooling around. Grandpa Reichheld was in the blacksmith shop in the back of the building. I noticed a coffee can on his workbench with some kind of liquid in it. There were some matches there. Pretending I was the blacksmith I lit a match, watched it burn and then to put it out I threw it in the coffee can. The instant it hit the liquid there was a fire. Scared me to death. Instead of calling him I ran out the front door, turned left and ran clear around the block about a quarter of a mile like a crazy moth that had just been touch by a flame, all the time hoping that when I got back the fire would be out.

It was. When I arrived back at the shop there was no fire, but Grandpa Reichheld was standing there waiting for me with the coffee can in his hand.

He should have been mad. I should have been punished. Instead he put his arm around me and said:

"Next time you're in trouble, call me for help." And then with a little smile he went on:

"That's what all the farmers do."

I never heard either him or my grandmother mention the son or daughter they lost. I think my sister Karen and I sort of took their place. They lived long lives. Long enough so that years later on a clear night they could sit and listen to their grandson on the radio station coming from Detroit. I could feel their presence. I was proud. I miss them to this day.

Dad was a pretty fair athlete in high school and he came to Detroit from that little town in Canada to try and play professional hockey. When that didn't work out he sold awnings for a while and then went into his own business manufacturing work clothes, jeans, coveralls, and when World War Two broke out everything was converted to making camouflage army uniforms for the boys fighting the Japanese in the Pacific.

Somehow my mother from Clinton, Iowa, and my father from Canada met and ended up living in Detroit. At the age of about 4, I started to get sick. Everything kids get once like measles, mumps, chicken pox, scarlet fever I had 3 and four times. I was in bed most of the time for maybe two or three years until one of the doctors figured out that if they went in and got the tonsils that would stop it. He was right. I had been in bed so long I had to learn to walk all over again. After all that my immune system was so strong I have hardly ever been sick again.

I grew up in northwest Detroit on St. Marys between Greenfield and Southfield and Puritan and Fenkel, went to Cooley High, Michigan State University, and Wayne State University. While in high school I was very active in music. Sang in the school choruses, took part in all the school concerts, took sax and piano lessons and sometimes was practicing when I'd rather be outside playing ball and other things.

My sister and I went to St. James Methodist Church only two or three miles from our house. I think we walked there. It's hard to remember now. I know by the time I was 16, I was driving there. At fifteen I met someone would have an effect on me for the rest of my life.

Best I can remember I was in a Sunday School Class or church social event. I was always the guy who ended up playing the piano. Nothing fancy, just enough to get by, to this day I can remember looking up from the piano one Sunday night and there she was.

Pretty, honey blonde, and the most beautiful eyes first staring at me then at the piano, then back at me. My hands froze, I asked her name, "Ann", she said. "Yours?"

At 15 years of age I was stricken. Blown away. Does this happen to all 15 year olds? Ann lived about three miles from me in another school district so she had attended a different grade school, but we were both going to Cooley High and immediately took to each other. Soon we were "going steady." We were both "in love." Around school we were an item.

If anyone would see me alone they'd ask, "How's Ann." And vice versa when they'd see her.

Al (Lee) and Ann.

She had a friendship ring I gave her on a necklace for all to see that she was taken. We were "going steady". We were both active in music all the school choirs and choruses. We were president and secretary of them. Had our pictures taken next to each other in all the yearbooks.

Al (Lee) and Ann.

We went everywhere together, spent time on the weekends, each other's house, constant companions, did all the things that 16, 17, and then 18 year olds do together. Ann's mother and father were wonderful people who always welcomed me into their home. Ann's mother played the piano. There was one in her home.

Ann knew my parents as well. There were family picnics, outings, and trips. We were a couple and everyone knew it. She was part of my family and I was of hers.

Ann was a brilliant student. Very smart, very popular, and she knew how to study. She was always on the honor roll; we were both members of the "Ensemble", a group of the best singers in school. And Ann was an officer of our senior class.

I was not a great student. Homework was something I just couldn't get into. I got by. Barely. One day while practicing for the

Christmas concert at Cooley High, Fern Robinson, a wonderful old music teacher and head of the music department called my name and told me that I was going to narrate the story of the birth of Christ. That was my first job as an announcer. I loved it. Getting up in front of all those people was no problem and when I did…I was hooked. She liked what I did and I wanted more.

Cooley High School in the mid 50s. My first public speaking part. I still remember it.

"The Angel Gabriel was sent from God unto a city of Galilee called Nazareth to a virgin espoused to a man whose name was Joseph of the house of David. And the virgin's name was Mary."

How I wish I could go back and talk to that boy. Warn him of things to come. Tell him to wait for certain special people in his life.

Not long after that Mrs. Robinson suggested to a few of us that we audition for a radio chorus at WJR in Detroit. WJR was a 50,000-watt radio station affiliated with CBS. Every Saturday they originated a half hour program called, Make Way For Youth. The director or the program was Don Large, a wonderful and kind little man with bright sparkling eyes, a terrific smile, a musical genius who had a great way with young people. The program was live on the network and featured the best school age musical talent in Detroit. Some great performers came out of that show and went on to Broadway, recording, and even the movies. Go to the Internet sometime and look up the name Maureen Bailey. She was one of us. What a career she's had. And it all started on the same show.

Ha! Where did I go wrong?

Well, I auditioned with others from Cooley and to my surprise I made it. Soon a few of us were driving to WJR once or twice a week in the evenings to rehearse and again on Saturdays for the live show. I was part of that program for years. It was a defining chapter in my life. Live studio orchestra, big voiced announcers, soloists, and our own small groups of four or five singing specialty numbers. Those were the days when I first caught the fever, radio fever. I remember all of it so well.

In the summers we would tour Michigan by bus singing at various places and even doing the CBS program live on Saturdays. I can still hear the opening song:

> "Make Way For Youth Will Be Our Theme Today
> Make Way For Youth Is On The Beam Today...."

That was my introduction to Radio. The people. The studios. The atmosphere, the feel, the anticipation, and tension when the microphone was on. I loved it. Never had any thought of doing it for a living, but I loved it and the people who were in it.

After graduation Ann enrolled at Kent State University in Ohio. I was headed for Michigan State University in Lansing, Michigan. My grades were not good enough to just be automatically accepted. I was never good at studying for long periods so I had to take the entrance exam. No one was more surprised than I was when I passed it. So, I was off to Lansing in my little old used blue Ford coupe. The car was a present from my dad upon graduation from high school. It even had "blue dots" in the taillights. Blue Dots were the big thing then. Very cool.

Ann was at Kent; I was at MSU. We wrote, talked on the phone, I even drove to Kent State a couple of times to see her. It wasn't the same. We were 18 and 19 now, pretty much grown. Still had feelings for each other and missed each other. I know I missed her.

Classes at State turned out to be easy for me. Cooley had been very good at preparing us for college. My biggest problem was finding a job. WKAR was the Michigan State owned radio station. They paid announcers two dollars an hour. I auditioned and failed. The next quarter I tried again. Same result.

I really don't remember how it happened or why, but Ann transferred to Michigan State and now I tried even harder to find a job that paid enough to keep me there. Al (Lee) and Ann together in school again. It was different now though. There were 15-20,000 students on campus. She had her classes; I had mine. I missed her.

I was invited to pledge a fraternity. That was a big deal then. I mean if you were a member of a fraternity you were really in. I was a pledge. The lowest of the low, but soon the time was up, we went through Hell Week and I was a full-fledged member of Phi Delta Theta. Didn't help me with announcing staff job though.

Then a break. A notice on a bulletin board announced that Tom Weber (Wayber) a professional announcer from WWJ Radio in Detroit was coming to the WKAR studios to do a series of about 26 half hour radio dramatic show called These Great Lakes. The notice was an invitation to audition for acting roles in the series.

I jumped on it, auditioned, and because I could change my voice and play character parts I got a job. $25 per show. I was in the big bucks now! Hey I was going to Michigan State, my girl was there now, I was a "Phi Delt" and I had a job in radio. What could be sweeter than that?

A month or so passed and then on May 17, 1954 a terrible call from home. Harry Keeler, my Iowa Grandfather had suffered a heart attack and died. Even to this day I choke up when I think of that call. He was the best friend I've ever had. There was a heart attack some months earlier. Afterward he wrote a letter to me at Michigan State. In it he said he hoped to recover soon and when he did: "Maybe you and me can go fishing in one of those big blue water lakes up north there. I hear that water's so clear you can put your hand in and still see it." He never had the chance, but every time I go fishing, every single time, no matter where it is in the world, I put my hand in the water and think of him. I loved him and miss him to this day.

Mom and Dad picked me up and we drove to Iowa. It was a quiet drive and a sad few days. Once back in East Lansing I called Ann. Couldn't find her around so the next night I wandered over to her dorm to see if she was maybe gone home for the weekend. It was about 9PM. The front lawn of the dorm was crowded with the girls and their dates hugging, holding hands, and kissing good night. As I crossed the street I noticed someone who looked like Ann and a guy kissing on the lawn. I soon realized that the girl didn't look like Ann. It *was* Ann.

Certain things happen in our lives that stay there in our minds, like a picture, never to be dimmed. That was one of them. I can still see that picture, then, at that moment it was the most traumatic event in my life. Al (Lee) & Ann. A couple since early in high school. No longer. I turned and walked. Fast!

Not a great week.

Ann and I remained great friends, but our time as a couple had passed. She transferred from State and landed at the Harper Hospital School of Nursing in Detroit.

Dad was paying my tuition but the Great Lakes Series was over and I couldn't make financial ends meet. I left State, transferred to Wayne University in Detroit and moved back home with Mom and Dad.

I auditioned for the announcing staff at WDET-FM, Wayne State University Radio and made it on the first try. Problem was they considered it a training ground and it wasn't a paid job.

After that a series of part time jobs in radio around town while I was going to school kept me in spending money. I worked in the control rooms pushing the buttons and running records for the DJs and program hosts. My very first job was at WCAR in Pontiac,

Michigan a suburb of Detroit at 1130 on the dial owned by an eccentric by the name of Hy Levinson. It seemed everyone in radio started out there. And almost everybody was fired from there at one time or another. I learned later that being fired from there was like wearing a badge of honor.

I worked all day on Sundays playing the taped church programs, running the commercials and just filling in the spaces. There was a red phone in the studio. It was actually red in color. It had no ringer or bell though. Right in back of the phone on the wall was 1 humongous red light bulb with the words: "150 Watts" emblazoned in large black letters. It was connected to the phone. No one knew the number except top management of the station. If they wanted to call in there had to be a light instead of a bell. If the microphone was on you could hear a bell…but not a light. Logical right?

As long as I was there I had never seen that phone used. Never saw what the light would look like. It just sat there like a silent warning that if you messed up it would certainly interrupt your life and the voice on the other end would definitely not be calling to wish you a happy day! No one wanted to ever see that phone light up and to my knowledge no one ever had seen it.

Every Sunday there was a 30-minute time period where no program was scheduled. I had to play records and announce them. No personality though, they said. Just give the name of the record and play the next one. It was exhilarating. I was actually on the air! There was an open mike and the voice that couldn't make the announcing staff at Michigan State was on the air! Ha, I loved it. I didn't think anyone was listening though.

Well, one Sunday I found out there was at least one listener. I had just started a record called "The Wabash Cannonball." Remember now this was Sunday. My program instructions were to play music that was to be quiet, relaxing, and peaceful. The Wabash Cannonball started out with a loud rebel yell, four or five banjos that sounded like they were coming from an amplified Hillbilly heaven, a steel guitar, and some real honest to goodness bluegrass singers with loud thin country voices.

Within seconds of the time I put that record on the Red Phone lit up. The light was blinding. The room was one huge flashbulb. It looked like the Los Alamos testing of the atomic Bomb! Enough light to destroy anyone's cornea for life I thought. It was flashing red! Long flashes then off for a second, then another long flash. As the Cannonball was getting wilder, the light was filling the room with red. I grabbed the phone, but couldn't hear a voice. Then I realized that the speakers there in the studio were so loud it would certainly blow out the eardrums of the person on the other end and that if there was a voice there no one could hear it. I killed the speakers in the studio and heard a female voice yelling " GET THAT RECORD OFF THE AIR".

It was Mrs. Levinson, the wife of the owner of the station. I said, "Yes, yes Mrs. Levinson". I was going to let it end, not say anything on the air and just go on to the next record. After a few seconds I heard her again: "I SAID…GET THAT RECORD OFF THE AIR…NOW!!!!".

Her wish was my command. I reached out, grabbed the arm that held the needle and slowly dragged it across the record making a long ear piercing scratching sound. All live on the air. The sedate Sunday morning radio station went from the up-tempo, head banging Wabash Cannonball to what seemed like a scratching, screeching, washboard sound to dead silence. Nothing. Radio's worst enemy. Dead air. Then, after about 15 seconds, as if the last 3 minutes never happened, something by a classical stringed quartet was playing so softly you could hardly hear it.

Through all that the loudest noise I heard was afterward on the other end of the phone when without another word, Mrs. Levinson just hung up!

The call from Mr. Levinson came a few days later. I was out of a job.

Chapter 6
WJLB

SOMEHOW I MANAGED TO HIRE IN AT WJLB, the ethnic and minority radio station in Detroit. Again, my job was to sit on the control room and run the records and commercials for the DJs and personalities who had their own individual programs. I was in one room with all the electronic equipment and they were in another. It was a typical old time radio studio with a large double paned glass window half the size of the entire wall. I could see them through the window and hear them either from the speakers or in a set of headphones I wore. And what a diverse lineup there was.

First, there was the Polish program. Now please don't take me wrong here. I don't have a prejudiced cell in my system, but what a deal this was for those Polish guys. I learned that the way it worked was that they bought the program time from the station and then went out and sold their own commercials. So, for the three hours they were on the air all the commercials were sold to Polish businesses that paid a hefty dollar for the commercial time. The station made out by getting the price they wanted for the airtime and the Polish Program got rich selling their commercials.

Hey, who needed to look at ratings, right? They had a captive audience. It was all broadcast in Polish! The music was Polish. The Announcers were Polish. The commercials were Polish, and all the listeners were Polish. Only part of the program that wasn't Polish was me! I didn't understand a word they were saying. Not one word. And I was the one who had to play all the music and commercials for them! At the right time and in the right order!

OK so to put it all in perspective I had the station log in front of me. The log is the daily list of programs, program times, commercials, where to find the commercials in the studio, and other scheduling information. Everything would run very cool unless those guys through the glass changed the order of what was to run. When they wanted a change they would push the button in front of them and start talking to me on the intercom in Polish! Because I didn't have the faintest idea what they were saying, there was trouble in River City.

After the Polish program was the German program. The German guy could barely speak English. He was about 5'6", around 280 pounds, and would come into the control room about 15 minutes before his show to give me the records and commercials to play. He was loyal to his listeners and his tastes. He was always smiling and happy. I could smell the same brand of German beer every day. I think I could have played God Bless America for the whole hour and he never would have known it.

My favorite person on the air at WJLB was Frantic Ernie Durham. Ernie was a very mellow human being. Always had smile. One of those people you could never say anything negative about and you never heard anything bad about. One of the great people in my life as you will see.

Ernie was on in the afternoon, a very important time for a radio station. Afternoon Drive Time. Everybody's driving home or somewhere and radios were definitely on. There were no cassettes, tapes, or CDs. Just radio. Ernie called himself ERNIE "D", played what we called Rhythm and Blues or R&B music and had the largest black audience in Detroit radio. Everyone African American person in town listened to Ernie. He was fun, laughing, happy, hip, friendly, and most of what he said Rhymed! I can still hear him...

"This is Ernie " D" on 'JLB
and after the commercials I'll be right back
with another smash hit from the top of the rack,
world renowned from Ernie DEEETROIT Town."

Ernie was IN baby! The world loved him. He had the biggest show, held the biggest in person appearances, had the biggest acts that wanted to perform for him, be on the radio with him. Hey, he was ERNIE "D" on "JLB and I was the one who got to work with him, play his records, commercials, and for that oh so short time I was the one behind the scenes who made it happen for him.

I loved him.

All the time I was working at WJLB and going to school I still managed to see Ann every now and then. We went out occasionally. A show now and then. Things like that. It was fun. Our lives were different now. We were friends and I knew it could never be more. Ann even invited me to come over to her school of nursing a couple of times and do my act!

Hey, no laughing now, but I did have an act. One of my favorite pieces to perform was a very popular comedy record at the time by Andy Griffith. Yes, the one and only Andy Griffith. It was called: "All It Was, Was Football". I had the words memorized and Andy, his accent, and mannerisms down pat. What a hoot that was. The nurses laughed and so did I. Ann laughed. One day while I was there Ann introduced me to Sami. I could see the two of them were more than friends. There is a look you know. The look of love. Sounds like a song cue. It was real to me.

I was picking up extra change in those days doing some narrating for commercials and shows. I had a gig at the Michigan State Fair narrating for the new Ford thunderbird. Not far from there was The Chevy Show with Warney Ruhl and his band entertaining Chevy people. Warney Ruhl had a top flight society band of about 20-25 pieces and played everywhere in Southeastern Michigan. During a break I walked over to see their show. And that's when I saw her.

Patti Brown was the band singer for Warney Ruhl. She was a beautiful brunette with sparkling eyes and an engaging smile that made you stare. I wasn't the only one staring either. And she caught me. She caught me staring. Ha. But she smiled back at me. I had never seen a smile like that. It was soul piercing. It invaded me. She had a personality on stage to match the smile and beauty and voice that were all the star of the show.

It was just like those bands at the old walled Lake Casino. The band would play, Warney would swing the baton back and forth, and every now and then Patti Brown would get up from her chair, step to the microphone and mesmerize everyone in the audience. I had to meet her. After a day or two I got up enough nerve and did.

Patti was stunning and a great band singer. I was still reeling from the years when it was "Ann & Al" though. Patti and I got to know each other in a hurry. We dated, had fun, and talked about the future. I met her parents and family. Most of them were talented and some were professional musicians. All were nice people.

Things between Patti and me became too serious too fast. I was one confused guy. I was working on the radio, but it was a small job. I was going to school but not getting anywhere. I was working on Wayne Radio but not being paid. And all the time the threat of being drafted into the Army just at the wrong point in my career was staring me directly in the face. Then, one day in a weak moment I decided not to wait for the Army. Going in was inevitable so I beat them to the punch, went downtown and advanced my draft. It meant I would go into service right away. Get it over with I thought.

Choices.

Then, without being totally sure I asked Patti to marry me. Did I love her? Yes. Was I still thinking about Al & Ann? Yes. Patti accepted though and we planned a wedding to take place as soon as the eight weeks of Basic Training was complete.

Choices.

My Mom and Dad were shocked at my decisions. Army and Marriage? Both at the same time? To further complicate matters, Patti was catholic and there was all that business about promising to bring up children in the catholic church etc. I agreed to that.

Choices.

I went into the US Army in February of 1957. We were bussed to Ft. Leonard Wood, Missouri. We called it the armpit of the earth. Each barracks had a coal burning stove. The first night there I had the honor to be assigned the position of Fire Guard, standing in the room with the coal burning stove and shoveling coal all night. The next morning was Sunday. We still had no uniforms, just what we wore from home. It was very cold, 33 degrees and raining, five thousand new Army recruits stood on the parade field. No raingear, most had no jackets, all were shivering and wondering what in the world they had gotten themselves into.

There was a large covered parade platform with powerful lights inside and a half dozen sergeants standing warmly under cover. They were smiling and dry. We were frozen and wet. Into the microphone the spit shined Master Sergeant bellowed: "Alright, I wants all the mens who's goin to church fall out to the left."

About 30 guys did. That's all. Seeing this the Sergeant proclaimed: "Alright, I want four thousand mens for kitchen cleaning detail. NOW how many men's is going to church?" So that Sunday everybody went to church. Ha. Some of them for the first time in their lives.

After a few days I shipped out to Fort Carson Colorado. It was cold, barren, and miserable for two months. Everybody got through it though. The fat ones got thin, thin ones put on pounds, the arrogant became humble, and we all became soldiers.

Patti and I were married as planned.

After another eight weeks in Arkansas in clerk typist school I was assigned to Fort Eustace Virginia. I was a supply clerk now. It wasn't bad though. It was a 7 to 5 job.

As usual I needed money and one Saturday I drove around looking for radio towers. Found one too not far from the Army Post in Newport News, Virginia across the river from Norfolk. There were only a few cars in the lot and I went in.

Because it was Saturday only a hand full of people were there. One happened to be the owner. Hey what did I know? I walked into his office, he looked up surprised, I introduced myself and asked if he had any part time jobs open.

I think he liked my moxy. He said he had Saturday and Sunday open and that if I could walk into that empty studio over there and make him an audition tape he'd consider it. See, he didn't think I would know how to run the equipment and he might have been right but they had the same gear that WJLB in Detroit did so it was a cinch. I did a 15minute tape in 15 minutes and handed it to him.

The next Saturday I was on WGH AM & FM, Newport News, Portsmouth, and Norfolk, Virginia. I was back on the air!!!

That next February our daughter Dawne was born in the Army Hospital at Fort Eustace. She was beautiful. Perfect. Patti and I were in the Army with a new little girl and flat broke. Army pay plus part time radio didn't make it. Patti moved back to Detroit where she could live rent free with my parents and start singing with the band again to make us enough to live.

I moved to a one room flat on the Campus of William and Mary College in Williamsburg.

Nineteen months after I went in I was released early to go back to school and start my life.

And what a start it was!

Mister Sinatra

I saw Frank Sinatra in person 7 times. Each time with more anticipation the last. No need to explain here how his performances affected me. The world's best popular music. Cole Porter, Irving Berlin, Gershwin, scores of others. All played by the best musicians on the planet, led by the likes of Nelson Riddle, Billy May, Axel Stordahl and Count Basie with Sinatra center stage and the audience in his hand. His control.

People have asked me so many times, "When you were on the air why did you always call him Mister Sinatra? Ha!

Well, the first time I met Frank Sinatra in person was at the Sands Hotel in Las Vegas. No, I didn't go back stage or meet him in a casino. Nothing like that.

I was in the men's room! The casino men's room! These four guys walk in and one of them takes his place at the urinal next to me. Understand that in the men's room, guys never look at the guy next to them. I don't know why, but this time I did. Uh not down. Up. Looked right at the face of the guy.

And there, next to me was Frank Sinatra going to the bathroom, proving that he was human!

I was a young smart guy in those days and I said:

"Hello Frank."

Without looking at me he said quietly:

"The name is MR. Sinatra."

I didn't say anything.

In a minute I was next to him again washing hands. Two guys handed him towels, some lotion for his face, and whatever.

After his remark at the urinal I kept looking away.

I felt a tap on my shoulder. When I turned around there he was, this time with a face-breaking smile. And yes the eyes were totally the bluest.

I said something cleaver like:

"Nice to meet you Mr. Sinatra."

He laughed, gave me five and said:

"Kid, to you the name's FRANK."

With that he and his entourage turned and left. When he got to the door he turned, looked at me, pointed his finger, and winked!

Since then to me on the air or off he has always been MISTER Sinatra.

Chapter 7
BACK IN ACTION

BACK THEN THE LAW SAID IF YOU WERE DRAFTED INTO THE SERVICE you were entitled to your same job or a better one when you were released. So, there I was back at WJLB in Detroit.

Same Polish Guys, same German Guy, same confusion, same Ernie D. One thing was different. They gave me the all night shift on the weekends. Midnight to 6 Friday and Saturday night. For six hours I played music and for 5 minutes every hour read the news.

This was a real hoot. Six straight hours and I could do, say, and play anything I wanted. Six hours! I was sure no one could be listening. Here's where I could learn and make all the mistakes right? Oh there were phone calls now and then, but not many and I never put them on the air. In those days if one off color word escaped over the air it was over for whoever was responsible and I needed that job.

One night I wanted to see if anyone was listening and I gave out one of the phone numbers that came directly into the control room. It was exactly what I expected. Over the next few minutes there were three or four calls. The all night show night show on a 500watt radio station. 1400 on the AM dial. Couldn't be listeners.

Next night at about 2:30 in the morning I opened the microphone and said something about a problem I had with management at the station and from now on, I said: "please never call this number". And I gave out the number of another direct line into the control room that, if called, would light up five more numbers.

"You are not allowed to call this number. It is forbidden. Do not call this number now or in the future. The station and the phone company will not permit it…period. The number doesn't even work! So don't call"

As soon as I got off that kick five lines lit up and stayed that way for six hours almost every weekend for months. Never gave it out again. Didn't have to. Met some great people on those phones. Weird ones too. And that could be the topic for another whole book!

I was going to Wayne University, working at the station and making a small hourly wage, nothing more. It was time to try and move on.

The only station I knew to call was WJR where I had spent younger years singing in the Make Way For Youth Chorus. I took an audition and was told they would keep it on file. Next day I met with Frank Gaal, the program director of WJBK, one of the big contemporary rock stations in Detroit. He thanked me and said he'd call if anything came up. Sure. But four days later he did.

He said the all night DJ was gone and they needed a replacement. Would I come to the station, do the all night show that night and in the morning if the General Manager liked what he heard I would be hired. If not, they would pay me for the night and move on. Nothing to lose I thought. Why not?

I arrived at the station about ten o'clock that night. Frank Gaal was there with his secretary/ program assistant to meet me and show me how to run their studio equipment. Frank was an affable man whose background was in news and journalism. His assistant was a striking girl in her mid twenties. To protect her identity I will call her Mary. I arrived at the station about ten o'clock that night. Mary was there to show me how to run the controls in studio. Remember this was 1959. Cassettes and tape cartridges with commercials and jingles on them weren't invented yet. The control board had 10 or fifteen knobs or volume controls. If you want to get technical, potentiometers or "pots" as we called them. Each "pot" controlled the volume of one device. Each had an "on" or "off" switch. One for each turntable, microphone, and individual reel-to-reel tape machine. The commercials were all on large 16-inch records or discs. The jingles and other production sounds were on the large tape machines we could see through the studio window in front of the "board" and in the next room. Those machines were noisy, had to be isolated from the air studio, and were operated by remote control. It was a good setup. Mary was a good teacher. After an hour or so I was confident I could handle it and was as ready as I would ever be. At midnight I started some instrumental song for an opening theme.

Now let me explain that for all the time I was on WJLB I always used my real name, Allan Reicheld (RY-keld). At the instant I turned on the microphone and started to talk at WJBK, a competing station, everything seemed to be in slow motion. While I was talking I realized that if I said my real name on the air, if anyone from WJLB was listening and, if I didn't get this new job I would be fired.

My real middle name is Lyle. In a split second, but with detailed thought while I was actually talking on the air I decided to eliminate my last name and invert my Middle and First name. So, it would be Lyle Allan. All this thought was going at the same time I was talking. But then, I realized that this combination wouldn't work either. Lyle Allan is a tongue twister. You try to say it. Lyle Allan. Too many Ls. So, live on the air and without thinking I said: "This is……Lee Allan". And that's the name people have known me by for decades. A spur of the moment blurted out name...that stuck.

The next day at WJLB during a break for the news, Ernie D hit the intercom from his studio, smiled through the glass, looked at me and at me and said these words:

> "As I listened last night to the radio....Daddeo
> I heard the mellow sounds
> going round and round
> From a man named Lee
> Whose initials you see
> Were realeeeee.....
> Allan Reicheld!!!"

Of all people, Ernie had heard me on the other station. He just smiled, came through the door and quietly said: "Did you get the gig man?". I told him I didn't know yet.

Twenty minutes later there was a phone call from WJR. The chief announcer Charley Park said there was a job for me if I wanted it. If I wanted it! The 50,000 watt voice at 760 on the dial and there was a job for me? It was an announcing job. Read the commercials and give the call letters. It was a straight announcer's job. I asked him if I could call him in the morning and he said fine. An hour later there was another call.

The GM at WJBK liked what he heard and the job offer was there too.

One station, WJR was an adult station with an older format, Tiger baseball, Lions football, and still had a live studio orchestra. The other station WJBK was modern, played the most popular music and had terrific ratings. For me it was a fork in the road. Yogi Berra, the great New York Yankee catcher once said:

> "When you come to a fork in the road, take it!".

It wasn't until fifteen years later that I learned that the morning after he heard me on the other station, Ernie D, one of the most respected broadcasters in Detroit called the president of Storer broadcasting, owner of WJBK radio and personally recommended me for the job.

Ernie Durham is now smiling and rhyming in heaven.

Oh yes the fork. I took it. I was new all night man at WJBK. The next night Mary was there to help me through the new routine. She left at about 1AM. On the way home, walking on a nearby Detroit street she was murdered.

Elvis Presley

The first time I met Elvis Presley was in Detroit's Fox Theater. The second time was just a for few moments in Memphis. I was one of a crowd and all we did was shake hands.

The first though was when I introduced him to a cheering, screaming packed house at the Fox Theater in Motown in 1957. He was new, fresh, electric, and at the same time sullen, dark, and mysterious. Elvis was known for his swivel hips and how he moved everything below his waist.

"Elvis The Pelvis" they called him.

On his rare television performances, even on the Ed Sullivan show the censors wouldn't allow any camera shots below the waist. My, how times have changed!

I was asked to be one of 4 MCs at the Fox that night. Elvis was emerging as an idol; the King's reign was beginning. Heartbreak Hotel was big and Elvis was new.

I was back stage. The producer told me I was going to introduce him to the screaming throng out front in the seats.

"Just go out there and say: Ladies and Gentlemen, Elvis Presley."

Just as I was getting ready to break through the curtain I heard a voice behind me say:

"Hey what's your name?"

I turned to answer and there he was. Elvis in all his glitter smiling, eyebrows raised waiting for an answer.

I said: "Reicheld. Name's Alan Reicheld." I hadn't changed it to Lee Alan yet.

At that the producer threw me the cue. I parted the curtain and faced a few thousand teenagers, all going berserk. As loud as I could I said:

LADIES AND GENTLEMEN...
ELVIS PRESLEY!!!!

No one heard me. The noise was deafening. They all knew what I was out there for. They didn't hear me but they knew what I said. Ha!

The curtain opened, the lights blazed from every angle in the theater and Elvis was on.

Before he started to sing, as I was leaving the stage and through all the noise and excitement, Elvis sidled over to me, put his arm around me and loud enough for me to hear he said:

Thank you Mister Reicheld.

Elvis called ME Mister!!!

I only met Elvis three times. All before 1964.

He always remembered my name!

Chapter 8
A NEW KIND OF RADIO

THE FIRST THING I LEARNED AT WJBK IN DETROIT was that I didn't know a thing about radio. At least this kind of radio. There was a format. Like a script. A plan. There were rules to follow.

Play lots of music. Give the time, temperature, call letters (name of the station), dial position, your name, promote the other shows, and play music. Lot's of music! Play more music than the other stations and tell the audience you're doing it.
"You're Talking Too Much"
"SHUT UP AND PLAY THE MUSIC! "
They even had musical jingles singing the name of the station.

>   Aahhhttt Fifteen Hundred On Your Sound Dial
>   Twenty Four Hours A day
>   It's The Sound Of Music With A Built In Smile
>   On W J B K
>   On W J B K
>   (Shouting) DETROIT!

I was on the air from midnight to six Monday through

Saturday and followed a guy by the name of Tom Clay who was on from seven to midnight. I'll never forget him.

We broadcast from the same studio. Clay would close out his show and before the last bit of his closing theme song was finished he was up and out of there and I was in his seat ready to start. I would do the news at midnight and then start my own show.

Tom Clay was 35 years old, thin, good looking with long wavy blondish hair. His soft throaty deep voice fit the look. He wanted to be a movie actor. To me he looked like James Dean. I learned later that's exactly who he wanted to be like.

He was the number one rated night time air personality in Detroit with a huge audience. When he talked, every teenager and young adult in town listened. Tom Clay was their idol. One minute he was totally nuts on the air. The next he was swallowing the mike talking so softly you couldn't hear him in the studio but on the air he was very close and very personal. Tom Clay understood how radio worked, how to create pictures in the mind of the listener. How to pull at the heart strings, to evoke emotion from strangers on the other side of the speaker, how to make them love him. He also knew how to follow the rules, do everything the format dictated, and still do his thing on the air. I was fascinated just watching him.

Each night when I entered the studio there were two or three guys sitting there with Clay. Actually, no matter when I arrived at the station there always seemed to be a few visitors in the studio. Most of the time Clay would ignore my presence, but occasionally would introduce me to his guests. I soon learned they were all from the music industry. They were in the business of promoting records. Their job was to get people like Tom Clay and others on the radio who had large audiences to play the records owned by the companies they represented. They were commonly called Promotion Men or Women. Get the records played. That was their mission. Whatever you have to do, get the airplay.

Almost every month Tom Clay would prove to everyone just how powerful he was on the radio. There was a large armory on the east side of the city owned by the state and used for national Guard activities. The hall would hold about three thousand people standing up. Every month or so Tom clay would rent the Light Guard Armory and announce to his audience that there was going to be a Big Old Ball there on a certain Saturday night and he would be there in person. The record promotion people would bring any recording artists who were in town to the event and Tom would promote that as well.

Clay filled the place. Every time he held the dance there it was jammed with teenagers who wanted to be part of it. Admission was a dollar, Tom paid the rent and expenses and kept the rest. A good legitimate business and proof that Tom Clay was King of the Hill in Detroit.

People still insist that they saw me sitting 70 feet in the air on a lighted restaurant sign near that armory one night waving at all the traffic on 8 Mile Road. The same 8 mile road that was recently featured in a movie. It wasn't me. It was Tom Clay, the promoter, the inventor, a guy who knew what radio could do and how to use it.

I was watching him and learning.

The others on that station, Tom George, Clark Reid, Don McLeod were very well known household names. Good people with good careers. They were talented communicators who all loved what they were doing. The format was contemporary, and we played only the most popular music. There was a list they called Forumla 45. Everyone played from that list and then we could play other records of our own choice.

Each week there was one record on the list that was selected by the station as a future hit that had to be played once every hour for a week. Those were the orders from management. Play it once an hour around the clock. In every city, town, and village across

America the Disc Jockeys and other air personalities replaced the drama, comedy, and pathos of the old radio shows. Listeners considered them to be very personal friends, companions who were there with them in their homes and cars every day. Compared to today there were only a few stations to choose from. All on the AM dial. Nobody listened to FM. Radios only had AM on them. FM would not become a factor until 1967 when the FCC forced it to happen. A very few stations and the personalities on them held the whole radio audience captive.

There were no computers. There was no Internet. Radio and television were the entertainment pulse of America. Everyone was watching. Everyone was listening. What a target they could make for the politicians! And that's exactly what they became. The target. And radio was the bullseye!

Chapter 9

RIGGED QUIZ SHOWS & PAYOLA

By this time everyone in America had a television set and they were glued to it every night.

Gunsmoke, Wagon Train, Have Gun Will Travel, Ed Sullivan Show, Maverick, Mr. Lucky, Milton Berle, Perry Mason, and one that is still on the air, the Price Is Right.

The biggest programs though were the new prime time quiz shows. Names like Tic Tac Dough, The 64 Thousand dollar Question, and others. These shows were still pretty much all live and the night after they were broadcast they were water cooler conversation and on the tip of every tongue. Then suddenly, someone blew the whistle. Politics was in it now.

Headlines. There was a senate investigation. The nation was stunned. The favorite quiz shows were rigged they said. Contestants were being given the answers. The long pauses before they answered, the beads of sweat on their brows, the worried looks were all an act they said. The public was being duped and the companies that produced the quiz shows and the networks themselves were fair game.

At the same time Disc Jockeys and the stations they worked

for were also under investigation. They called it Payola. The music industry was paying DJs under the table to play their records on the air. Pay for Play. The government called it something else.

Commercial bribery! An ugly term.

I won't dwell on the TV shows here. But the quiz shows were rigged. Answers were given in advance and in the end a lot of people paid a price for it. If you're interested, there's a movie about it. Oddly enough it's called: "Quiz Show". Rent it and watch it. It's accurate. Names and all.

In major cities all over America those Promotion Men and Women were paying DJs to play their records. The law says you can't do that. It is bribery. And if you're on the public airwaves you can't take money to play something or say something unless you actually announce that you were paid to say it or play it.

That makes it a commercial. Law simply says that when you're paid for something on the air you have to identify the sponsor. Ever notice the political ads?

"...paid for by the committee to elect John Doe".

Disc Jockeys were being paid off by music companies to play their music. The stations they worked for were in jeopardy of losing their licenses. We were all required to sign affidavits that affirmed we had never taken money or anything else in return for favors to anyone. Some couldn't sign. Many couldn't sign. Tom Clay was one of them.

Clay was the target of an avalanche of complaining by music people who were trying to play the game honestly. They went to station brass accusing him not only of taking money, but actually having a rate card of sorts. So many plays of a record for so much money. Like that. Station execs got tired of hearing it.

"Where's the proof?", they said. "Prove it or forget it."

They did.

Tom Clay did a lot of remote broadcasts. One of his frequent remotes was done from a local amusement park. "Tom Clay from Edgewater Park." One night in mid- summer Tom was doing his remote broadcast. The station carried Detroit Tigers Baseball. After the game started, Tom was approached by a music promotion man, a little man by the name of Harry Nevins. They got into Tom's car. Nevins asked Tom to play one of his records. Tom demanded five hundred dollars to play it. Nevins objected, but Tom persisted. He said he couldn't play favorites. It was five hundred or no play and that was it. Nevins pleaded. Tom wouldn't budge. The conversation ended. Nevins left. The car door slammed.

Nevins was wearing a wire.

Earlier in the day, frustrated with more accusations and no proof, the program director of the station challenged Harry Nevins. He insisted that Nevins put up or shut up. Nevins agreed. They outfitted him with a wire recorder. It was right out of a James Bond movie. His tiepin was the microphone.

Harry Nevins went to Edgewater park that night, confronted Tom Clay and got it all on the wire. Later, after midnight and while I was on the air, the program director transferred the wire recording to tape and made copies. He mistakenly left a copy in the control room.

I still have the tape.

Tom Clay was confronted with the evidence and fired. I was called at home and told to come to the station and do Clay's show, but not to mention Clay's name. Next day there were headlines and Clay's picture. He admitted everything and actually held a news conference to do it.

That was only the beginning. Other big names in Detroit, New York, Chicago, LA, and every other city in the US were falling like dominoes. Some had excuses. Some said they were "consultants" for the record companies and never took money to play music. Some were advisors to music companies, they said, and were paid to take part in weekly conference calls judging the potential popularity of new records. Some stations refused to hang their people out to dry. Most were fired by stations without backbone enough to stand by their people. Fact is before all this publicity, and just like the quiz shows, nobody considered it really wrong. It was common practice for some. Even the stations themselves were doing it, corporately!

Remember that record I said the station selected each week? The one we had to play once every hour? The station was paid to play it! No announcements were ever made that it was paid for. It was corporate payola pure and simple.

It was a major scandal, a big mess. It was all over the newspapers. Literally every day there was another casualty of the investigation somewhere in America. Fired. Banned from the industry. People were going to jail over this. People I knew. We were all warned to never, but never say anything about it on the air. Never mention rigged quiz shows and absolutely never ever say anything about payola. Period.

And I didn't. I didn't even think about saying anything. For about four weeks anyway. And then . . .

Chapter 10
BIG MOUTH

WELL YOU SEE IT WAS THIS WAY. The newspapers were full of it. They were loving this. Eating it up. Reporting everything they could about rigged TV quiz shows and radio stations and DJs in deep trouble.

Newspapers and other print media are the natural predators of electronic media. They compete for every advertising dollar out there. It was a field day for anything printed and they didn't miss a trick.

I didn't have anything to say about anything. I was just a little all night guy trying to make a living. The big guys, and unfortunately in those years there were literally no women on the air in local radio, had their mouths taped shut. Pick up a newspaper and it's smeared all over. Turn on the radio and you'd believe you were on another planet. Nothing reported even in the newscasts. Radio and local television were oblivious.

Meanwhile I was bouncing from radio show to radio show. Tom Clay was gone and then the afternoon drive time personality, Don McCleod, was dismissed. Don had been very good to me when I came to the station. I listened to him, liked him, and respected him.

Don was the afternoon "drive time" man on 'JBK.
"McLEOD'SVILLE USA"
Monday – Friday, 3pm to 6pm

He had a warm, hip personality, and a way of reaching right through the speaker and grabbing your attention. I was listening and learning. Don had a crippled hand. I don't remember exactly, but I think it was deformed and he may only have had one finger and a thumb. What I do remember is that he could pick out a record, throw it on the turntable and cue them to the starting point better than any of us.

I learned a lot from Don McLeod.

Once when he went on vacation I sat in for him on a remote broadcast from Dexter Chevrolet on 8-mile road in Detroit. There I was in the showroom substituting for Don McLeod. Ha! For a week or two I was the afternoon drive time man. What a trip. Me? The afternoon drive time guy on the big station in town? How did THAT happen?

Anyway, after he returned it was nearly three weeks before he said anything to me. I thought he was upset. Finally, he cornered me one afternoon and said with a careful smile on his face:

"Hey....I heard you did a good job while I was away. Too good! Next time make a few mistakes, ok? I need the gig."

I'm sure he was joking. At least I think I'm sure.

He loved radio and loved being on the radio. His firing was a bum rap. I'm not going into what was happening there except to say that I'm convinced he really wasn't involved in that mess. Don thought he was doing the right thing and absolutely nothing wrong until the politicos rewrote the rules.

Don was my friend, but that didn't stop me from getting the call. "Come into the station this afternoon, do Don McCleod's show, but don't mention Don McCleod's name." And I did. And didn't say a word about anything.

Sooo… there came a time when I was temporarily doing my all night show for a change and at about three in the morning after reading a newscast that totally ignored the ongoing scandal I turned on the microphone and started to talk.

I was sick of reading about everything in the newspaper and then the on the air, pretending nothing was happening. I don't remember my exact words but there I was, alone in the low light of the studio in the middle of the night, talking into an open microphone. If it hadn't been for my experiment with the phone number at my former station I would've believed that no one was listening but I knew better.

I knew all about rigged quiz shows and I said so. Quiz shows had been rigged and contestants had been given answers from the beginning of time. Having contestants that knew nothing and just stood there saying, "duh", would've been uncomfortable for everyone and a death knell for the programs themselves. This was show business, not a courtroom, I said. The mike was still open and I was still talking.

To prove it, I said, "I was actually on a rigged quiz show myself". I went on to explain that I went to Cooley High School in Detroit and my senior trip to Washington DC and New York part of our class visited a live network television quiz show called Break The Bank.

The host of the show was Bud Collier, a tall man in his 40s with a terrific voice who also had a show in prime time called "To Tell The Truth" and another show "Beat The Clock." Years earlier on the radio he had been the voice of both mild mannered Clark Kent and the man of steel himself Superman. I was really impressed.

Before the show the producer came out and selected contestants from the audience. I think at the urging of some of the class members who were a little shy my girlfriend, Ann Hutchison and I were chosen to represent our school on the show. Just before we went on the producer told us out category was, songs with the word "one" in the title. Then he said something like: "If the first song that we played was called "One Kiss" would you know that was the first song that we played? Well, I guess! He continued with, "then if the next song we played was called One Meat Ball would you know that was the second song? And so on. He was giving us the answers.

The show was live and suddenly there we both were on national television talking to Bud Collier himself. He told us what our category was and asked the first question. Neither one of us knew what the song was so the answer: "One Kiss" was blurted out. It was right. Then the second question was asked, and the third. We got them all right and were winning money, but time was up. They asked us to come back. It was Friday so we had to stay the weekend in New York. We spent most of it in record stores looking for songs with the word "one" in the title.

Monday came and we were the first ones on the show. This time though they didn't offer the answers. We were on our own. They played the first song, told us the title and asked what Puccini Opera it was from. Opera?! I knew nothing about opera. I was totally blank. Then Ann looked up at him, blinked her eyes a couple of times and quietly said: "Madam Butterfly"? Bud Collier smiled and said: "that's Right!"

While the audience was applauding I nearly fell off the stage. Madam Butterfly? Where did she get that answer? Some thirty years later she told me she saw the sheet music sitting on her mother's piano just before she left home. Hey, now I had visions of buying a brand new car and driving it home from New York. That didn't last long. Next question asked us for the name of the song. I recognized it but couldn't come up with the name and we were done. We won $500 and went home.

The song was called Johnny One Note. It haunts me to this day.

Well, the point was answers were given to us, no different that what was going on today, I said on that open mike. After more running off at the mouth I looked at the clock. A cold chill went down my back.

I had been talking for over 20 minutes! I paused, turned off the mike and played solid music for the next half hour.

Chapter 11
HEADLINES

I DIDN'T SAY ANYMORE. Just ran the station format. Call letters, time, temperature, etc., until 6AM and I was finally off. Tom George, the morning man came in, said his usual cheery " Hey Lee what's up?" and took over. That was a good sign I thought. At least he didn't know what I said.

WJBK radio was on the second floor of a large free standing building at the corner of 2nd and Bethune in downtown Detroit. Television, WJBK-TV Channel 2, occupied the first floor. As usual I took the back stairs to the parking lot in back of the building. It was November and still dark at this time of the morning. When I opened the door leading to the outside there was a man standing there with one of those big newspaper type cameras pointing at me. The flashbulb went off like an explosion. I was blind for a minute. He said, "Hey Lee, Thanks" and took off. I thought, "This is great. Finally getting some publicity". Got in my car, drove home and went to sleep.

The ringing phone woke me. That was back when phones had loud bells. I looked at the clock. It was one in the afternoon. The program director at the station wanted to see me right away.

Probably to do someone's program again I thought. As I left the apartment I picked up the paper laying on the porch, got in the car and threw it on the front seat and froze!

The headlines said something about the president and trouble overseas. Below that was my picture and in big bold headline letters:

DJ ADMITS PART IN RIGGED QUIZ SHOW !

I just sat there for a minute. Finally I got up enough nerve to read the story. It wasn't good folks. It was all there. Problem was they printed what I said. Never mind that I was in high school at the time. Or that Ann and I only won $500. I was going to throw up any minute.

Not only did I open my big mouth, but some guy at the newspaper was listening, wrote the story, broke speed limits to get to the station at 6AM, took my picture and got in all into the paper before his deadline. Wonderful!

As I said before the newspapers loved this whole scandal and I now I was in it. There were three major newspapers in Detroit at that time. I didn't even want to look at the other two! And then that phone call from the station. How hard was that to figure out?

The general manager's office was huge. Mr. Lipson was a small man with a big desk. And a bigger chair. In a meeting he definitely had the advantage, especially one like this. When I walked in all I saw was a big newspaper wide open and my picture staring back at me. He was behind the paper. He didn't say anything and the paper didn't move. For a long time the paper didn't move!

Must be a slow reader I thought. I stood there. Finally, he just deliberately and very slowly crumpled the paper revealing his face. It was a bright crimson and looked like it was going to blow up any minute. He took his glasses off, looked directly at me and tried to say something. His mouth opened. His lips moved, but no sound came out. He looked like Ed Norton of The Honeymooners in pain. He tried again. This time there was sound escaping but it was just a noise like a little growl. Finally he succeeded.

"Did you say this?" "Yes Sir", I said. "All of this?" "Well, most of it I guess."

Mr. Lipson proceeded to chew me out from one end to the other. He was not loud. I think the word is controlled. He was controlled and making great effort not to pick up something and throw it at me. Normally, he had a high voice. Except now it was higher and he spoke in a quiet monotone. Quiet, controlled, and monotone. That's the worst kind. I knew what I had done and was really just waiting for him to say I was fired. But he didn't say it.

After what seemed like hours in front of him, and after a few more times when his jaw moved but nothing came out, he finally just told me to never say anything like that on the air again and then politely but firmly said: "I am now throwing you out of my office. Get out of here and stay out." He then raised the newspaper back in front of his face making sure I could see my picture on the front page again. I didn't want to look at that anymore, so bruised and beaten, I left with my job intact! But it wasn't over!

Connie Francis

In 1962 I considered Connie Francis to be the most popular female singer in the world. Personally, I never liked her voice on the ballads she sang, but I really loved the up tempo tunes like: "Many Many Tears Ago" and the rest.

I will never know how we pulled it off, but that same year Connie made an appearance on Club 1270 television with Joel and me. She had an entourage with her the size of an army platoon and communicated to us only through them. Her performance was taped in midweek and was to be inserted in the show on Saturday. She lip-synched to the records and was very good.

I was the designated interviewer that day. As soon as the camera was on, Connie changed before my eyes from a standoffish introvert to a vibrant smiling personality. She was absolutely radiant with smiles, conversation, and just glowed. As soon as the camera was off she withdrew to her "people". I thought it was me that she didn't like, so we only talked when were both on camera and taping.

The entire appearance only took about an hour. When it was over her platoon said goodbye to everyone for her. Then, as we walked up the stairs from the studio to the control room where their coats were stored…

Connie Francis turned to me smiling, shook my hand and without a word transferred from her hand to mine a hotel room key.

No, I don't know the answer to your question. I never tried to use it!!!

Chapter 12
FIRED!

JAC LEGOFF WAS A GREAT TELEVISION NEWSCASTER IN DETROIT on WJBK-TV Channel 2. In other words, downstairs! He, along with the rest of the broadcast world was under strict orders not to say anything about rigged quiz shows or payola on the air. He was curious though how I said what I did, landed on the front page of the newspaper and still had a job. Ha! So was I.

When I told him of my meeting with Mr. Lipson, Jac asked if he could use my office. My office? It was the record library, a big room longer than it was wide with a glass pane in the door. Once inside with the door closed I could see him through the glass reading something. He was pacing back and forth with a script in his hand reading it out loud. Reminded me of Mr. Lipson. Mouth moving but no sound. He was rehearsing something for the six o'clock news.

At five minutes to six Jac emerged from my "office", and raced down the hall to get to the studio in time for the opening shot. I went into the television master control room and watched. In those days instead of making the news TV reporters just reported the news. So the six o'clock news was only 15 minutes. Maybe we should go back to that.

I watched. Jac LeGoff was beautiful. Always smiling. He was very popular, good looking, soft spoken, well liked and respected by everyone and was rated the number one TV newscaster in the city. Everyone paid attention to Jac. He was sort of the Walter Cronkite of Detroit.

That evening as his 15 minutes drew to a close the camera dollied into a tight shot of just his head and shoulders. The background was black. He looked up into the lens and started. It was the script he'd been rehearsing in my "office".

Basically, he said that quiz shows were entertainment and had been altered from the beginning of time. He said giving some help at the beginning of a contestant's time on a show should be treated no differently than if the show made some of the answers so simple that no one could miss. Ever watched "Who Wants To Be A Millionaire"? Instead of giving contestants the answers the first few questions are always so easy, a child could answer. Rigged? No! Controlled? Yes! As for payola, I think he said that gratuities in some businesses have been around forever. The buyer in a large department store receives a gift from a supplier, people are taken to lunch, and others get tickets to shows or samples of a company's product. Jac did not condone criminal activity. He made his point though and as the camera drew closer he looked directly into the lens, raised the first finger of his right hand and said: " So, let he who has not sinned cast the first stone".

The next morning there was a telegram from Storer Broadcasting. Jac LeGoff was fired.

Chapter 13
FUROR

ONCE AGAIN THE NEWSPAPERS DELIVERED THE MESSAGE.

"CHANNEL 2 FIRES LeGOFF".

It was a ten alarm fire. The station switchboard burned up. No one had ever seen anything like it before. They had to bring in extra help just to handle it. Jac LeGoff, one of the world's nicest guys caught in the controversy. I thought a reporter's job was to report. Not to be muzzled. Storer Broadcasting caved in to their own fear and nearly ruined the career of a wonderful man. They had already done it to others on all of their radio and television stations.

About three weeks later I had another call from the station. "The boss wants to see you." I checked the paper as I headed for the car. No headlines this time. No problem. I had been waiting for this call.

Things were quieting down around town a bit and with all the sitting in I had been doing for the big guys on the station who were losing their jobs I was sure Mr. Lipson was finally going to give me one of those prime times and my own show. I felt a little guilty about it though. I mean there was Don McCleod, Tom Clay, and over on the television side Dale Young who had a TV dance party like Detroit's version of American Bandstand. They, along with Jac Legoff had all been fired and here I was driving to the station to take one of their jobs.

Mr. Lipson was sitting in that big high chair again. No newspaper this time. "Morning Lee." he said. "Lee, for budgetary reasons we're cutting back the staff and dis-continuing the all night show. Going to be all on tape from now on. Engineers will just play it." I waited for him to tell me about my new time slot.

It never came. "Lee, I'm afraid you are no longer suitable for our programming purposes. Yesterday was your last night on WJBK. You can pick up your check at the front desk."

Lipson allowed no questions. I was stunned, and gone, another victim of the purge, but an innocent one. I expected the newspaper to run the story, but I was shocked at what I saw.

The story recounted what I had said on the air a few weeks before, all about me being on a rigged quiz show while a senior at Cooley High, but there was something else.

They reported that the station had received a telegram from an organization that called themselves "The Guardians Of The Public Morals".

They quoted the telegram saying: "…by his own admission he had taken part in a rigged quiz show and had proven he was not an individual to hold a responsible position with a station of already proven high integrity."

It went on to threaten, "to notify the papers and the House committee for legislative oversight and possible boycott all products advertised over your station. Station officials would not comment."

No one at the station would answer my questions, nor would they show me the telegram the newspapers talked about. I had a suspicion as to the source of that telegram, but I couldn't prove it. I went to AFTRA, the union I was forced to join when I went to work at WJBK. I told them that it was time now for them to prove the worth of their union. "Get me my job back", I told them. It was useless. They wouldn't even look into it. No more of those unions for me!

Years later, Clark Reid, one of the DJs who wasn't fired during that slaughter told me that the rest of them thought I was a company spy. They thought that I was a mole and the reason some of them were getting fired. Unbelievable! Well I know where that telegram came from. It was actually the brainstorm of Tom Clay. He suspected that I was instrumental in his firing, sent the telegram to the station hoping they would fire me too. He got his wish.

I was on the street.

I did nothing except talk about this on the air. It was wrong of me to violate their policy, but that's all I did. They fired me and made it look like I was involved in the mess that was going on nationwide. I was devastated, hurt, and sure that the publicity would kill any future I might have had, so I drove around. Aimless. Thinking. Worrying.

I ended up at Baker's Keyboard Lounge, a local bar and restaurant. As I was ordering something a large man sat down next to me. I was in shock and in no mood to talk with anyone when he said: "Hey, are you Lee Alan?" Without looking up I just nodded my head and then saw a hand about the size of my leg extended into my face as the voice said: "Mickey Shorr Lee, I'm Mickey Shorr". I looked up. Way up. Sure enough it was Mickey. One of the biggest names in Detroit radio and at six foot five and nearly three hundred pounds one of the biggest men I had ever seen.

Mickey had been fired too from WXYZ. He and I shared our stories and talked a long time that day. It was the beginning of a love-hate relationship that lasted until his death nearly 30 years later.

Crazy Guggenheim

The two most popular non-singers who appeared with us on Club 1270 while I was on the show were Frankie Fontaine and the man himself Cassius Clay before he became Mohammed Ali.

Frankie Fontaine? Well, he was only fairly well known at the time for his ignoramus character he called "John L. C. Sivoney". Don't remember him? Yes you do! If you were alive then you do. A few years later Frankie took his act to the Jackie Gleason show and changed the character's name to

CRAZY GUGGENHEIM, the happy fool who always showed up with Gleason's "Joe The Bartender".

Remember?

There would be Joe behind the bar wiping glasses with a white towel and singing some old song as only Gleason could and Guggenhiem would appear. Joe would look up and say:

"Hi Ya Craze...."

Guggenheim (Frankie) would look into the camera, cross his eyes, give us a fool's smile and say:

Hiiiii Ya Joe!

It was hilarious.

Anyway, when I had him on Club 1270 naturally I wanted him to do the character he made famous. Five minutes before he went on he refused. Frankie said the only way he'd do it would be if we would pay his going fee. No pay – no way.

We couldn't pay.

He didn't do the character and without the smile, the crossed eyes, and the voice, no one knew who he was.

Chapter 14
MICKEY

I WANT TO INTERRUPT MY STORY HERE TO TELL YOU about one of the most unforgettable people I have ever met.

What a guy! What a character. What a genius. Mickey Shorr!

If you're ever in Detroit you'll see some small yellow buildings with MICKEY SHORR emblazoned across the front. In Dash Car Stereo. That's what they sell and all sorts of other gadgets. Most people these days think that MICKEY SHORR is just the name of a business or a building.

Not so. Mickey Shorr built that business and was one of God's special people.

Mickey Shorr was about 30 years old when I met him that day. Before I worked at the station that had just fired me, Mickey had already been a radio personality on that same station, WJBK, had been fired from there and moved on to WXYZ where he had been caught in the scandal and had just been fired again.

Mickey was a big man with a 6th grade education and big ideas who made a big noise on the radio in Detroit. When he was on the air there was no mistaking him for anyone else. He was loud, exciting, funny, friendly, and spoke another language that only his listeners could understand. Radio people didn't understand Mickey or recognize his talent. Radio management didn't. The advertising community didn't.

None of them understood that Mickey Shorr was a unique phenomenon that never should have left the airwaves and could have made all those 41 long suits in the front offices a lot of money. He eventually did anyway…another way.

"Heyyyy Good Buddies", Mickey would say.

And when Mickey gave the time of day on the radio he had everyone doing math in their heads. No one ever gave the time the way he did. That was his gimmick. What was the Broadway show that had a song called: "You Gotta Have A Gimmick?" Well Mickey had many.

"Heyy.. Good Buddies, it's A Nickel and a Sawbuck Before the Bewitching". What?
Or " "It's Two Over Two Dozen After a Five Spot". Just picture yourself tuning in the radio and hearing that! What was that guy saying? A Sawbuck what?

In Mickey Shorr time, "A Nickel and a Sawbuck Before the Bewitching" is 15 minutes to midnight. And "Two Over Two Dozen After a Five Spot" is 22 minutes after 5 o'clock. That was Mickey Shorr.

"Pavolia" he would say. "Pavolia."
Whenever he was on the air and signing off he would say: "PAVOLIA"

One time I asked him what Pavolia meant and he said: "Well, it means take it slow. Take it easy. Walk the peaceful walk. Make it all count. Love you."

He later explained to me that the way he gave the time was a gambler's language he picked up in the crap joints across the Detroit River in Windsor, Ontario Canada where some friends of his operated illegal casinos. I think his friends were mob connected but not Mickey. Mickey knew everyone and everyone knew him.

That's the language they used. "But I never gambled", he said. Mickey picked it up, used it on the air, and it made him a unique voice that all the teenagers loved.

Mickey didn't let the firings stop him.

As a kid of seven he made tamales and sold them in back alleys. In his teens he lied about his age and did comedy routines in burlesque houses. Later, Mickey and his brother Jack Shorr started a car seat cover business. "Shorr's Seat covers". The two brothers did their own television commercials and became famous for them.

In the commercial Jack Shorr might answer a ringing phone at SHORR'S SEAT COVERS and on the other side of the split screen there was Mickey laying down in the sand in a desert somewhere, nearly dead of thirst. "Jack", he would say. "Jack, it's me Mickey" (who else?)

Jack: Yeah Mickey

Mickey: Jack, I'm stranded out here in the desert. Outa money. Need money Jack. Can't get home.

Jack: Sorry Mick. What do ya want me to do?

Mickey: Cut all the prices of all the seat covers. Slash 'em all. The prices Jack. Not the seat covers. Don't slash the seat covers. Cut the prices. That'll get me enough to get home...

Jack: But Mickey, when I get the money how do I send it to you in the desert?

Mickey: Minor details Jack. I'll get there somehow to pick it up. (What?) just zero out those prices for two days only and you'll figure it out.

Jack: Right Mickey...I'm always the one that's gotta figure it out...

Then Jack might get up from his chair, walk in the other

room and there would be Mickey lying in a pile of sand on the floor! Never was in the desert at all.

And so on. TV commercials for Shorr's Seat Covers. Funny, ridiculous, effective, and they made Mickey a celebrity. And that's how he ended up on the radio.

After he was fired from the radio, from WXYZ, and after I met him he moved to California and sold pots and pans out of the trunk of his car to support his wife May, his daughter Debby and two sons.

The firings never stopped Mickey Shorr.

In the 60s, Mickey moved his whole family to Chicago and WSDM-FM where he was as Program Director of the station owned by the Chess brothers of Chess records. It was his job to get enough listeners so the sales force could convince advertisers that buying commercials on the station would get them business in their stores and for their products.

Now this was an FM station in the 60s. Until 1967 FM was nothing. No big listenership because there were practically no FM radios in cars and almost none at home. Stations were simulcasting. That is to say the AM stations that also had FM transmitters were broadcasting all their programs on both stations at the same time.

If you're old enough you'll remember that stations used to identify themselves by saying: "WLS AM & FM, Chicago," etc. In 1967 in one of their better moves, and there haven't been many, the Federal Communications Commission ruled that all radio stations that had both AM and FM stations in markets of more than a hundred thousand people had to start broadcasting separately. They had to use their FM stations or lose them. And furthermore radio manufacturers had to start making all radios with both AM & FM. I'm not going further into radio history here but, well HELLO! That was the wake up call that changed radio forever.

And there was Mickey Shorr right in the middle of it all programming a nothing FM radio station in the 60s at the beginning of this FM revolution. Know what the genius did? Know what he put on the air to fight the big guns?

Women!

There were no women at all on the radio at that time in that decade and Mickey Shorr hired all women Disc Jockeys and blew the town away! All Girls they called it. Not suggestive either. Couldn't be in those days and shouldn't be now. Mickey was the first to do it. The result? WSDM became the top FM station in Chicago going away.

WSDM! No wonder the listeners remembered the call letters and where it was on the radio dial.

      WSDM! Mickey's genius called it

      W

      S (SMACK)

      D (DAB IN THE)

      M (MIDDLE)

      SMACK DAB IN THE MIDDLE – WSDM.

Wow!

Now here's the kicker. Mickey did all this before 1967 and the FM station still became a top station! What was the line in the movie Field Of Dreams? "If you build it they will come." Mickey built it and the listeners came.

From there I'm not sure what he did. I think he was in Florida for a while, but eventually back in Detroit where he and his wife, May found a small storefront and started "Mickey Shorr's Tape Shack." They had cassette tapes and two or three "In Dash Car Stereo" units that they demonstrated.

They had no money to buy lots of inventory so when they sold one, Mickey or May would run out and buy another to replace the one they sold.

The business grew quickly and they moved it to an old gas

station. Mickey painted the building a bright yellow with his name in gigantic red letters:

MICKEY SHORR and a big red heart. And there he was back on the radio. This time he was doing his own commercials. They were sixty-second versions of his old radio shows and he was saying that because his prices were so low they called him THE BIG HEARTED SLOB! "Just look for the yellow shack with the big red heart."

In those days I was in the advertising business and worked for Mickey doing his advertising. He was a tough taskmaster and could get very volatile. Same as I could. I'll never forget the first commercial I did with him. I was supposed to have scripts ready for Mickey. The problem was we got to the studio and I still didn't have anything written. My mind was a blank.

Mickey walked in looked at me and said: "OK, where's my script?" I said: "Hey Mick, who needs a script? How long have you and I been on the radio? Really, do we need a script? What for?" Before he could recover from this dumb statement I turned on the tape machine and the microphone and said:

"This is Lee Alan with Mickey Shorr of Mickey Shorr's Tape Shack, Woodward,. Just north of the zoo. Mickey, why do they call you the BIG HEARTED SLOB?

It was as if I had pushed a magic button. Mickey's eyes lit up, I could see the wheels going around, his mouth started going and he said:

"I don't know Lee maybe it's because one time Sammy Davis Jr. said: "Mickey, you're the only guy I know who can wear a $2,000 suit and still look like a slob." But looks aren't everything Lee and if you come to my tape shack I'll sell you anything you see so far below the competition it'll make you head swim."

And so on. Mickey went on to build many more locations. We became great friends.

Mickey Shorr loved radio. Really loved radio. He told me more than once he would give up all his business success if they would just put him back on the air.

Just let him do his show again. They never let him.

After four heart attacks he sold all his "Tape Shacks" and he and May moved to Tampa-St Pete in Florida. Instead of retiring he opened up a sandwich shop and his genius made him another fortune.

When he was in business in Detroit, Mickey Shorr spent millions of dollars on radio and Television. Gave the radio industry millions in business.

Nobody financed him or helped him with that business. He and his beloved May did it together on their own.

Like most creative geniuses, Mickey Shorr was a perfectionist. He was honest, loyal, emotional, hilarious, and tough. Mickey fired me as his advertising agency two times. I was devastated. Then the phone call would come. "Hey Lee", he would say. "I need some advertising and fast, you got time?" And we'd be working together again.

In 1981 I had a physical scare. While talking on the telephone one morning in my office I was having trouble pronouncing words. My mouth felt stiff and just wasn't responding to what I wanted it to say. I thought I was having a stroke. I called my wife who said she thought it was something else but said I should call the doctor right away. I did. He told me not to drive, but to get to the hospital right away. Examination by a neurologist proved that I was not having a stroke, but had contracted something called Bells Palsy. Within two days the entire right side of my face was paralyzed! I couldn't close my eye. The paralysis prevented me from speaking clearly. To be understood I had to literally hold my right upper lip in place. My voice was also affected.

When Mickey Shorr arrived at my office a few days later I

was feeling sorry for myself. "Lee, I've got to get these commercials done for the store." I told him I'd call a couple of announcers to do it. "Hey listen I can't afford to pay you and other guys too. You do it." I tried to tell him I couldn't. I sounded different. Couldn't say the words properly. Mickey would have none of it. "Just get in that booth and do the commercials Lee I don't have time for this."

Mickey wasn't being mean. It was his way of saying that he didn't care what my condition was. He wanted me to do this and he was telling me to stop feeling sorry for myself and just get on with life. That was Mickey.

Thomas Edison said: "Genius is 1 percent inspiration and 99 percent perspiration" That was Mickey. He was a free spirit who never told anyone more than he thought they needed to know. May was no exception. Through all his hard days and the volatility that accompanies genius and creativity, his wife stuck with him, he was her Mickey to the end.

In 1988 there was a reunion of all the radio people in Detroit history. This was radio. These were his colleagues and friends. Mickey wanted to come. He desperately wanted to be there. He was going to come. He had to come. He wanted them all to see him. He belonged there. He was a legend among wannabes. His doctor told him he needed a heart bypass operation first so he went into the hospital.

He underwent the surgery on a Friday and died on Saturday. He never got off the table. He was only 61 years old.

He never got to the reunion.

I was there. All of Detroit Radio was there.

And they all got up and said nice things. They all praised him.

All the people who benefited financially from his genius and from this man's friendship praised him. The same ones who, while he was alive, wouldn't let him back on the radio. The listeners were deprived of hearing this gifted man. Today because of his former business and creative genius, people think Mickey Shorr is only a building.

Later there was a wake for Mickey. I made a tape and played it there.

I loved him and I miss him.

PAVOLIA Mick………PAVOLIA!

Mohammed Ali

Our Halloween show on Club 1270, ABC-TV in 1963 had Marvin Gaye, Hank Ballard and the Midnighters and Cassius Clay (Before he became Mohammed Ali). Playing the idiot fool as usual I came out dressed as a Ghost. Cassius had just released an album called "I Am the Greatest". It was hilarious. Most of it was all about Sonny Liston, how he was going to "whup the big ugly bear", and the entire cast and crew of the show were doubled up laughing as he floated like a butterfly roaming all over the set reciting his "greatest" material.

All the time he was moving and dancing I was behind him in my Ghost outfit mimicking him and dancing like his shadow. Now and then he would suddenly turn around and shoot some left jabs and combinations my way just barely missing. He played to the audience, mugged the camera, ran up the stairs off the set to the control room, disappeared for a few seconds, and reappeared. All the time I was close behind waving my arms like I was scaring him...or somebody!

That night he was on my radio show reciting the same Greatest material.

A few months later Cassius Marcellus Clay in fact "whupped that big ugly bear" Sonny Liston, became the heavyweight champion of the world, joined the Muslim Religion, and changed his name to Mohammed Ali.

It was only then that someone pointed out to me what that Halloween appearance looked like to some people. Think of it. Cassius Clay, a black Olympic Gold Medallist from the south dancing around a TV studio followed ever so closely by someone covered with a white sheet and a hood with holes for eyes and mouth.

A black man with a white shadow in a sheet! Now what's wrong with that picture?

I'm sure he realized what it looked like. But he was gracious, funny, fun loving, and a master psychologist. Sonny Liston was totally psyched out.

He was, is, and always will be...THE GREATEST!

Chapter 15
WKMH RADIO

Leaving WJBK radio turned out to be the best thing that ever happened to me. Next stop WKMH Dearborn, Michigan. Station call letters stood for Knorr, Mccoy, & Hanson. Never met Mccoy or Hanson, but I new Mr. Knorr. Among other things he was an owner of the Detroit Tigers Baseball team in those days and was kind, interested, and thought what happened to me at WJBK was a joke. I'll tell you why in a minute. Well at least in a few sentences.

WKMH Radio meant only one thing. Robin Seymor. The consistent big name in Detroit for years had been Robin Seymor. I mean everybody knew Robin. "Bobbin' With Robin." He was a very powerful and bright personality, and the consummate professional at his craft. We all called him the Bird.

As I understand it when the Payola scandal happened, Robin got with Fred Knorr, they did what they had to do and got on with life. Period. I cannot say here what involvement Robin had except that he told me had an interest in the record distribution business and when all this happened he sold it. End of story. Robin was clear of any trouble and Mr. Knorr stood behind him.

The broadcast industry lost some talented people as a result of this purge by a publicity seeking, anything to get elected, senate investigation. Yes, some of the air personalities were crooks. Most weren't. Most were underpaid young men who loved what they did. Their listeners loved them, depended on them for parts of their day, grew up with them. And now they were gone. L.A., New York, Chicago, Detroit, in every city in the nation jobs were lost, lives were ruined. It was needless.

It was a classic case of employers covering their rear ends and not protecting the innocent people. To be safe they threw everyone out. Baby with the bath water. Good and bad. In the end the public lost, the same people that those Washington clowns were supposed to be protecting. Radio and TV stations lost. They lost their audiences, public trust, and advertising revenue. And a lot of radio and TV people never worked on the air again.

Robin Seymor was a survivor. He was smart, witty, and knew how to promote and make money. And after I interviewed with Fred Knorr I was on the same station with The Bird. He was on in the afternoon and I was on at night.

The program director, responsible for everything that was on the air was Larry Fisher. A smiling, smart, easy to get along with guy who said: "Lee, you're on from 7PM to Midnight. Say anything you want, play the station list of songs, and just don't get us in trouble".

WKMH became a training ground for me. A place where I could be wild on the air and not get in trouble for it. It was a small station with a big voice, and a very bad broadcast signal at night. That's when I was on and I loved it.

Chapter 16
THE HORN

ON THE AIR AT WKMH WAS A WHOLE NEW THING FOR ME. The studio was old. Equipment was a little outdated, but it worked. Robin Seymor did everything he could to help me. I was a little nervous when I first met him but he soon showed me the class guy he always was. No more "all night shows" for me. Seven to Midnight was the prime time for any new DJ to be on. Here's why.

Let's go back to the late 50s for a minute. FM radio wasn't even a thought in anyone's mind then. Only AM. FM wouldn't become a factor until the late 60s when the Federal Communications Commission ruled that radio stations in large markets that had both AM and FM stations had to broadcast separately from their AM stations. Until then stations simulcast all their programming on both AM & FM. When the FM rule was passed in 1967 FM suddenly became another world of radio adding literally hundreds of "new" stations. It forced manufacturers to add FM to every radio. Until then most radios had only AM stations built into them. So in every major city in the United States the AM dial had only a few stations. That gave the listener only a few choices. And that made the people on the air very powerful people. A very few reaching very many.

Chicago, New York, L.A., Miami, wherever there was radio there were only a handful of stations in any market. In Detroit, from left to right on the AM dial was WJR at 760, CKLW at 800, WWJ at 950, WCAR at 1130, WXYZ at 1270, WKMH at 1310, WCHB (forget where), WJLB at 1400, and WJBK at 1500. That's all. WCHB and WJLB were ethnic stations, not listened to by the general audience.

What about Television? Same thing. UHF television was something nobody knew anything about. To get it you had to have an extra adapter installed on your TV set. So, in all the big cities there were only three or four stations. In Detroit your TV set had Channels 2, 4, 7, Channel 9 from Canada, and Channels 50 and 56 if you had that adapter. That's all. Four stations and two that practically no one could get. Not too hard to become a TV star in those days. All you had to do was get on.

Boring enough so far? What it all meant was that if you were on radio or television and even breathing you had a substantial audience.

I was on, breathing fairly well thank you, and what's more I was on at night when all the young people were listening to their radios. Remember, there were no FMs, no cassette players, tape players, nothing. If you were listening to anything you were listening to a record player at home or to AM radio.

There I was on WKMH with a poor broadcast signal at best, playing music, reading the news, making mistakes, and starting to get reaction from a captive population listening to AM radio. That's not to say there wasn't competition. There was. I was the little guy on the dial. The big guys had all the listeners. I was just fooling around and the station allowed me to do it. They figured that nighttime was a throwaway for advertising revenue anyway, so they let me do my thing.

Jonathan Winters was my favorite comedian. One night I

was on remote at a drive in restaurant. I will never forget Pandy's Drive In. It was winter and about ten below zero outside. I was broadcasting from a tiny mobile trailer with a large glass window in front so the traffic could see me. All the records and commercials were played back at the station by Jerry Bennett, my producer. I had a microphone, a telephone hookup so I could talk to the producer and that's it. While the songs were playing we would talk and decide what was going to happen next. There was a space heater with a wood stove. About every 20 minutes I had to go in the back and put more wood on the fire. Real show business right? Ha! Kind of like the guy in the circus who follows the elephants with a shovel!

Anyway, there I was on the air at Pandy's Drive In when suddenly while I was talking live on the air I hear this other voice say: "Oh do we have to sit here for this?". And then a silly laugh. I reacted as best I could and then another silly laugh and: "There's the Dummy Again". Jerry had found a Jonathon Winters record, was listening to me and inserting Jonathon bits into whatever it was that I was saying. And that was the beginning. I came back with wild remarks like (at the top of my voice): "The only Dummy is the one talking when I'm not". Or "Waittttt a Minuuuttteeee....."

It was getting real warm in the trailer. I thought it was just the extra energy on the show. Jerry had a terrific sense of humor and every few minutes there was something new from Jonathon Winters. "Sixteen and still talking like that, that's pathetic", I would react, we'd play a song, talk over the song, throw things on the floor, whatever. Then I realized why it was so warm in there.

That space heater overheated and a fire started in the back of the trailer. I was forced to run for my life. Records were still playing on the air, Jonathon Winters was on with his wild remarks, station jingles were playing, recorded commercials were going, but I wasn't. They called the fire department and the trailer burned to the ground. Ha, it was the hottest show in town that night. Sorry!

If you ever went to Pandy's Drive In Detroit you had to have Melted Cheese With Chili and Onions. Maybe that's what started the fire.

Fantastical!

The next night I was on remote there again. What a night that was! Jerry was at his best with the wild tracks of Winters, I was yelling, laughing, running back and forth, going outside leaving the microphone on so you could hear me at a distance. Wild! Then all of a sudden I said something that would stay with me for the rest of my life. Even to this day.

I said " This Is Lee Alan ON THE HORN"!

What I meant was that I was on the radio. On the Air. Or the telephone. Like talking On The Horn. Well, it stuck. I kept saying it more and more. Then back at the station Jerry Bennett found some old sound effects that he would play whenever I said "On The Horn". Car Horns, Tubas, Moose Calls, Duck Quacks and so on. After a while, instead of saying they sounded terrible, I said they were fantastic.

They all had a wonderful tone!

The phrase started way back in college when I was pledging a fraternity. As a pledge I was the lowest of the low, and had to answer their fraternity house-phone with the longest speech in the history of the world. "Hello, this is Michigan Beta of Phi Delta Theta, the oldest fraternity on campus. Our national chapter was founded in Miami, Ohio", and on and on for what seemed about another hour and ending with: "This is Lee Alan so forlorn at your service ON THE HORN." Somehow on the air that night it just popped out. And it stuck!

A few weeks later a music promotion man by the name of Curley Dimetro came to the studio and gave me an actual horn. It was a silver Pakistani Taxi Horn that curled around itself a couple of times and had a big bulb on the end. Squeeze the bulb and you play THEEE HORN!

The sound was meant to be loud and it was. If I blew The Horn into the directly into the microphone without warning to anyone at the station the force of the sound was so powerful that it could possibly set off a reaction at the station transmitter serious enough to blow us off the air. I had to always remember to blow the horn away from the mike; never into it. Never! Well, almost never!

After a few nights of blowing Thee Horn, people started asking about it. Where did it come from. How long have you had it? What does it look like? Some were saying it sounded terrible. Like a sick Moose, one said. So, the legend of The Horn was about to be born.

 The Horn Remembers...

Del Shannon

Del Shannon was an absolute delight on our shows and off. He was a positive, smiling, music master and loved by all who knew him. Who could ever forget that falsetto voice soaring to impossible heights in "Runaway", "Hats Off To Larry", Little own Flirt, and Keep Searchin' We were very good friends and we ended up together in pursuit of the original interview with the Beatles at the Deauville Hotel on the beach in Miami, Florida. We always kept in touch. Every now and then the phone would ring and Del would be calling from somewhere. "Hey Horn", he would say. "Want to go find those Beatles again"?

Years later when his popularity was eroding in the United States Del Shannon was a king in Europe. Tens of thousands flocked to his shows. Then on the night of February 8, 1990, Del's wife Bonnie returned to their home in Santa Clarita Valley, just north of L.A. and found him collapsed in a chair with a bullet in his right temple and a .22 caliber rifle by his side.

Shot himself they said.. Friends said he was suffering from depression and taking heavy doses of Prozac. Not a good thing. The world lost a nice man and a great and powerful entertainer. I lost a dear friend.

Prozac.

There was Prozac in my family for a few years.

I believe it contributed to a personal tragedy of my own.

A different kind of tragedy.

Chapter 17
LEGEND

REMEMBER THE JACK BENNY RADIO PROGRAM I talked about in Chapter three? Benny was my favorite radio comedy program of all time. Remember the part about the vault deep under his house where he kept his money and the guard who was there? Well, listen to this. Oh I forgot this is a book. Listen to a book? Sorry, for a minute I thought I was on the air.

The Horn caused so much talk around town, and yes even among grown adults at the station that I had to explain it somehow. I mean when they asked me how I found it or where it came from I couldn't just say some guy in the music business just wandered in one day and threw it on the desk. That wouldn't have been very interesting. So I started creating the story of The Horn; what it was, where it came from, how valuable it was. Each night there was something a new.

- It took 40 years of research to develop the fine tone of The Lee Alan Horn
- The Horn was manufactured in Pakistan by a Pakistan watch-maker.
- It was made of pure Aborganite . . . . Aborganite??

- Everybody knows what Aborganite is, right?
- The fine tone is in the key of F-Sharp. And it is!
- The Horn is insured with Lloyds of London for over 7 million dollars.
- When it's not on the air The Lee Alan Fine Toned Horn is in the vault.
- Inside the Vault The Horn is guarded day and night by 17 Pinkerton Men.

The idea for the vault came from the old Jack Benny program. Hey, if that vault was safe enough for Benny's money, then why not The Horn? Interestingly enough in all these years no one has ever made the connection between Benny's vault and mine.

And so, The Legend of The Horn...was born. No rhyme intended there. Sometimes it just happens though. Sorry Ernie Ha! In months to come I would take The Horn with me on personal appearances.

Everyone sort of clamored to see it. Wait till you hear that story. To this day people know and ask about The Horn. And incidentally it does have a WONDERFUL TONE! They even call ME The Horn. My tone is questionable though.

Chapter 18
JACKIE AND BERRY

THINGS WERE CHANGING. I knew it. Those same people who used to hang around Tom Clay's studio at WJBK were now waiting for me when I arrived at the station in the afternoon to put my show together. Record promotion people. They worked for the music companies and their only job was to make friends with the popular air personalities and get their music played on the air. If you didn't have an audience or your show didn't mean anything you never saw promotion people.

They had an uncanny sense of what was happening. Radio stations subscribe to rating services. The ratings show the size of the audiences and the relative popularity of the stations and their personalities. Our jobs on the air always depended on ratings. The promotion people never needed ratings. They already knew what was happening. They knew who was important, and who the public was listening to, and those were the DJs, the personalities they needed the airplay from. And now they were hanging around me.

Things were different now. I mean different from before the payola purge changed everything. Prior to the senate inquisition disc jockeys pretty much played the music they wanted to. Oh, stations had programming lists of music, but the jocks played their own selections too. That's what got them in trouble. Promotion people whose job was to get airplay did everything they could to get it.

They paid people on the air with money, favors, trips, presents, furnished houses, cars, dinners, TV sets, diamond rings, shares of stock in their companies, lunches, parties, and yes women, sex, and lots of it. Now that all those DJs had been fired things were different right? Wrong!

The promotion people were still there. The record companies still needed airplay and the promotion people still needed their jobs. When I was doing the all night show at WJBK I never heard anything from them. After a few months at WKMH I knew something must be happening. Promotion people were hanging around waiting for me and some of them were ready to offer anything within their means to get records played. Payola was still there. The ones who were involved were just more careful.

One of the music people who was constantly there with a handful of records was a young black man from Detroit. His name was Berry Gordy Jr. Every week there was Berry sitting in the lobby of the station with something new that "was going to be a SMASH". Nobody really paid much attention to him. We all knew he was a good writer. Berry was writing the hit songs for Jackie Wilson among others. Berry's own records though; the ones he produced were not very good. That's just my opinion.

As I said, Berry Gordy Jr. among other things was a good songwriter. Some say that money from the songs he wrote for Jackie Wilson were the real reason that his Motown Empire got started in the first place.

Jackie Wilson was an extremely talented performer. His honey laden tenor voice thrilled millions both black and white. But he was a tragic figure as well. It was the well-known story of crooked management; mob controlled handlers, drugs, booze, and women. Lots of women.

When Jackie made up his mind to be a solo act he was involved with Al Green, manager of Della Reese, Lavern "Tweedly Dee" Baker, and others. Green made a deal with Decca records to sign Jackie, but only one day before the signing, Green died. Green's associate and friend was a man by the name of Nat Tarnopol who took over where Green left off and finally signed Jackie to Decca's subsidiary label, Brunswick.

Then came the hits. Reet Petite, Lonely Teardrops, and more. Many of them written by young Berry Gordy Jr. Meanwhile Tarnopol talked Decca bosses into believing he could bring more artists of Jackie's caliber to Brunswick and was given fifty percent ownership of the label in return. Jackie was busy with more than singing. Harlean Harris a stunning fashion model and Jackie became an item. They were together and everyone knew it. At the same time Jackie was romancing Harlean, he was seeing another woman, Juanita Jones.

February 15, 1961. Jackie and Harlean arrived very late together at Jackie's New York apartment. Juanita was there. Waiting with a gun. She shot him twice. Jackie, now seriously wounded, grabbed the gun and stumbled downstairs to the street into the arms of a policeman who rushed him to a nearby hospital. Although he survived, he lost a kidney. The second bullet, lodged near his spine could not be removed. He carried it the rest of his life. Jones was never charged.

The rest of his stormy career is legend and tarnished. Drinking, coke, uppers, coupled with paranoia overtook Jackie Wilson. All the while his managers and handlers were pilfering his earnings and keeping him broke. At one point he became a recluse. Staying in his apartment for weeks, not getting dressed. Drinking day and night.

In 1970, after a fight with neighbors, Jackie's eldest son, 16 year old Jackie Jr., was shot dead. In the end, Jackie was able to free himself of the shackles of Nat Tarnopol, but not soon enough. His life, professionally and personally was one tragedy after another.

Once, in 1960 the promo man from Brunswick, Jackie's music label, invited me to be his guest to see Jackie perform at the Flame Showbar in downtown Detroit. The Flame was a famous watering hole for the very hip in town, but a mob handout as well. Jackie Wilson at the Flame was like having Sinatra at the Sands. Total dynamite. I went.

Not only was the place jammed with the rich and famous and not so, but the traffic outside was a parking lot. So many cars that their lights turned day into night for blocks. Small crowds of people gathered at the curb, under the streetlight posts, all dressed to the nines. Hey this was Jackie's town and Jackie was here. You had be somebody to get in too. Not just anybody. Somebody had to know you or forget it.

I was with the Brunswick record people so we skated past the 250 pound giant trolls in shiny mohair suits who were guarding the front door and were ushered to a large ringside table. The club was very glitzy, white table cloths with tiny glowing lamps that looked like candles, low light from above, waiters dressed like they should be, a fabulous stage filled with band instruments looking down on a dance floor waxed so well that when you looked down you could see your whole body looking back.

I won't take the time to describe the show except to say that Jackie Wilson was electrifying. Surrounded by two-dozen black and white showgirls and backup singers, his voice, his moves, his eyes, his way absolutely incited the audience and grown women both back and white were screaming, laughing, and crying all at the same time. Lonely Teardrops, Reet Petite, To Be loved, one after another all Jackie's songs and all written by Berry Gordy Jr.

Sitting at the same table with me that night, were some of the major movers in the music business. Their names have faded and mean nothing to anyone now, but then they were royalty. Among them was Nat Tarnapol, Jackie Wilson's manager and thief. Out of his earshot he was known as Nat "The Rat" Tarnapol. Mob controlled and out for one thing…himself.

When the show finished to thunderous applause they asked me if I wanted to go back stage and see Jackie. I had met him a number of times before but always at the station or lunch, never here in his own element where he was king. Backstage we went. I can see it to this day.

They were all naked. All those girls on the stage with Jackie? All naked now. All changing clothes, removing makeup, mingling with backstage visitors and oblivious to some of us who were staring. If that wasn't enough some of them were in various states of greeting their men friends. And some of those friends were getting naked too! What I saw that night would compete with any porn site on the Internet. Except for a small towel Jackie Wilson was also naked. "Lee. Hey Baby thanks for coming. How was it Lee? How was the show? Saw you down front. Great to see you here. Heard you're playing my records Lee. As always, thanks Baby."

I thanked Jackie Wilson and got out of there. Never went back. The Flame Showbar. It was English for Sodom and Gomorrah.

On September 29, 1975 Jackie Wilson, the voice that had thrilled millions suffered a heart attack while performing at the Latin Casino in Cherry Hill New Jersey. There was brain damage. He was a vegetable for almost nine years until he died on January 21, 1984 at the age of 49.

Nat "The Rat" Tarnapol ended up owning the record company and all the money.

Fifteen hundred people attended the funeral. Jackie Wilson was buried a pauper in an unmarked grave in Detroit. Later a headstone was donated by Frank Sinatra in honor of Jackie's memory.

Berry Gordy Jr. wrote nine hits for Jackie Wilson and from what I know that gave him the seed money for Motown. That's what convinced him to start it all. A music explosion that would be heard and recognized around the world.

Chapter 19
GORDY

ONE DAY BERRY GORDY JR. SHOWED UP AT THE STATION with his usual armload of records. I liked to think that all these guys were there to see me, but the one they really were after was Robin Seymor. Robin was still the biggest man in town and when he played a song on the air, if it had any chance of being a hit, it happened. Everyone listened to Robin. Well, on this day Robin wasn't around and Berry Gordy gave me his pitch on his records, thanked me and left.

    I threw them on the pile of other records I had received for the week. Understand that every week there could be hundreds of new single records. All represented by someone in the music business. They were promotional copies provided at no charge to all of us. "Not for sale" copies. It was impossible to listen to them all.

    I have often thought what kind of a collection I would have if I had kept just one copy of each. Not only single records, but LPs. Remember LPs? They were free too. Thousands upon thousands of them over the years.

    Later that week I was working at my desk, preparing for my show and listening to new releases when one of Berry Gordy's records caught my attention.

The introduction to the song was just the group singing by themselves with no band or instrumental accompaniment underneath. Except for that part I thought the rest of it was the best I had ever heard from Berry Gordy.

I called and told him the intro needed some strings or horns or something. Three days later he brought me a new version. Same record, except now there were saxophones under the group at the beginning. I played it on the air. Then the whole station started playing it. There was a call from Berry.

"Lee, don't play that record anymore", he said. That same group had recorded for another record label in Chicago that was now releasing some of their old songs. Berry was afraid his new record would get lost and die.

I refused to take it off the air. So did everyone else. It didn't die. It started Berry Gordy Jr. on his meteoric rise. The group was The Miracles. The song was Shop Around.

Chapter 20
SOCK HOPS & TEEN DANCES

IN THE LATE 50S AND EARLY 60S THE BIG THING TO DO ON THE WEEKENDS was going to record hops. Today they remember them as "Sock Hops". Back then I never even heard the term. They were called record hops. And they were everywhere every weekend. Grade schools, high schools, dance clubs, special dances. They were not concerts, shows, or sock hops. It's got to sound bizarre now to today's generation right? "Hops". What pictures does that conjure up? People hopping around. Bouncing up and down. What kind of brainless fun would that be?

I don't know why we called them record HOPS, but that's what they were. Understand that even though the public thought all of us on the air were millionaires, the fact is there were only a very few making enough to survive. The rest had to have another way to earn more money. That was the reason so many got caught in the payola purge. Stations not paying anything. Using the glamour of being on the air and the local celebrity it brought as their excuse not to pay enough. DJs just found other ways. One of them was the Record Hop.

If a school was going to have a Hop, someone would call the

station and book a DJ to do run it for them. The DJs had all the latest records, would line up a local band to play, and would actually come to the school and MC the whole thing. There were dozens of them every weekend. More. And here's where the music business came in.

Recording artists were always on promotional tours to promote their records. The Promo guys in town needed to get airplay so those artists, big and small were brought around to all the Record Hops at no charge to anyone! And they all came. Think of it. A small school dance might have The Supremes, Temptations, Stevie Wonder, Rolling Stones, and others appearing at their "Hop". No charge. The acts were brought to dance and most times would "lip Synch" their records. You know what that means right? The DJ would play the record and the artist would just mouth the words. If the sound system was good it looked and sounded great.

All the DJs were doing them for the extra money. The amount they made depended on how big their name was. Someone like Robin Seymor would get more than someone doing the all night show somewhere. It ran anywhere from a hundred to four or five hundred dollars a night. Very big money in those days. Two of those a week plus your radio station salary and things were smooth.

I never did many record hops. Couldn't. I was on the air at night. But there were opportunities.

Once in late 1960 I was approached by three policemen from Redford Township, Michigan. They had been holding Record Hops at the local UAW 182 Union Hall. They were planning something bigger and wanted me to promote it on the air and MC the event. I said no. They kept after me. I decided to give them a price they would absolutely refuse. "Six hundred dollars", I said. They agreed. "Six Hundred it is".

The dance was to be held at the Riverside Roller Arena in Plymouth Michigan in a few weeks and they wanted to know could

I get a night off from the station and do it? I needed the six hundred and besides I had never done this before. I agreed. Instead of paying me more money the station had already agreed to allow me a little slack now and then. I did the dance.

Riverside Arena could hold about three thousand people for a dance. I promoted it for about three weeks. I said it was a big dance, there would be bands etc., and of course I would be there in person. Understand now that I had never appeared at any of these things.
Never.

I mean I had been on the air at WJBK and now WKMH for a couple of years, but I was not a household name. I was a crazy man on the air to be sure. Blowing horns, throwing things at the studio walls, breaking records on the air. Turning the turntables off, letting them freewheel and slowly run down until they sounded like a low growl on the air. Pulling needles across records. All wild and nuts! The ratings were showing that I was beating WXYZ Radio. That was the big station, but I thought sure that was a fluke.

The dance started at 7PM on a Saturday night. There were no special big name acts in town so it was going to be some local bands and records, and me. That's it. I convinced the three police to hire another guy to actually spin the records so I could to my act without having to stand there and physically play the music. The record spinner was a friend of mine who also worked at the station. He started at 7PM when the place opened. I arrived at 7:30 and couldn't believe my eyes.

First off, I couldn't get any closer to Riverside than about two blocks. Traffic was backed up everywhere. Stopped. The people knew they weren't going anywhere so they were all standing outside their cars in the middle of the streets laughing, talking, and waiting for a miracle to clear the way. I parked where I could and schlepped my way to the dance. People were lined up 8 deep trying to get in. Inside the first thing I saw was a total mob. A sea of people trying to dance but when one moved they all had to move the same way. They were stacked next to each other like dominoes. If one falls they all go. Standing next to the door was a man in uniform. His shirt said: "Fire Marshall". I wanted nothing to do with that so I worked my way around the edge of the floor to the stage. The music was loud and despite the crush everyone was having a ball. Literally!

Pretty soon I was recognized by one and then all. There were loud screams and applause. As I got up on the makeshift stage people were yelling; "LEE – LEE – LEE – LEE". "Hey Lee, where's your Horn. Hey Lee". You couldn't hear the music anymore, just the people. I soon realized that all this commotion was for me. And that was the first time I ever looked into their eyes. My listener's eyes.

I had never seen more than one or two of them at a time. In a store, on the street somewhere. Never like this. They weren't just yelling. There was love in that room. I could feel it and I could see it. They hugged me, shook my hand, wanted me to say some of the things that I'd been saying on the air. They hung on every word. Where did all these people come from and why were they so excited about seeing me? That night I realized the power of radio and what happens when you love your audience and they know it. And I did love them, then and now.

The night was a blur. First thing I knew the dance was over. I played the last song, a slow dance so they could all hold each other and let it end. Before they left I was mobbed. Nicely mobbed. Hugged, patted on the back, touched. It was new and thrilling to me.

I went to the office where the police promoters were counting money and talking. When I entered the little room there were about 12 people there. "Hey Lee, how'd it go?", said a burley guy seated at the only desk in the room. The others were sitting on kitchen type chairs just laughing and talking. It was obvious to me that everyone was happy with the turnout. "Fantastic Lee, we had a full house. Great show Lee".

I didn't know a soul in the room except for the policeman with the money and now no one was talking to me, not even acknowledging my presence. I guessed that the others were police too. There was something strange going on here. For the last three hours hundreds of people were lined up just to talk with me. In this room, except for the big guy behind the desk I could have been invisible. Next to the big guy were neat stacks of money from the night's box office and a large gun.

I thought the gun was because of all the money. I said, "OK. Everything was good and thank you very much." And he gave me $100. "A hundred dollars? Our deal was $600! What's going on here?" I said. He put his hand on that gun and said, "You better take the hundred and leave. These guys here will help you to your car. Wouldn't want anyone to take it away from you." He kept his hand on the gun and just let it move toward him a little. I decided that I had no friends in this room and left. Fast.

That dance and those hoodlums disguised as legitimate police would come back to haunt me.

Fabian

Fabian caused total chaos when he appeared with me at Walled Lake Casino and on Club 1270. Thousands crammed the Casino and they were all in hysterics. He sang:

"Turn Me Loose. Turn me loose I say...."

But the crowd was so frenzied no one heard him.

The next time I saw him was thirty five years later I was in Birmingham, Michigan a central point of the Woodward Cruise that draws nearly two million people. In front of a theater there was a large crowd of young to middle aged girls around a red convertible. When I approached to see what was such a big deal about the red car I saw that it wasn't the car at all. Seated behind the wheel was Fabian himself signing autographs and being ogled, touched, and hugged. In all those years nothing had changed.

I made my way through the throng and said:

"Hey, you still look the same".

Fabian looked at me for a moment and said:

"Lee Alan – you don't look the same at all – you look younger"!

Now you know why I love Fabian? Ha! He always tells the truth!

Chapter 21
MICHAEL

ED HARDY WAS A HULK OF A MAN IN HIS EARLY THIRTIES and the news director of WKMH. Another young radio newsman on his staff was Tom McIntyre; a strong willed journalist who was serious about his work, but always had a terrific sense of humor. Within two years all three of us ended up best of friends working at WXYZ.

Before then one afternoon a week or so before Christmas at WKMH the three of us were sitting around in the office talking about nothing as usual when I happened to ask if either one of them had an idea of what I could do on the air for Christmas eve. I always read the true story of Christmas, but I was looking for something to add. Without hesitation Ed reached into a worn brief case, pulled out an envelope and said: "Here, if you want a reaction read this!." "What is it?" I asked Ed.

"Lee, when I was in the Marines I was stationed at the San Diego Naval Base. One Christmas a Navy Chaplain read this to 5,000 Marines. Look it over"

Ed went on to explain that he was assigned to a Special Forces unit that was responsible for handling events like these and broadcasting them on the Armed Forces Radio Network. In the envelope was a copy of a letter written by a young Marine home to his mother. The Marine, named Michael was hospitalized in San Diego after being wounded in Korea. He had given a copy to the Navy Chaplain who in turn contacted all the members of the boy's patrol who were with him that day and also the Sergeant in charge. In the letter Michael tells his mother what happened to him on that lonely, frozen battlefield. I was so impressed with Michael's letter that I read it on the air that Christmas Eve. Today, the Sergeant and the patrol members themselves will all tell you that this is a true story.

After reading it on the air I had a thousand or more requests for copies within four days. That was the first year. Since then I have read it on some radio or television station every year during the Christmas season. Literally hundreds of thousands have asked for a copy. Millions have heard it.

About six months before writing this book I finally recorded my own reading of the letter and have now released it as a CD version, just the way it was heard on the radio.

I simply read the letter at Christmas time and let it stand on its own. For the first time I have printed the letter word for word here for you to read and keep. Oh yes, Michael, the sergeant in charge of the patrol, and the patrol members themselves are real people. As I write this chapter, Michael himself still lives.

You be the judge. Here it is. The story is the letter. A copy of the original. As written to his mother from a hospital bed.
A Letter From Michael:

Dear Mom:
I wouldn't dare write this letter to anyone but you, because no one else would believe it. Maybe even you'll find it hard, but I've got to tell somebody. First off I'm in the hospital. Now don't worry you hear me? Don't worry. I was wounded but I'm OK

you understand? OK! The doctor says I'll be up and around in a month. But that isn't what I want to tell you.

Remember when I joined the Marines last year? Remember when I left how you told me about Michael The Archangel? You really didn't have to tell me that. Ever since I can remember you always told me that poem about Michael, the Archangel. When I got to Korea I started saying it. Remember the poem you taught me?
"Michael, Michael of the morning fresh court of Heaven adorning."
You know the rest of it. Well I said every day. Sometimes while I was marching, sometimes resting, but always before I went to sleep. I even got some of the other fellas to say it.

Well, one day I was with an advance detail way up forward of the front lines. We were scouting for the Commies. I was plodding along in the bitter cold. My breath was like cigar smoke. I thought I knew every guy in the patrol when along side of me comes another marine I'd never met before. He was bigger than any marine I'd ever seen. He must have been 6 foot four and built in proportion. It gave me a feeling of security just to have such a buddy near.
Anyway, thee we were, trudging along. Just to start a conversation I said: "Cold ain't it." And then I laughed. Here I was with a good chance of getting killed any minute and I was talking about the weather. My companion seemed to understand. I heard him laugh softly. I looked at him.
"I've never seen you before. I thought I knew every guy in the outfit."
"I just joined at the last minute." *He replied.* "The name's Michael."

"Is that so." I said surprised. "That's my name too."
"I know." he said. And then went on..."Michael. Michael of the morning...."
I was too amazed to say anything for a minute. How did he know my name and the prayer that you taught me? Then I smiled to myself." Every guy in the outfit knew about me. Hadn't I taught the poem to anyone who'd listen? Why now and then they even called me St. Michael..

Neither of us spoke for a time. Then he broke the silence.
"We're gonna have some trouble up ahead!"
He must have been in fine physical shape for he was breathing so lightly I could hardly see his breath. Mine poured out in great clouds.
There was no smile on his face now. Trouble ahead I thought to myself. Well with the Commies all around us, that's no great revelation.

Snow began to fall in great thick globs. In a brief moment the whole countryside was blotted out and I was marching in a white fog of wet sticky particles..
My companion disappeared.
"MICHAEL!!", I shouted in sudden alarm.
I felt his hand on my arm. His voice was rich and strong.
"This will stop shortly."
His prophesy proved to be correct. In a few minutes the snow stopped as abruptly as it had begun. The sun was a hard shining disc. I looked back for the rest of the patrol. There was no one in sight. We lost them in that heavy fall of snow. I looked up as we came over a little rise. Mom, my heart stopped.
There were seven of 'em. Seven Commies in their padded pants and jackets and funny little hats. Only there wasn't anything

funny about 'em now. Seven rifles were aimed at us.

"DOWN MICHAEL!" I screamed and hit the frozen earth.

I heard those rifles fire almost as one. I heard the bullets. But there was Michael. Still standing. Mom, those guys couldn't have missed! Not at that range. I expected to see him literally blown to bits. But there he stood, making no effort to fire himself. He was paralyzed with fear. It happens sometimes Mom, even to the bravest.

He was like a bird fascinated by a snake. At least that's what I thought then. I jumped up to pull him down. And that's when I got mine. I felt a sudden flame in my chest. I often wondered what it was like to be hit. Now...I know.

I remember feeling strong arms about me. Arms that laid me ever so gently on a pillow of snow.

I was dying! Maybe I was even dead! I remember thinking: "Well, this isn't so bad."

Maybe I was looking into the sun. Maybe I was in shock. But it seemed I saw Michael standing erect again. Only this time his face was shining with a terrible splendor.

As I say, maybe it was the sun in my eyes, but he seemed to change as I watched him. He grew bigger. His arms stretched out wide.

Maybe it was the snow falling again, but there was brightness around him like the wings of an angel. In his hand was a sword. A sword that flashed with a million lights.

Well, that's the last thing I remember 'till the rest of the fellas came up and found me. I don't know how much time had passed. Now and then I had a moment's respite from the pain and fever. I remember telling them of the enemy just ahead.

"Where's Michael?" I asked. I saw them look at one another.

"Where's who?" asked one.

"Michael. Michael, that big marine I was walking with just

before the snow squall hit us."

"Kid," said the sergeant. "You weren't walking with anyone. I had my eye on you the whole time. You were getting too far out. I was just going to call you in when you disappeared in the snow. "

He looked at me curiously.
"How'd you do it kid?"
"How'd I do what?" I asked, half angry despite my wound. "This big marine named Michael and I were just..."
"Son", said the sergeant kindly " I picked this outfit myself and there just ain't another Michael in it. You're the only Mike in it." He paused for a moment. "Just how'd you do it kid?
We heard shots. There hasn't been a shot fired from your rifle. And there isn't a bit of lead in them seven bodies over the hill there!"
I couldn't say anything. What could I say? I could only look, open mouthed with amazement. It was then the sergeant spoke again.
"Kid", he said gently.
"Every one of them seven Commies over the hill there was killed....
by a sword stroke!"
As I say it may have been the sun in my eyes or the cold or the pain, but that's what happened.
Love,
Michael

Wherever I go people ask me about the Michael Story, a simple letter written by a young marine home to his mother. I have read it on radio and television for over forty years. As I said it was given to me in 1960 by my dear friend, ex marine and news director at WABC radio in New York Ed hardy. Every year wherever he was in the world at Christmas time Ed would always call me to talk about the Michael story.

A few years ago the calls stopped. Tom McIntyre whom I have mentioned a number of times in this book, called me to say that Ed had died somewhere in Oklahoma while serving as press secretary to the governor there.

Ed believed Michaels letter.

I believe Michael's letter.

I have often wondered what I will say to Michael, the Archangel when I meet him in heaven face to face.

Before I say anything at all I'll guess I'll just ask Ed about that.

He got there first.

Ann Margaret

In 1961 I PROMOTED A SHOW AT Detroit's Light Guard Armory. One of the visiting stars that week was Ann Margaret. The 19-year-old Swedish born drop dead gorgeous beauty had already been a star in television's "77 Sunset Strip for over two years when she hit Detroit. She was here on a promotional tour and most of the cast was with her including Roger Smith, her future husband.

When she walked out on the stage in front of about 2,000 teenagers I was literally unable to speak. I had seen her on television yes and she was attractive, even beautiful, but in person she was indescribable. I had never seen a woman with that personal charisma and aura.

She didn't say a word!

She didn't sing!

She just stood there in the most sexy and alluring way before a stunned audience and me. I admit I was staring.

Then without warning she walked toward me, put her arms around me, came as close as two people can get to each other, put her arms and everything else around me and kissed me.

The audience reacted by tossing pennies on the stage. Hundreds of pennies. I have never seen an audience react like that. Never before, never since.

I met Ann one more time about twenty years later while in Las Vegas. She didn't remember me. Until I mentioned the pennies that is.

Ha! I got another kiss.

Oh yes, that first kiss? I felt it for a month…

Chapter 22
MOREY'S

MY TIME AT WKMH WAS PASSING QUICKLY. I was learning, meeting new people, it was fun, the show was becoming more defined, crazier, funnier, serious, romantic, and I could feel the audience growing. I was still broke.

One day as I was getting ready to go on I read about a new nightclub in New York named after a hit song by Joey Dee and the Starlighters. The song was, "The Peppermint Twist." The club was, the Peppermint Lounge. Joey Dee was playing there. It was the biggest thing in New York. I had an idea.

Not far from the radio station there was an old part of town on a major street lined with bars and restaurants. I took a night off and went there. Friday night in the city that was becoming known as Motown, home of the Detroit sound, the Rock N Roll capital of the world and there was no one home. These places were deserted. I went from bar to bar, restaurant to restaurant. Only a few people in every one. Far cry from New York I thought.

It was about 11 o'clock when I walked into Morey's Bar. Pretty run down. Needed paint. I had to look closely to see the name. Light bulbs in the sign were burned out. From a distance it looked like M_REY's B_R. "Who owns this place?", I asked the bartender. "I do, but not for much longer". "Name's Lee Alan", I said. "That so? Mine's Joe. Yeah I listened to you before", he said. "Aren't you the one with that crazy Horn?" Morey's Bar was almost surreal, a picture right out of a Frank Sinatra song, a lonely saloon that had seen better days. One guy playing clinkers on an old piano. A place waiting to die. "No people anymore", Joe said. "There could be", I told him. "There could be."

I told Joe about the Peppermint lounge in New York, and how I thought it could happen here. "In this old place? No way." He said. But I kept after him. " Put table cloths on the tables, hang a thousand LP covers on the wall, keep the drink prices low, and hire a band."

"Hire a band?", he said. "I can't even afford to pay the rent. A band?". "Not just any band Joe. There's a great band called The Royaltones. Hire them. And oh yes, change the name of this place." "Change the name?" Joe was laughing now. He thought this was all a joke. Here he was going broke with four customers on a Friday night and I was telling him to fix up, paint up, decorate, and hire a band.

"The Twist ", I said. "Joe, do what I tell you and this will be the most popular "in" place in town. Change the name to "MOREY'S ROYAL TWIST LOUNGE"

"What do you get out of this", he asked. "A dollar at the door", I replied. It was then he nearly fell on the floor laughing. "People paying to get in? You're outa your skull." I finally convinced Joe that he had nothing to lose. I would do the advertising on the radio, he would handle the place, and my brother in law would occupy the little ticket both and I would get one-dollar admission. It was a deal.

Joe did what I asked him, hired the Royaltones, I did the advertising along with Dave Prince, a colleague of mine and a month later it happened. Detroit's first and only Twist Club.

At one time it had obviously been a beautiful nightclub. Not now. Inside the entrance door to the right was a window in the wall with a slot at the bottom like a theater ticket window where they must've taken the cover charge. Opening the inside door revealed a large room with about a 150 or so tables. Beat up tables with four bad chairs at each one. Tables were empty. To the right was a bar. A long old fashioned bar with what looked like an antique top that could seat maybe 75 people.

Beyond all of that was an empty dance floor gleaming in a low light and a stage big enough for 10 or 15 performers or a small band.

There was a piano there. An old man was playing. There were four people sitting at the bar, no one else. I sat down and looked at the place again. This was perfect I thought. If we do this right it could be the biggest thing in town.

Opening night was about 10 degrees and snowing. The lines of people stretched around the entire block and into the parking lots. All adults over 21 years old. My brother in law was inside the ticket window taking a gladly paid dollar for every person. We could've charged ten dollars that night. Morey's was transformed. Bleached white tablecloths on every table covering up the past, refinished chairs, LP covers all over the walls with pictures of popular artists including Joey Dee, Chubby Checker, Sinatra, Mathis, hundreds more. George Kay and his fabulous Royaltones had been hired and were all set up waiting to go. The air was electric. Joe, who didn't believe that this was going to work was behind the bar going crazy because he didn't hire enough bartenders.

Morey's Royal Twist Lounge was a phenomenon. The twist was big and now Detroit had it. Wednesday through Saturday night and to get in you had to know somebody or stand in line outside. Always jammed. Always exciting. It lasted for months until Joe decided to raise prices and until he decided he no longer needed me.

I don't really remember how the whole Morey's thing ended for me, but it became not fun and like all owners who don't know about marketing Joe took over and it died. This time for good. Morey's became an old bar again and the Royaltones moved on.

Chapter 23
TROUBLE

THE STATION I ALWAYS WANTED TO WORK FOR WAS WXYZ. Everybody wanted to work there. That was the big station. The station that in earlier days had originated the Lone Ranger, Green Hornet, Challenge of the Yukon and now had the best and highest rated and highest paid people on the air. WXYZ was owned by the ABC network and along with WXYZ-TV was located in Broadcast House a new state of the art facility in Southfield, Michigan.

WXYZ was number one all day. On the air in the morning was Fred Wolf, a professional bowler turned radio and TV personality. Fred was the most popular guy on the air in morning radio. Down to earth, simple approach, loved what he was doing, and a voice so distinctive no one could mistake it for anyone else. I can still hear him" "GIT IT OUTA BED"!!, he'd say. He called his morning coffee "Swamp Water". He was the first one ever to do a remote broadcast. Wasn't far though. Just out to the front porch of the station. Fred was also on television. He was MC for wrestling, the Gold Cup Hydroplane Races on the river, and his own network program, Championship Bowling. Everybody there was on television. What an opportunity it would be.

Following Fred Wolf was Marty McNealey, formerly the morning drive time personality at WJR, a 50,000 watt clear channel station in Detroit. The station I had been singing on as a kid years before.

Paul Winter a Doctor of Philosophy with precise pronunciation and a honey smooth voice was on in the afternoon.

At night opposite my show on WKMH was Joel Sebastian, a tall, blonde, handsome, native of Detroit who could mesmerize anyone with his deep voice and a sort of cute and sweet way he had about him.

All night was Don Zee, the perfect all night air personality. They called him the Zombie and he was an all night awake guy with a fun way about him and a very wry sense of humor. On the weekends was Fred Wiess, a silver haired gentleman announcer with a golden voice and a heart to match.

I had always dreamed of working at WXYZ. Fat chance though. With that lineup of professionals, and each number one in their time slots. They were the New York Yankees of radio. Well, I always have been a dreamer.

One afternoon out of pure frustration with my financial situation and the new management at WKMH I picked up the phone and called John O. Gilbert, WXYZ Radio Vice President and General Manager. After the operator answered and I asked for Mr. Gilbert I thought how stupid I was for doing this. Calling the GM of WXYZ? Why GMs all have secretaries didn't they? Guards who stop people like me from even getting through. I hadn't given anyone my name yet and was just thinking about hanging up when a voice came on the phone and said: "Hello, this is John Gilbert".

I nearly swallowed my tongue. "Hello", he said again. Quickly I said hello and told him it was Lee Alan calling. Realizing that he wouldn't know me from any other thousand people I was about to explain when he said: "Lee, nice to hear from you. What's up?" Huh? He knew me! Well, I stammered that I was working at WKMH and well, I was wondering if there was a time when I could maybe come over and...Gilbert interrupted, "Lee, we just brought Joel Sebastian over from Chicago and I am so blessed with this line-up I don't have anything open right now but keep in touch, OK? I said OK and we both said goodbye. Unbelievable. I actually got through and talked with the GM of WXYZ!

The owner of WKMH radio Fred Knorr, the man who believed in me, took a chance and hired me, died suddenly at his Florida home. Scalded himself to death in the bathtub.

Morey's was over.

I didn't get along with Frank Maruca, the new program director or the new Vice President, Walter Patterson. They wouldn't pay any more money and frankly they didn't like me and didn't want me there. I was at a dangerous point too because I started thinking I knew more about radio than they did. So there I was on the air playing what in those days was rock music, and what today we call oldies. At midnight WKMH turned into a jazz station.

Jim Rockwell was the all night personality and broadcast from a studio in the Sheraton Cadillac Hotel in downtown Detroit. WKMH was licensed as a Dearborn radio station and maintained studios in the Sheraton for the soul purpose of being able to identify itself as a Detroit Station. It was more important sounding with "Detroit" in the station identification and better sounding when selling to advertisers. The FCC required that a station properly identify itself with its call letters and location at certain times twice an hour. The proper identification for this station was: WKMH AM & FM, DEARBORN. Well that didn't sound very impressive so with the studios in downtown Detroit we were ordered to use the following ID and when we said DEARBORN we were always told to say it quietly. Like this: WKMH AM & FM Dearborn : WITH STUDIOS IN THE SHERATON CADILLAC HOTEL DETROIT.

Sounds a little silly now, but then it was orders.

So, there was Jim Rockwell the greatest expert on the subject of jazz music I have ever known alone in very cool atmosphere in the Sheraton Hotel downtown. Each night when I ended my show, Jim would do the news at midnight and take it on an all night ride from there. His audience was mammoth and loyal.

One night not long after I started at the station instead of playing the normal Rock Music all the way to midnight I started the half hour at eleven thirty by playing Frank Sinatra. Let's look back at the year for a minute.

The most popular songs being played on the air were: El Paso by Marty Robbins, The Big Hurt – Toni Fisher, Mack The Knife & Beyond The Sea – Bobby Darin, Theme From A summer Place – Percy Faith, Cathy's Clown – Everly Brothers, Alley –OOP – Hollywood Argyles (How 'Bout That One!), and so on.

There was no Frank Sinatra anywhere. So, I started playing Sinatra. Not the big beat hip swingin' Sinatra, but the soft meaningful torch songs. Sinatra with Nelson Riddle and his Orchestra, Sinatra singing the music and lyrics of Cole Porter, Berlin, Jimmy Van Heusen and Sammy Cahn. I played the music with lyrics and feelings of the love thoughts and life experiences we've all had but don't know how to express. "I Only Miss Her When I think Of Her", "Just Friends – Lovers No More", "What's New…How Is The World Treating You".

Frank Sinatra every night for a full half hour ending what was a wild rock radio show. Eleven thirty to Midnight every night. " I took a trip on a train – And I thought about you", "Where Or When", "A Cottage For Sale", "None But The Lonely Heart". Most all were soft, very deep, very sad, very dark. No one ever sang them like Sinatra. Another went:

I'm sentimental so I walk in the rain

I've got some habits even I can't explain
Could start for the corner, turn up in Spain
Why try to change me now....
So let people wonder, let 'em laugh, let 'em frown
You know I love you till the world's upside down
Don't you remember I was always your clown
Why try to change me now...

And then one night not long after I joined WKMH I played a song that people ask about to this day. Everyone asks! Wherever I go the second most asked question is about that song and why I played it.

Nelson Riddle and strings that cried with emotion and Sinatra singing. I always started it talking over the quiet instrumental introduction by referring to the number of days I had been back on Detroit Radio counting from the day I was fired by WJBK. Like this:

IT HAS BEEN EXACTLY 120 DAYS NOW
THAT I HAVE BEEN BACK ON DETROIT RADIO
AND SOMEHOW …….I'M STILL A GLUM ONE…

Sinatra: I'm A Glum One
                  It's Explainable
                  I Met Someone
                  Unattainable,
                  Life's A Bore
                  The World Is My Oyster No More

As I played the song I spoke the words a split second before he sang them and then over an instrumental interlude I said:

"I'VE FLOWN AROUND THE WORLD IN A PLANE
DESIGNED THE LATEST IBM BRAIN

>   WITH QUEENS I'VE A LA CARTED
>   BUT SOMEHOW, I CAN'T GET STARTED WITH YOU."

The song finished with Sinatra Singing:
>   And with Queens I've A La Carted
>   But I Can't Get Started
>   With You.......

Then I always said:
>   IF TONIGHT I HAVE SAID OR DONE ANYTHING
>   THAT OFFENDED ANYONE IN ANY WAY
>   IT WAS UNINTENTIONAL.
>   IF I HAVE SAID OR DONE ANYTHING
>   THAT MADE YOU LAUGH,
>   MADE YOU CRY,
>   MADE YOU SAD OR MAD, EVEN AT ME
>   THEN FOR THAT BRIEF PERIOD OF TIME
>   YOU FORGOT ABOUT YOUR PROBLEMS
>   AND THAT WAS INTENTIONAL
>   AND I WILL TRY…AGAIN TOMORROW NIGHT.
>
>   WATCH HOW YOU DRIVE THAT AUTOMOBILE NOW
>   AND DON'T YOU DARE
>   TURN IT INTO A COUPLE OF TONS OF DEADLY
>   WEAPON
>   AND STAY TUNED NOW FOR JIM ROCKWELL
>   AND ALL THAT JAZZ

Sinatra would repeat:
>   And with Queens I've A La Carted
>   But I Can't Get Started
>   With You.......

And I always ended saying:
>   LEE ALAN

LOVE YOU
YOU'RE BEAUTIFUL
GOODNIGHT

That ending made a bigger and longer lasting impression on hundreds of thousands of people than any ending of any radio program in Detroit history that I know of! I say that not out of ego, but just fact. To this day as I write to you more than 40 years after I first played it a dozen people a day ask me about that song and why I played it. Especially why I played it!

I have never revealed the reason. I don't intend to

Again, Fred Knorr was gone, Maruca and Patterson refused to pay any more money, and my big mouth telling them they were all wrong with their programming ideas didn't help. Morey's was over and so was I. Fired again and no job hopes in sight.

Dwight Eisenhower

I met President Eisenhower at the Detroit Auto show in 1960. I was broadcasting on remote from there on WKMH radio. For those familiar with Detroit, the auto show that year was at the Detroit Artillery Armory on 8 Mile Road. Yes the same, as Eminem's 8 Mile Road.

The President appeared with his entourage and walked directly toward my broadcast booth within two feet of me and smiled that famous smile. This great military General, Supreme Commander of the Allied Forces in WWII, and of the invasion of Normandy, D-Day was now in his last days of his second term as President of the United States.

My impression? I expected this historical giant to be exactly that. A giant in size and stature. He wasn't. He was only 5'10". He appeared short.

When we shook hands he looked directly at me.

He had the bluest eyes I had ever seen.

And he smiled. The smile was like the sun and bigger than his face.

All these years his slogan was:

I LIKE IKE Now I knew why.

Chapter 24
THE JOURNEY BEGINS

THIS TIME THERE WAS NO QUICK FIX. I was married to Patti, had a two-year-old daughter Dawne, a house payment, and no job. There were only eight stations in town that counted and I had already used four of them up. Two of them, WJR and WWJ were older style straight radio stations with no future for me, WXYZ was not a possibility, and the other one CKLW was Canadian and couldn't hire any more Americans.

    Just when I was considering going back to school and getting some kind of job, any job to bring some money in there was a phone call. The voice on the other end of the line identified himself as the program director of WCPO radio in Cincinnati. There was an opening there in the morning drive time. Would I be interested and if so would I please send him an audition tape? How did he know my name and phone number? For the moment I didn't care. I needed work and it looked like I'd never get it in Detroit. At least not now.

    I sent the tape. Only a days or so later he called again. Would I like to work at WCPO? It was just that fast. Too fast. No in person interview, nothing. Two phone conversations and a job offer. Sounded strange to me, but I said yes packed my car to the ceiling and headed out. The station paid for a motel until I could find an apartment and I started on the air.

I was the new "morning man" on WCPO in Cincinnati. It was a big job. Morning drive time anywhere is a big job. The deal was that once I got started and was comfortable I was to have my own television show on their sister station WCPO-TV Channel 9. I had to get up at 4:30 to be on the air at 6AM. I didn't know the town. I didn't know about the people. I didn't even know how to pronounce the street names. It was awkward and uncomfortable. I had no feel for what I was doing. Everything was strange to me. When I went home there was no home. It was a motel room. This was not going to be fun.

It was Friday. I had been on the air in Cincinnati for three days. I was at the motel regretting everything and talking with a friend of mine from Detroit who had also been shipped out of town. Dick Rakovan was a promotion man for DOT records who had been transferred to Buffalo, New York. He was calling me from HIS motel room.

"Are you as lonesome as I am"? I said. "Yeah, tell me all about it", Dick said.

Now before I go on I want you to know that people in the music promotion business knew everything. They knew what was happening in every radio station in America. They knew about every Disc Jockey (I hate that term), how popular they were, what their job status was, and more importantly who was leaving what station and going where. The music promotion network was better than Western Union then or Email on the Internet today.

Dick Rakovan continued: "At least you're going back home", he said. "I'm stuck here in Buffalo". "What're you taking about Dick?" I said. "Cincinnati is not home and I don't like it one bit".

"You don't know about it, do you? Lee, you're going back

to Detroit. You're going to work for ABC radio. WXYZ. At least that's what I heard". I had known Dick for a while and he knew how much I wanted to work for WXYZ. Everyone in this part of the country wanted to work there. WXYZ had their pick of the litter.

"No chance Richard", I said. "I talked with them a couple of months ago. They just brought Joel Sebastian over from Chicago and their lineup is set. I heard it from John Gilbert himself". Dick went on, "OK man, I'm just telling you what I heard. And my sources say that WXYZ is making a move and you're part of it". We laughed a little, talked some more and hung up. Two guys feeling sorry for themselves. At least that's what I thought then.

Lyndon Johnson

March 31, 1968. The Vietnam War was raging. Protests were taking place everywhere in the country. Robert F. Kennedy had announced for the presidency and was running in the primaries. Dr. Martin Luther King Jr. was carrying on his fight for civil rights and equality. The pressure was on President Johnson from every part of this country and the world.

I traveled from Detroit to Chicago and the national Association of Broadcasters convention.

From the Oval office in the White House at 9pm on March 31, 1968 Lyndon Johnson spoke to the nation and said in part:

"With America's sons in the fields far away, with America's future under challenge here at home, with our hopes and the world's hopes for peace in the balance every day, I do not believe that I should devote an hour or a day of my time to any personal partisan causes or to any duties other that the awesome duties of this office – the Presidency of your country.

Accordingly, I shall not seek, and I will not accept, the nomination of my party for another term as your president. But let men everywhere know, however, that a strong, a confident, and a vigilant America stands ready tonight to seek an honorable peace- -and stands ready to defend the cause—whatever the price, whatever the burden, whatever the sacrifice that duty may require."

Goodnight and God Bless All Of You.

The next day, April 1, 1968 as I approached the headquarters hotel of the NAB convention in Chicago I noticed uniformed men with guns on some of the buildings. When I reached the block where the hotel was I was searched by men with suits and little pins in their lapels. I realized then that The President had flown there that morning and was speaking to the convention.

When I reached the hotel entrance it was roped off from the front door to the street on both sides of the walkway leading to a line of long black limousines. I had no choice but to stop and wait.

Within about 15 minutes there was a flurry of activity near the hotel entrance and suddenly there, coming out through the door was Lyndon Baines Johnson, 36th President of the United States.

He paused at the top of the three steps leading to the sidewalk. Only a few months short of his 70th birthday the President looked at least a hundred years old. He was very tall. His color was gray, almost ashen. The lines in his face were embedded. Pronounced. The world was on his case and it showed,

Then he descended the steps, turned left toward the velvet rope on my side of the door. There were a few hundred people there. I was in the front. As if being guided by some unseen force or thought he walked directly to where I was standing, looked down at me, smiled, shook my hand and said: "My name is Lyndon Johnson, what's your's? Are you here for the conventions? I answered yes sir and told him my name."

Without saying anything to anyone else he turned and walked quickly to the waiting limo. They were gone in a few seconds.

Three days later on April 4, 1968 Martin Luther King Jr. was murdered in Memphis.

Two months later on June 4, Robert F. Kennedy was shot by Sirhan B. Sirhan.

He died June 6.

I had seen what war and the Presidency could do to a man.

Chapter 25

THE CALL THAT CHANGED MY LIFE

ABOUT AN HOUR AFTER DICK HUNG UP THE PHONE RANG AGAIN. "Lee, is this Lee Alan?" the voice said. "John Gilbert WXYZ in Detroit. How's the new job Lee?". No way to believe this one. John Gilbert calling me? Got to be a joke going on here.

Huh, Must be Dick or one of his guys in Buffalo. I played along.

"Fine, fine Mr. Gilbert. Just started, but fine so far. How's your new job in Buffalo? Ha!" And then I laughed, and he heard me. "Buffalo?" he said. "Lee, this is John Gilbert in Michigan. Lee are you planning to be in Detroit tomorrow?" This was not a joke! I had only heard his voice once before in my life when I called him from WKMH, but this was the real John Gilbert. I think I was stuttering now.

"No, actually tomorrow I am apartment hunting". "Lee, you don't understand", he said. Are you planning to be back tomorrow and in my office at about 3PM?"

Me in his office? Tomorrow? What did Dick just tell me on the phone? "Lee you're going back to Detroit."

My mind was racing. A call to me in Cincinnati from

WXYZ? How did he know where to call? I'd only been here four days. Nobody knew how to reach me except for Dick Rakovan, my wife, and people at the new station, WCPO. When I came out of my daze I heard Mr. Gilbert on the other end of the line.

"Lee, Lee, are you still there? What about it? Are you coming home tomorrow?" "Yes! Yes Sir, I was planning to be there the whole time. Not looking for any apartments tomorrow. Bad day for apartment hunting, I always come home every weekend". What was I saying? I hadn't even been here for one weekend yet. I was babbling and he knew it. He laughed and said: "Great, Lee. See you tomorrow at 3. You know where my office is?" Was he kidding? Broadcast House! Broadcast House? In my sleep I could find it. "Yes, Mr. Gilbert I think I can find it." I don't remember how the conversation ended. I grabbed some things and started the five-hour drive home.

I never turned the radio on. Not even once. All I did was think.

The nice little house on St. Marys street in northwest Detroit was just big enough for my Mom and Dad and my younger sister Karen. My room upstairs was so small you could hardly turn around in it. Just enough room for my small bed on the right as you entered, a small side table on the left and at the end of the small space a dresser with a fold down desk top and on the dresser was a radio.

On the way back I thought about those days there at home. My Dad who worked so hard to make his industrial clothes manufacturing business a success, but was strapped with an alcoholic partner. Starting with nothing but some ideas and a partner who had a legal background, Dad built it into something large and worthwhile only to have it begin to erode because of his partner's addiction to booze. I can remember as a boy working at Dad's factory in downtown Detroit. The building was located at 743 Beaubien. It's still there just a block or so from Greektown. To get there I had to take a bus to his partner's house and ride with him to work. Many times when I got there breakfast was on the table. A fifth of scotch. That was his partner's breakfast. Dad's business was being destroyed by the boozer but there was no way to buy him out. All Dads' money was tied up in the business. So he approached a supplier. Norman Shulevitz, owner of Cadillac Overall Supply. Shulevitz agreed to buy Dad's 50 percent partner out, but demanded another percent giving Cadillac Overall Supply controlling interest and leaving Dad as president of his company. Dad agreed. Sometime later, at the age of only 56, Dad suffered a minor stroke. His new partners used this as an excuse, declared that he was no longer able to run the company, and forced him out putting this nice man into an extended, deep depression.

I thought about my mom, who in mid life rolled off the bow of my Dad's speedboat catching both hi speed propellers across the chest. She miraculously survived and spent months and months recovering only to be a changed person. She was fun, jovial, and happy before, serious and different afterwards.

And the little radio in my room. It was my window to the world. That's where I first heard WXYZ. As I said earlier, that's where my Lone Ranger came from and The Green Hornet. Sergeant Preston and his dog King. Ha! If you're old enough to remember or know anything about the legend of the Lone Ranger, here's some trivia for you.

Fran Striker created The Lone Ranger. In the very first story a posse of Texas Rangers are ambushed by the Butch Cavandish gang. The Rangers are all killed, except for one. John Reid, whose brother Dan Reid lay dead with the rest, survives. He is discovered by Tonto, a Potowatomi Indian who nurses him back to health. Finally, when John Reid comes out of his coma he asks about his companions. Tonto tells him: "All dead". "My brother Dan, what about my brother?" Reid asks. "Him dead too", Tonto answers.

"All Rangers killed except you. You….. LONE RANGER."

John Reid vows to avenge the tragedy of his murdered brother and companions. To keep outlaws from discovering there is a survivor of their massacre he must disguise himself and dons a black mask. About every other week the story includes The Lone Ranger's nephew, Dan Reid.

Fran Striker, the writer who created The Lone Ranger also wrote The Green Hornet. The Green Hornet, whose real name was Brit Reid, was sort of a modern day Lone Ranger who also wore a mask, also had a sidekick. a Philippino named Kato, and instead of a white stallion, rode in his sleek car named The Black Beauty. Get the similarity? Lone Ranger, Mask, Indian sidekick named Tonto, a fast white stallion named Silver, silver guns with silver bullets, and The Green Hornet, mask, Philippine sidekick, a fast car named The Black Beauty, and a gun that shoots gas, knocking his opponents out, but never killing them.

OK, here's the trivia. How was The Lone Ranger Related to The Green Hornet?

Answer:

The Green Hornet's real name was Brit Reid, son of Dan Reid Jr., Son of Dan Reid Sr., brother of John Reid, the real name of THE LONE RANGER. So, the Lone Ranger is the Green Hornet's great, great uncle!

Is that fun or what? I loved that little radio. My world was in there. My idols and friends were in there. Anyway, sorry I got off the story but I always thought that was so cool.

As I drove back to Michigan I remembered listening during those days. I thought about the legacy of that station and the people who were there now. They were all the best on the air. What could John Gilbert want, and of all people why did he call me?

The next day I drove the 15 minutes from my home to Broadcast House. It had taken me over twenty years to get there.

Chapter 26
THE MEETING

BROADCAST HOUSE, SITUATED ON ABOUT 10 ACRES in Southfield Michigan, housed both WXYZ Radio and WXYZ Television Channel 7. Both were owned and operated by ABC, The American Broadcasting Company.

Set back at least a hundred yards from the road across an immaculate lawn with landscaping to match, Broadcast House was built to look like a Georgian Manor. I was nervous the second I turned into the property and followed the winding driveway around the lawn to the small visitor's parking area in front of the building. The entry way had double doors leading to a foyer with a high ceiling, perfect period furniture, and a smiling lady behind a reception desk tastefully designed not to look like a reception desk.

"Yes, may I help you/", she said.

"Yes, my name is Lee Alan and .."

"Oh yes Mr. Alan" she politely interrupted " Mr. Gilbert is expecting you. Just take that hallway there. His is the third office on the right." Mr. Alan? Huh! I'd been called many things before, but never MR. Alan. And Mr. Gilbert was expecting me?

Now I *was* nervous.

I followed her directions and entered the office. It was an outer office where his secretary normally resided. This was Saturday though, and it was empty. I was just about to knock on the only other door I could see when it suddenly opened and there standing before me was an ABC Vice President. John Gilbert was a thin very good-looking man with a smile from ear to ear.

"Lee, welcome Lee. You made it. How was the trip? Please, come on in. Coffee, Coke? Good to finally see you". Too many questions. Too impressive. Too much. My mouth opened but there was no sound. Now I knew how Mr. Lipson felt back at WJBK when he tried to talk but nothing came out. Mr. Gilbert seemed to understand.

"Lee, sit down. Make yourself comfortable. We have some ground to cover here but first I just want to thank you for driving all that way to get here today." I managed something like, "Thanks, but I appreciate the chance to meet with you". Or something dumb and trite. This was really awesome. I was actually sitting in the office of the Vice President of WXYZ RADIO!

Mr. Gilbert continued: "Lee, I can see you're a little taken by all of these surroundings. You're not alone. It affects everyone like that. I've been here a couple years and I still feel; the same way." He was smiling, and talking in an excited tone. "Here I am the General Manager of the number one radio station not only in Detroit, but in this part of the country and, the place is legendary. Historic! Lee", he said pacing back and forth in front of me, "we are in the radio station that created The Lone Ranger, The Green Hornet and frankly I still can't believe I even work here, let alone run the place. This is really The New York Yankees of radio." By this time I was out of it. Gone! I was going to need an EMS unit and smelling salts any minute.

"Think of who I have up there on the air". For the first time I figured that the actual studios must have been on the second floor with executive offices on the first. He went on, "Fred Wolf in the morning. Flat out number one and a legend in his own right. Paul Winter, Joel Sebastian, Don Zee, Fred Weiss. The ABC companies all over the world are behind me, the programming of the ABC radio network, and (laughing now) all I really have to do is show up for work". As he rattled off the names of the guys on the air I noticed that one was missing. Must have been a mistake I thought.

"Lee, I watched your ratings when you were at WKMH".
I started to make an excuse telling him that the signal power of that station was so small that it would be hard for anyone to have good ratings, but before I could get that out he was already past it,
"You were coming dangerously close to us, even with that small signal over there". He went on,

"Lee how'd you like to come to work here."

I didn't hesitate. I said, "How much do you want me to pay you?"

He laughed and said, " The night show".

"No problem" I said. " I've done all night shows before".

"No Lee, not the all night show. The NIGHT show. Seven to midnight"

Gilbert explained that Marty McNealey was leaving. Joel Sebastian would move from nights to afternoon drive, and Paul Winter moves from afternoons to midday. "Like to you to start Monday", he said. I was speechless. Then I remembered my job in Cincinnati.

"Don't' worry about it". He said. "It's all handled". I was still speechless.

"Handled'? I managed

Then he dropped the bomb.

John Gilbert explained although they wanted to hire me when I left WKMH, there were some doubts about my humility and willingness to take direction and get along with management.

"Lee, we got you that job in Cincinnati", he said. "We wanted to see if you would take a job that was out of town, leave home, go through the problems of getting there, looking for new surroundings and starting over again in a strange town. You did it Lee. It was a test. It was great. They already know you're not coming back". They have your replacement ready to start Monday. Funny thing is they tried to talk me into leaving you there. The really liked what you started".

This was too much for me in one day.

"There's just one problem, Lee", John Gilbert said, this time with a serious look on his face. "Joel Sebastian has a dance that he does every Friday and Saturday night at Club 182. He broadcasts from there live from 7 to 10 and then does the stage show at 10 o'clock. His 10 to midnight segments are on tape. He records them in the afternoon. Lee, if you go on at night, you'll be broadcasting from Club 182 Saturday nights too". I still hadn't heard the problem.

Those dances are owned by three Redford Township Policemen who don't want you out there. They say you caused them some problems over at WKMH. They don't think you'll do the job for them.

Well, there they were again. I had no choice but to explain the situation to Mr. Gilbert. I told him the whole story. Riverside Arena, the capacity crowds, traffic jams, the police promoters, the $600 they promised, the $100 I ended up with, and the gun that convinced me to leave. They were parasites using their badges of authority to build a business. They rented the hall, hired DJs who could bring the records and the crowds, recording artists, and bands for nothing. And when it was over, hiding behind their badges and using their influence, took the money and ran.

Mr. Gilbert listened intently. "Three thousand people! You had three thousand people out there"? "Rest couldn't get in", I said.

"Fantastic. Listen Lee, after what they pulled on you can you go out there and broadcast from their Club 182 dances and really promote for them". "No problem". I said.

John O. Gilbert, Vice President of ABC Radio came around from behind his desk, offered his hand to me and said: "Lee, welcome to WXYZ".

I'm not sure, but if I fell over from shock - I don't remember getting up.

Jerry Lewis

I met Jerry Lewis the comedian, actor, writer and former partner of Dean Martin when Jerry came to Motown to open and promote his movie, the Nutty Professor.

I was selected by the movie company to go to a dozen theaters where the movie was playing and introduce him to the audiences. I drove to the first movie theater and met him just before it was time for me to go on stage, warm up the audience with some of my antics and introduce Jerry.

He was very cordial, but seemed uncomfortable with all this. Talking to an audience in front of a movie screen I mean. Anyway it went well. I went out there, got them going a little and introduced Jerry. He turned on, and the audience was laughing the whole time.

There were about 11 more theaters to get to before we were finished. All went really well. The more we did this the better it was. Finally we arrived at the last theater. It was June, nine or ten at night and it was dark. The theater was a drive in. There must have been 5 or 6 hundred cars. Each one had a speaker hanging from the window so the occupants could hear the sound. I went out on the stage into a blinding spotlight and talked to the cars. It was hot and there were hundreds of bugs flying around in the lights. Ha! That was an experience itself.

Then, I introduced Jerry Lewis. As before, he came bounding out looking and sounding like the Nutty professor character. While he was talking he suddenly stopped, grabbed his ear, and let out a Jerry Lewis yell that I think you could hear for miles. At the same time he leaped into the air and came crashing down onto the stage. I was laughing. Everyone was laughing. Horns were blowing, Car lights were flashing. It was the funniest I had seen him.

But Jerry Lewis wasn't laughing. He ran from the stage yelling:

"GET THIS DAMNED THING AWAY FROM ME…..GET IT AWAY!" We realized he was serious. No comedy now. He was terrified. Jerry Lewis was rushed to the nearest hospital where the doctors removed a June Bug the size of a quarter from inside his right ear.

A week or two later he wrote me a note. It read:

"If I ever come to Detroit again…. Don't …."BUG"…. me.

I saw him once after that as he was getting ready to do his "Jerry's Kids" Telethon. He remembered my name. I liked Jerry Lewis.

Chapter 27
DAY ONE

WXYZ WAS THE BIGGEST, FASTEST, MOST THRILLING RIDE OF MY LIFE. As I write these words I relive them. It could never be duplicated. Ever. My colleagues in radio, my counterparts in other cities have stories. Exciting stories, but none to compare with what follows.

I can see it all, feel it, and touch it as I write. I want you to know that this is very emotional for me and at times, extremely painful. I loved radio. I loved being on the air. I loved the performers I worked with, the music people, the exhilaration; I loved what radio could do. With sound and imagination anything from the Grand Canyon to crawling inside a thimble could be created. Sound. It was all in the sound. People on the radio today use the microphone like it's a giant megaphone. They don't understand what radio can do. I loved it all, and chill that went down my spine when I knew I was on a major station and the microphone was open. But above all I loved the audience. If you were one of them, even though we may never have met, I loved you. I love you now. Nothing will ever match the exhilaration of being on the radio talking, and performing for you.

Before we begin this journey I want to give you a sense of

where the world was when I started with this wonderful radio station.

The year is 1961. John F. Kennedy had been president only four days. There are 178 million people in this country. The average salary is $4,743. Bread is 19 cents a loaf, butter is 81 cents a pound, gas is 26 cents a gallon, a new Corvette costs about $2,600, you can buy a Ford or Chevy for as little as $1,600.

The number 12 song on the Billboard music charts is Shop Around by the Miracles. Remember how it started?

Other new records being played:
> Where The Boys Are - Connie Francis
> Are You Lonesome Tonight - Elvis
> Calendar Girl - Neil Sedaka
> Wonderland By Night - Bert Kempfert.

At the movies we were watching Exodus with Paul Newman, The Apartment, Psycho, and Ben Hur. And in Motown, Berry Gordy is getting hot.

My first show on WXYZ was something less than spectacular. I had no idea what I was doing and for the first time in my life I was nervous on the radio. On top of it I learned that my first night was to be broadcast from a paint store. A Paint store!

A remote broadcast designed to get people to come to the store and buy paint. Really exciting right? Wrong!

The store was only open until ten. I was on till midnight so my first words through a microphone on WXYZ were uttered on tape. I had to record the 10 to midnight segment, the last two hours of my first show so when the store closed at ten we would leave the site and the engineers at the station could roll the tape. Even though I had left I was still on the air. Recorded, but on the air. It meant I could listen to myself on the radio in my car as I drove home. Listening to myself on my first night. Now that was a scary thought!

I had to record those two hours at one thirty that afternoon. Monday afternoon. My first day. The only person I knew was John Gilbert. I was a stranger to everyone else. Or so I thought.

I was at the station Monday morning by 9AM.

The visitor's parking area in front of the building was off limits. Employees parked in back. The driveway snaked around the building. On the left was lush landscaping. On the right were large overhead doors used by trucks to get things in and out of the television studios on the first floor of the building. Just as the driveway took a sharp right, heading for the rear of the building there was a cluster of beautiful, large, mature pine trees that surrounded what I later learned was a Green. An actual Golf Green that the president of the company had put there as part of this wonderful, awesome package known as Broadcast House.

The back of the building was just as awesome as the rest of it. Executives had reserved spaces and parked head in under an overhang nearly touching the back wall of the building. Highest ranking on the left. The first spot was reserved for John F. Pival, President, WXYZ Incorporated. Next to him the sign read John O. Gilbert. Then the rest. There was a large metal door in between two of the reserved spaces that lead to the central engineering room for both radio and television. I would become very familiar with this entrance, but I am getting ahead of my story again..

Next to Mr. Pival's space and three steps up was the back entrance to the building. Leading away from the porch a covered walkway went about 30 yards, turned sharply to the right, and ended at the entrance to a small house done in the same Georgian Manor architecture as the main building. This was the cafeteria. Upstairs there were meeting rooms. This was a panacea. Right out of a dream.

I entered the main building. A small waiting room revealed a nicely dressed woman with a large smile behind a desk that matched the décor of the building. "Yes, may I help you?" she said. I gave her my name and before I could explain anything she smiled even broader and said "Mr. Alan, welcome to WXYZ. Mr. Baker is expecting you." There it was again. "Mr. Alan". "That hallway to the stairs up to the second floor. Turn right. The program area is the second door on the right". I thanked her and followed the directions.

In his book "Wyxie Wonderland", Dick Osgood writes:

> "Bob Baker was a big Canadian from Fort William on Thunder Bay in Ontario. He breezed through school like a genius and began his radio career as program director of a very small station. By World War II he was in Toronto where he occasionally wrote newscasts for Canada's most listened to newscaster, Lorne Green."

Of course the Lorne Green Osgood refers to is the same one who ended up playing the lead role in television's Bonanza.

Baker joined WXYZ in 1950 as a record assistant, whatever that was, making $65 dollars a week. For Baker that was a raise. He'd been making $45 in Toronto. He was a big man, jovial, friendly, firm, quick minded, and knew something that virtually no one in radio today knows. He knew its history. He knew what radio was and how to use it. Baker joined WXYZ at the tail end of radio's days of live drama, comedy, and music shows when it was not unusual to have 20 or 30 people in a studio all at once acting, playing live music, or whatever. He was there when The Lone Ranger, The Green Hornet, and Challenge of the Yukon were still being produced three or four times a week. He was a man who weathered the transition from the old radio to the new. By 1961 Bob Baker was an authority on radio and now he was my immediate boss.

I climbed the stairs, turned right and entered the second door on the right.

Chapter 28
THE INNER SANCTUM

IT WASN'T BOB BAKER'S OFFICE AT ALL. The door opened to a large room that was ringed with waste high solid walls and glass from there up to the ceiling. Inside the glass were cubicles that each held two desks, chairs, phones, etc. They were the offices of the air personalities. The Disc Jockeys. Those offices were all empty. Fred Wolf was still on the air, but was broadcasting from his remote trailer, which on this morning was downtown in front of Science Hall on the Campus of Wayne State University. I remember seeing him there when I was a student at Wayne. I would often stand there watching him thinking I was nuts to even try getting into radio as a full time job. If I was going to make it I would have to compete with pros like Fred Wolf. Fat chance I used to think. Now here I was inside Broadcast House looking at one of the glass offices that could be his waiting to see my boss and his.

Fred Wolf was an amazing, unique man who was loved by everyone who ever listened to him. In 1934, 24-year-old Fred Wolf was working at Chrysler Corporation as a timekeeper. When this country went to war in 1941 he worked there as part of the team that built the Sherman Tank. Fred was also a bowler, a professional bowler on the championship team at the Stroh Brewery. He was one of the best. At war's end Fred was on his way up at Chrysler, but a painful problem with his back ended his pro bowling days. So he managed the team and at tournaments announced the players and the scores. Someone from a radio station heard him and suggested that he put some reports together, record them and see if it would fly as a short radio show.

On October 15, 1945, Fred Wolf went on the air at WXYZ with his bowling reports. The rest is history. The details of Fred's rise can be found in the book, WYXIE Wonderland, by Dick Osgood. Let's just say here that he was a star from the beginning. Fred Wolf ended up on WXYZ in the morning drive time, the most important money time on the radio. His success there was instantaneous and now legendary. Everyone loved "Freddie Wolf".

One morning in July, long before the move to Broadcast House, it was so hot in his non air-conditioned studio that Fred decided to do something about it. While the news was on he grabbed a chair and a small table, and ordered Harold Winter, his engineer, to hook up a microphone to a long cord. Fred was moving his show outside on the porch. Dick Osgood:

> "The change was not as simple as it sounds. Fred's records were run by Bob Baker in the director's booth of a dramatic studio and the turntables could not be moved. As soon as a record started playing, Wolf would remove his headset, race into the studio, and find out from Bob what the next record would be. The two also hollered back and forth through the open windows. Meanwhile, the porch microphone picked up all the sounds of the morning traffic".

And the traffic was blowing their horns to let Fred know they were listening and you could hear that on the air too. Broadcasting from the porch was so talked about and so successful that the station built a permanent hut on the front lawn with a big window in front so everybody could see him inside. They called it Wolf's Wackie Wigloo. Later they made a deal with a local mobile home dealer and built one on wheels. It then became Wolf's Wandering Wigloo. These were the first remote broadcasts by a Disc Jockey, a term that Fred hated, by the way. DISC JOCKEY. Can't say that I ever liked it either.

As I now stood in the bullpen area of the inner-sanctum of WXYZ Radio a small lady at asked if she could help me. Must have looked lost or dazed because I was. Her desk was covered with cups of what obviously was cold coffee. Pat Riggert was Bob Baker's secretary. "Yes, I'm here to see Mr. Baker", I said. "Name's Lee Alan". "Lee", she said. "Welcome, Bob's waiting for you. Go right in. That door there." I was starting to feel at home already. Pat was the first one to call me by my first name. I was no longer Mr. Alan.

Baker's office was small and the only one that didn't have glass walls. When I walked in his smile was so big I thought his face was going to break and he was talking a hundred miles and hour. He talked so fast that he glossed over some words like they needed to be in the sentence but were not important. He was going on about how he had listened to me on 'KMH, thought it was fantastic, how he recommended me to Mr. Gilbert and how it was his idea to see if WCPO offered me a job, if I would actually pack up and go and on and on. I found him to be a smart, all seeing, all knowing guy who loved his job and loved the people who worked for him. I was his discovery and he made me feel at home.

Within minutes I had an office, desk, chair, phone and all the other things offices have. The office had two desks. The other one bore the name Joel Sebastian. He wasn't there though and before I could settle in Bob appeared at the door waggling his first finger motioning for me to follow him. I was about to get a tour of the radio station I once dreamed of just seeing, let alone working for.

Radio's part of this complex was so well planned that there really wasn't that much to see. The nerve center was a large room with some complicated looking equipment that only the radio engineers could touch. And I mean that literally. WXYZ was a union radio station. The engineer's contract prevented anyone but them from operating or even touching certain things. This room was Master Control and it was their kingdom. We could watch, but that's all. There were large half wall glass windows on two sides and you could see parts of all the other studios. From here the engineer controlled the volume and sound quality of everything that left the station. Bob introduced me to the engineer on duty and we moved on. There were five small studios and one large one. Two of them just had a microphone, a switch to turn it on and off, two machines that played tape cartridges, and a set of earphones. The news was broadcast from these rooms.

The other 5 studios each had turntables for playing records, four machines that played tape cartridges, and a small control console from which the operator could start and stop the machines and control the volume leaving the studio. It was all fed to Master Control where the engineer had final say on everything. The engineers in Master Control could put any one of them on the air.

One other large room was a bullpen where the news reporters gathered news by phone or from the teletype machines that constantly typed out news from all over the world provided by news services like Associated Press, United Press International, Reuters or other services that the station subscribed to. The machines were so loud with as they all clacked out their information that they were isolated behind a glass window in their own little room. You could stand in front of the window and literally read the news minutes after it happened.

In addition to all the other news information, once an hour or so the news services would send out a complete newscast already complied into five or fifteen minute lengths. If the news people didn't want to do any local snooping for news on their own they could literally rip the newscast from the machine as it was supplied already written for them by someone at the news service, cut it in manageable lengths, get a complete weather forecast from the same machine, walk into the studio, read the newscast on the air and sound like they were just as authoritative as any network or large news organization. There was a term for it. RIP AND READ. If stations didn't pay much attention to their newsgathering they were called RIP AND READ operations. RIP the news off the wire, and READ it on the air. All stations had the clacking, constantly typing, news machines and all stations could RIP AND READ and sound just as good as anyone else.

WXYZ was different. Their news people worked hard at uncovering news, sending their reporters out on new stories, calling news sources, recording interviews and voices from the phone, writing news stories around their material and writing their own newscasts. The news services were used, but the stories were always rewritten. In keeping with the legacy of the quality of the station, everything in this news department was done well.

Bob Baker whisked me through the station, talking fast in his usual way and introducing me to the people as we went. I had listened to them all on the air for years. None of them looked like they sounded. No one ever does.

The tour completed, Bob showed me the record library, where at least one copy of everything the station played or had ever played was filed, and explained the format of the station. He handed me a loose-leaf book, guided me to one of the studios I had just seen, showed me how to operate the equipment and said: " OK Lee you're on your own now. You're on remote tonight from Victor

Paint from 7:15 to ten so you've got to record your ten to midnight segment now. When you're ready to go Louie there in master control will start the tape. Good luck", he said as he shook my hand and left.

The door closed behind Bob Baker. There I was by myself in the studio at WXYZ. Alone. I had music, equipment to play it on, a loose-leaf book full of commercials, racks with tape cartridges of station jingles and recorded commercials, station sounds, an engineer to help me if I got into trouble and a green light. I had a green light to open the microphone on the station I had listened to as a boy and begin.

The tools were all there. All I had to do was figure out how to use them. What to say and how to put everything together so that the station was happy and the listeners would tune in and stay with me. I just looked at everything for a few minutes. It reminded me of a keyboard on a piano. Everything just sat there as if to say: "I can play and do anything. All you have to do is press the right buttons".

I put everything in order, set the clock to read 10PM, called the engineer, Louie Shook in master control and asked him to roll the tape in exactly 5 minutes. My rocket ride with WXYZ was about to begin.

Chapter 29
5 – 4 – 3 – 2 – 1

"Tape is rolling", a voice yelled through the talkback speaker. Recording that first two hours was a scary thing. Thank God for Louie the engineer. I think"!

It was 1:30 in the afternoon, but it wasn't. The tape I was making was for 10 to 12 midnight. 81/2 hours later. So everything I was doing and saying was as if it were then. It meant that I had to refer back to things that took place the hour before that hadn't happened yet. And what about the music? Music that was going to be played the first three one hour segments from 7 to 10PM couldn't be played too soon again in the 10 to Midnight recorded segments. At least that was the normal way of doing a show. Listeners would soon learn that on this new "Lee Alan Show" nothing would ever be normal.

The tape was rolling and so was I. WXYZ had "Live News at Fifty Five" in those days, meaning that there was five minutes of news every hour at 55 minutes after the hour (or 5 minutes to the hour). All the other stations started their news exactly on the hour. The reasoning was that as they were starting their news we were back playing music and since more people wanted to hear more music than news, we would get all the music loving button pushers.

After the news, unless it was the very beginning of the show when I would play my theme song, the new hour was always supposed to start with a station jingle, a nice musical identification of WXYZ followed by the first record. That's what I was told to do. That's what the format was. Play a nice station jungle, then music. The one I chose went:

> It's the happiest sound for miles around
> It's the bright spot
> It's the right spot
> Double U
> X –YYYY -Zeee.

It was a very nice jingle.

The Jingles and commercials were on tape cartridges that looked something like audio-cassettes but bigger and were stored alphabetically in tall revolving racks near the turntables to make them easy to locate (see the studio photo). The clock counted down, 10 – 9 – 8 – 7– 6

I loaded the nice WXYZ Jingle into the cartridge machine, the record I placed on the turntable was a loud, up tempo big hit called Tossin' and Turnin' by Bobby Lewis. I cued it up to the start and waited for Louie, the engineer to say the tape was rolling.

Louie Shook was a very short man with a brush haircut, a major smile always on his face, and a cigar in his mouth. Unlit as I recall. He was known for being a nice, quiet, cooperative, smiling, happy man.

Understand now, that the engineer's job was to handle all the technical equipment and see that everything had the proper volume and blend. Their job had nothing to do with programming. Nothing to do with what was said or played. The engineer handled the overall sound and calibrated and watched the transmitter to make sure we were on the air with a quality sound.

WXYZ used what is known as a limiter-compressor, an electronic device built into the system so that if there was a sudden noise that happened too fast for the engineer to react, too fast for him to take the volume down quickly enough, the device would do it for him. After a loud sound was compressed by this device, what followed would be so low you couldn't hear it for at least two or three seconds. That was only for sounds that were on the air. For anything being recorded the engineer was on his own controlling it manually. If the a sound was too loud it would drive the equipment too hard and send the little needle measuring the volume into the next county possibly ruining the recording or even the equipment.

5 – 4 - 3

The nice WXYZ jingle was ready, the record was ready, I was nervous but I was ready and staring at Louie waiting to see and hear him tell me the tape was rolling. That would be my cue to start.

There were a couple of other engineers in master Control busy with the Paul Winter Show that was presently on the air in an adjacent studio. Paul was visible through another glass. I hadn't met him yet. Dick Kernen, the producer who played all his records and commercials, etc. was in the studio with him. Over in the newsroom, visible through another glass window I could see the reporters on duty, Dick Osgood and Porter Borne busily typing and on the phone. They kept the door to the clacking newswire machines closed to retain their peaceful atmosphere. I looked back at Louie. Two others had joined him in Master Control. One was my boss, Bob Baker. I didn't recognize the other man.

Louie's hand was raised in the air behind his head.

The clock still running: 2-1

Suddenly Louie's hand went from behind his ear to a straight arm pointing directly at me and he said loudly over the talkback speaker: "TAPE IS ROLLING". As he said it a number of things happened all at once and in quick succession.

In a split second, but it seemed in slow motion, here's what happened. While Louie was saying "Tape Is Rolling" I was reaching down on the floor to get The Horn. Remember the Horn? The Lee Alan Fine Toned Pakistan Horn? Well, no one here had ever seen it before this moment, or for that matter had ever heard it.

I was raising it to eye level directly in front of the mike. As I did this the first thing I noticed was the smile starting to disappear on Louie's face and the beginning of a strange quizzical look replacing it. It was sort of the type of expression you might see on a man's face after he has just stepped into an open elevator shaft and was on the way down. Fear. That's what it was fear!

I saw Louie's mouth open and start moving. It looked like it was forming an O. Or maybe a Nooooo!.

While I was still raising The Horn to the microphone, the other engineers in Master Control, hearing whatever Louie was saying, started a quick pirouette turning to look in my direction. Their mouths formed the same shape. All three of them with mouths like little OOOs.

At the same time all this was happening I was reaching for the little button that would turn the microphone on. As my hand approached the button the look on Louie's face defined itself as panic. The cigar dropped from his mouth to the floor, he and the other two engineers raised both their arms and waved them at me back and forth, palms forward in the air. Six arms giving me the Nooooo sign.

They saw The Horn in my hand, saw me punch the microphone on and punch the button next to it. That one opened up a large echo chamber so that anything that was on the microphone sounded like it was in the Grand Canyon. Before any of their yelling and hand waving could stop me, I blew the Lee Alan Fine Toned Pakistan Horn directly into the microphone with the echo chamber full blast!

When I blew the horn, the three engineers in Master Control all leaped to the control board to kill the loud sound. Bob Baker whirled around and started for the door leading to my studio. Dick Kernen, Paul Winter's producer turned his face to the glass with his nose smushed against it. Paul Winter came to the window as well. Only time I had ever seen him before this was on television. Osgood and Borne in the newsroom both turned and looked at the same time.

Everyone all at once. They all heard The Horn. The other man in the control room was the only one laughing. I could hear him right through the glass. The whole station was at a standstill. Following the Horn Blow I played the nice jingle:

"It's the happiest sound for miles around. . . .

But nobody heard it. I followed that with Bobby Lewis singing:

I COULDN'T SLEEP AT ALL LAST NIGHT
JUST THINKIN' OF YOU....

But nobody heard that either. The engineers didn't know what was coming in time to do anything and The Horn was so loud it buried the needles, distorted everything on the tape and blew out two speakers. They killed the sound and the nice jingle and Bobby Lewis were off in a silent realm.

Bob Baker burst into the studio. "What was that?", he said. I knew he had seen it and because I couldn't think of anything else to say I looked at him and said:

"That was the Lee Alan Fine toned Horn, made in Pakistan by a Pakistan Watchmaker", etc. His red face broke into a large smile and then hysterical laughter. Everyone was laughing. Even the newsmen, Dick Kernen sank below the windowsill and was doubled up on the floor. Paul Winter just shrugged and went back to his chair. All laughing. Not the engineers though.

Louie Shook was shook. He retrieved his cigar from the floor, rewound the tape and asked me to start over. I did. And again

I started with The Horn, only this time he was ready for it. They all were. The rest of the recording went all right I guess.

The next day Bob Baker called me into his office and showed me a slip of paper. It was a union grievance filed by the engineers that said:

"Recording aborted because of loud sour sounding horn blown directly into the microphone. This was done on purpose by Lee Alan, the new disc jockey who needs to know more about the equipment or the engineering department will not be responsible."

The Horn was the talk of the station.

Oh yes, the other man in Master Control who thought this was all too hilarious?

Hal Neal, President of ABC Radio who was visiting the station. In years to come I would hear him tell that story much better than I ever could in a hundred different ways. In time Hal Neal would be my benefactor in ways I had no way of knowing then.

From then on it was a real hoot to watch my friends the engineers whenever I would even reach for The Horn, let alone give it a Blow.

The broadcast that night, my first live show on WXYZ was from a large mobile home that was custom built for Fred Wolf. This remote broadcast facility was a far cry from Fred Wolf's microphone and card table of a few years ago.

When Fred was broadcasting there it was called Wolf's Wandering Wigloo a throwback to those days when Freddie bolted from the hot studio and broadcast from the porch. When anyone else was in it there was no name. On this night it sat outside the front window of Victor Paint somewhere in Northwest Detroit. Outside a large lighted sign told the world that this was:

W X Y Z – 1270

It was luxuriously appointed and furnished inside. One end was a solid clear pane of glass from desk height up to the ceiling.

Anyone passing by could see whoever was sitting in the window. There was a kitchen too. Well stocked with coffee, cold soft drinks in the refrigerator, glasses and dishes etc. Unlike the old WKMH I was not required to go in the back room and pile wood on the fire. Ha!

This was a professional set up all the way. No wood stove here. Instead there was there was always an engineer from the station to hook up the remote and keep us the air. In those days it was all done with telephone lines. The phone company would install a Class A phone line between the remote site and the station that would carry a better quality sound than a regular phone. So, when we were on the air we were actually on a phone line that was being picked up by the station and then broadcast. And remember it was AM radio. Not FM. Not stereo either. The sound was monaural and not the best quality. No one knew the difference though; all the stations sounded the same. It was the only game in town.

The radio personality sat in front at a table facing the large glass window. From the outside, and to passing traffic it looked sort of like a large television set that got stuck on the side of the road. There were speakers outside so a crowd could see the DJ and hear what was on the air at the same time. The engineer stayed in the back with his audio equipment.

The only thing that was broadcast from here was the voice of the DJ. Everything else, including the news, audio inserts from the network, phone calls from listeners etc., originated from a studio back at Broadcast House where a producer played the records, commercials, station jingles, and anything else that was recorded.

The remote DJ wore a headset with two earphones. In one was the sound of station on the air, the other was a telephone operator's earphone with a small mike that allowed him to hear and talk with the producer back at the station who was wearing the same type of headset. On the desk in front of him were the on and off buttons for his station microphone, a volume control for the speakers in the remote trailer, a volume control for the headset itself, and a small button that, when pressed, buzzed in headset back at the station. When the DJ pushed the buzzer that was the cue to the producer to roll the next record, commercial, or whatever was planned. Always in the back room of the trailer, the engineer's job was to see that we stayed on the air, to control the volume of the DJ's mike, and to make sure that no loud horns blew us off the air.

I was hired on Saturday. This was a cold Monday night in January. My show followed and hour and fifteen minutes of news and rather boring network programs from the ABC radio. I hit the air at 7:15 At that time in January it was already dark. Think of it. It was Monday night, cold, dark, broadcasting from the paint store, and my first show on the monster station. Are you ready?

No customers showed up that night in the store and no one stopped to see what I was doing in that remote studio. Just like the all night shows, I was convinced no one was listening. I had no idea what I was doing I'm sure it sounded like it. At 9:55 the station took over with "live news at 55" and I left. About half way home I realized that if I turned the radio on to WXYZ that wild tape recording session that I had that afternoon was on the air. I could listen to myself on the radio. I didn't have the nerve. I didn't listen. Instead I was doing my homework.

I was listening to John R. "Way down South in Dixie" (The Great John Richborg) on WLAC-1510, Nashville, Tennessee.

Over the years so many people wondered how I had such an uncanny "ear" for new music that became hits. I'm not sure I did, but John R. did. He was my secret weapon. John R. had the "ear". I had listened to him for years. He had a deep raspy voice with the southern accent to go with it and every new R & B record in existence. That night on the way home John R. played a song that actually made me pull over to the side of the road, turn the radio up and listen. The artist was Mose Allison. A black Artist playing the piano and singing a jazz lick I'd never heard the likes of. On top of that the words were way different than anything out there. They talked about strange and mysterious powers.

    Everybody's talkin' 'bout the Seventh Son
    In the whole round world there is only one
    And I'm the one. I'm the one.
    I'm the one, I'm the one
    The one they call the Seventh Son.

It went on: I can tell your future, It will come to pass
    I can do things for you, make your heart feel glad
    Look in the sky, predict the rain
    I can tell when a woman's got anther man
    I'm the one they call the Seventh Son.

  You've got to understand that all Disc Jockeys had the same tools. A radio station, microphones, jingles, all the same records were available. What I always looked for was a way to have something different. Something that either no one else had or that no one else could do. The Horn was one of them, certain records too. I'll point them out as we go along. Oh just one thing. Two years went by before I knew that Mose Allison wasn't black. He is a white jazz artist. His music is still available. I might be the only one who played his music on a white pop station. The Seventh Son. Still love it.

  Something different:

  Mose Allison and The Seventh Son. Remember, DJs were known for the music they played and what they said. This music would prove to be dynamite for me, and something I would play for the rest of my years on WXYZ. More about that later – Film at eleven. Ha.

Florence Ballard & the Supremes

I met Florence Ballard when the Supremes were starting out in the early sixties. She was bright, beautiful, and had an outgoing personality that could charm anyone. She charmed me. That's for sure. In my opinion Florence had the best in the group, but it was carefully kept in the background by the powers at Motown. The Supremes with Florence appeared with and for me more times than I could ever remember in the sixties. I liked all of them, but Florence was my favorite. It is said that because Berry Gordy Jr. had a personal focus on the Diana Ross, Florence was never given the chance to shine as a lead singer in the group and when Berry Gordy finally changed the name of the Supremes to "Diana Ross and the Supremes", Flo was devastated and started drinking. She was eventually fired by Motown and replaced.

The last time I saw Florence Ballard, she appeared at Detroit's Light Guard Armory at a benefit dance and show for Easter Seals in January of 1976. A few weeks later on February 21, she was dead of a blood clot in a coronary artery.

I recently had the opportunity to meet Michelle Ballard, Flo's daughter. She seemed unaware of her mother's legacy and didn't really know a great deal about her career or her music.

More than 5,000 people showed up for the funeral. Florence was my friend. She died still wanting to be the lead singer of the Supremes. I believe that Florence Ballard died of a broken heart.

Chapter 30
TUESDAY

AT 10 THE NEXT MORNING THERE WAS A PROGRAM MEETING of all the DJ air personalities, producers, some of the sales people and anyone else who had a bone to pick with what was on the air. After that first wild day on the job I still hadn't met anyone else who was on the air at WXYZ.

I turned into Broadcast house, down the long driveway past the cluster of pine trees to the back parking lot. The small waiting room at the back of the building was full of people. I was headed for the conference room; not paying attention to their faces when a tall beefy man stuck out his hand and said: "Hey Lee, great show last night". Was he kidding? That fiasco? And who was this guy anyway? "Lee, he said as we shook hands, name's Harry Balk. I'm Del Shannon's manager. Have you met Del?" "Well, uh", I was stammering now. Del Shannon was a gigantic recording star then. Hit records all over the place. When Del Shannon appeared anywhere he drew thousands of people, even in Europe. Remember "Runaway", Hats Off to Larry, and others?

"No I haven't met Del." As I said it from out of the crowd Del Shannon himself appeared with a big grin on his face. He was first. A line formed. Smiling people introducing themselves. They were all waiting to see the *important* DJs on the station; not me. One by one I met them. Del Shannon, The Shirreles, The Marvelettes, and a guy with the sunglasses whom I had met before, Roy Orbison. They were all accompanied by either their managers or the music promotion people. I was pretty much blown away by this time. I'm meeting people I'd only heard of before. A couple of them asked about brunch in the cafeteria after the meeting.

Then I noticed the time. Two minutes to 10. I made a bee-line for the meeting.

The conference room at Broadcast house was like something out of a movie. Warm, polished wood everywhere surrounding a table that seemed like it could seat 40 people. Well, it wasn't quite that big, but impressive it was.

And there they all were. All the reasons that WXYZ was far and away the number one station in this part of the country. The people. I recognized most of them. Near the back of the room was Fred Wolf. Before then I had only seen him from a distance or on television. And Fred was on television nearly every day. Standing next to him was Paul Winter, the man whose voice I had been trying to copy since I was a kid. Fred Weiss was there. Fred was the weekend guy and had been on television for years. No one could ever mistake his silver hair. Mr. Gilbert was seated at the head of the table, Bob Baker next to him. Sales people were there as well.

I must have looked pretty stupid standing there with my eyes out of my head looking at these icons of Detroit radio when a tall young looking blonde guy approached me. "Leeeeee", he said with a smile as wide as the room. "Joel Sebastian Lee, welcome aboard". I recognized his voice. What a voice. Honey smooth, and deep. Later, Joel would become the voice of the United Airlines commercials. Joel was the one I replaced in the 7:15 to midnight slot when management moved him to afternoons. Afternoon drive time was the second most important time on the station. It was a big promotion for Joel and now "Drive time" rush hour was his.

The next hand to shake was Don Zee, the all night man on the station. All night on WXYZ was different than those all night shows I had done. This was a very big show, had large overnight ratings and no one ever did an all night show like Don Zee. "Daddy Zee. Two Es if you please." From now on when I finished my show at midnight at midnight, Don Zee was next.

The whole lineup was there: Fred Wolf 6-10AM, Paul Winter 10-2, Joel Sebastian 2-6PM, me 7:15 to Midnight, Don Zee, and Fred Weiss on the weekends. Just as I sank into a chair to wait for the meeting to start another group of men came in led by Mr. Neal, president of the ABC radio stations and yesterday's laughing man in the studio when I blew the engineering department away with The Horn.

It soon became apparent that they weren't the only ones blown away.

Chapter 31
CHANGE

MR. GILBERT STARTED THE MEETING BY WELCOMING practically the whole station. They were all there. Standing room only. Sales, office crew, engineering was represented, Bob Baker's programming people and producers, on the air staff including the news department, and the group with Mr. Neal from New York.

I only remember bits and pieces of what took place that morning. I was still in shock that they even let me in the building, let alone work there. I had only read about things like this. And now here I am writing about it for *you* to read.

Mr. Gilbert started out by praising everyone in the room. The whole staff. The new ratings were out and WXYZ had made giant gains in audience and management was ecstatic over it.

John Gilbert was the type of person who always seemed to be jubilant and almost hyper. He went on about each individual air personality and what a great job they were doing almost to the point of embarrassment. Then he got down to the reason for the meeting.

Marty McNealey was gone. McNealey had been a big name in Detroit at WJR Radio as the host (DJ) of their morning drive time show, The Music Hall which later became the domain of the late JP

McCarthy. When he left and later joined WXYZ there was newspaper publicity. It was a big move for him. He had left a 50,000 watt clear channel station to join WXYZ. Well, in those days I would have too. Mr. Gilbert explained that Marty had moved to Chicago and, even though it had already happened, announced that Joel Sebastian was the new afternoon drive time personality replacing Marty. Then it was my turn.

He didn't make a big deal about it, but just introduced me and said that I had been on WKMH, had great ratings, and was now with WXYZ 7:15 to midnight. When he was finished with me a voice from somewhere in the back of the standing crowd was heard: "And he brought that horn", Charlie Kocher, the chief engineer added with a little laugh: "We should have the replacement parts by tomorrow for the tape recorder that horn blew up yesterday".

Louie Shook almost lost his unlit cigar again.

While some quiet laughter rustled through the room another voice: "Yeah I heard that that thing last night. If you want to put a Moose call on the radio why don't 'cha get a real one?" It was Fred Wolf. All in fun you understand. I think!

From the end of the table Bob baker laughed and said: *"Well, WE'RE all talking about it, let's see what the public does"*.

Mr. Neal: "Charlie, I was there when that happened yesterday. Wish I had a movie of it. Funniest thing I ever saw in a radio studio. Don't know about that horn though."

John Gilbert: "Don't let 'em get to you Lee. Great job so far and welcome aboard".

The people at WXYZ sensed that changes forced by payola would have an effect on the whole station. They were right. Within the past year two radio giants Ed McKenzie and Mickey Shorr had left, and guess what? Joel and I were their replacements. Joel was perfection on the radio, but compared to Ed McKenzie nobody knew him. And me? Compared to any of them I was anonymous!

The radio station, Joel and I, had to recapture the audience and hold it.

Yes I know John Gilbert had just announced that the station made gains in the ratings, but let me explain about radio ratings and why they're important.

In major markets (cities) radio ratings are generally being taken all the time. Ever get a survey in the mail, or a phone call to ask you about your listening habits? Well the methods don't really matter here except to say that ratings are usually published every quarter. So, by the time the ratings come out they're at least one to four months old. Unless stations order what we call "overnights" or something more current, ratings reflect the past, what listeners were doing as much as four or five months ago; not necessarily today.

Radio makes its money by selling time. Commercial time. How much the sponsor pays for it depends on how popular the station is with the demographic they are buying. The smaller the audience, smaller the rating, the lower the price or rate the station can charge for its time. Big ratings equal big audience equals big money.

Sorry to get into these boring parts, but it has a bearing on what was happening at WXYZ in those days.

Although John Gilbert was happy about the ratings just out, he knew they reflected the past, not the present. Those numbers came from surveys done when other people held the time slots. Not Joel Sebastian and certainly not Lee Alan; people who'd had left the station. McKenzie, Shorr, McNealey. The next two rating books could tell a different story and Gilbert knew it. We had no contracts in those days. No agents to represent us. We were at the mercy of our audience, and the ratings, and management.

Listening to Joel Sebastian that afternoon gave me an idea.

Chapter 32
THE FAMILY FEUD

BY NOW YOU KNOW THAT OLD TIME RADIO WAS AN INFLUENCE ON ME and played a major role in what I did on the air. So, here we go again back to The Jack Benny program.

There were many great radio comedians, Red Skelton, Milton Berle, Edgar Bergen and Charlie McCarthy (which one's the dummy?), Abbott and Costello, Fibber McGee, and Fred Allen were some of them. Allen was all time master of the ad-lib. I have listened to his radio show tapes over and over. He and Jack Benny were the best of friends, but even back then they understood that without listeners and ratings nothing stayed on the air and that if you can create something that will make people talk about you, they'll will tune in and listen. Controversy works!

On December 30, 1936 on national network radio Fred Allen made a crack about Benny's violin playing. He said something about Benny's playing being bad, maybe something to the effect that Benny's violin was the only musical instrument in the world that had a permanent scratch and when Benny played, it was nails on a chalkboard. Something like that. Allen was serious, or at least he sounded serious. There was nothing funny in his voice when he said it.

Later that same week on his network program, Benny picks up on this and answered him. Something like he heard what Fred Allen said on his program about the violin. Maybe Benny said something like the permanent screech and scratch in Fred Allan's voice shouldn't even be on the air.

The Benny-Allen feud was on!

A feud that would become famous was born. And it continued for years.

Hearing Fred Allen's remarks, people would tune in Benny to see what he was going to say and then back to Fred Allen the next week. Once again, off the air they were the best of friends but the radio feud was on. It sounded serious and the audience believed every word. Everybody was talking and more importantly they were listening; more all the time. Fred Allen's ratings went through the roof, so did Benny's.

For some reason that famous feud and the massive listening audience it brought for the two comedians had stuck with me.

I heard Joel Sebastian that afternoon read some letters from a few fans who said they were sorry Joel was taken off the night show. Jokingly, Joel said that I, Lee Alan, purposely went to WXYZ management and took his job.

That night, Tuesday night, I went on the air and in a serious tone said that I had something "very personal to say about Joel Sebastian", and I would do that "Friday night at exactly 8:30 so join me here at this spot on your radio dial for a big meeting and I'll tell you what I have to say about Joel and this whole thing".

For the next two nights I repeated said the same thing. "Friday night at 8:30," I kept saying.

Joel started getting phone calls and letters from fans who: "Just wanted to tell you what Lee Alan was saying on the air and that they would listen Thursday night and report back to him on what was said". Joel said things on the air a few times too. He said he was: "sorry that Lee felt he had to go to my boss, that he needed that night show so bad that he'd go to any extent to get it", and so on.

The Alan-Sebastian feud was on.

Joel and I were not friends then. We'd only known each other for a few days. I only knew him from listening to him and also that he graduated from Redford High School, the Arch Rival of Cooley where I had gone.

To this day I know very little about Joel Sebastian. Everybody liked him, but I'm not sure very many really knew him. Joel's wife was an attorney. Word was that Francis had no use for Joel's profession as a Disc Jockey. Teenagers loved Joel and he was invited to do sock hops at high schools and other commercial places all the time. His dance card was full and he made big money doing them. In those days five hundred to a thousand a week was big money and Joel made that much just doing outside appearances. He was cordial, easy to get along with, non controversial, loved his audience, and on the air his honey voice mesmerized the listener. Joel Sebastian with just an all round good guy. I can't think of one thing Joel ever did to upset anyone. Except me!

Not only did we go to rival high schools, but also we went to rival colleges. He went to the University of Michigan, and I to Michigan State. We had one thing in common. Joel and I belonged to the same college fraternity, Phi Delta Theta. So, once the feud thing was over if you were listening in those days and heard us calling each other "Brother Joel" and "Brother Lee", that was the reason. Fraternity brothers from different colleges.

Joel Sebastian and I never really became friends. On the radio, yes. In the workplace, yes very nice. But down deep he never liked me and as I think about it today, I can't blame him. More about that later.

Actually, Joel was a little reluctant to get into this "feud" thing but he went along with it. At first, when he heard me say what I did on the air, even he thought I was serious.

The feud heated up.

"I didn't need Joel's job", I said on the air. I'd: "even trade with him; take his afternoon job", I went on. This was the dumbest, most obvious game ever. Anyone in the business knew that's exactly what it was, a game. The listeners thought we were serious.

Music moving, everything rocking, fast pace, fast talk, Jonathon Winters wisecracking, Horn blowing, commercials, jingles playing, phones lit up with callers, throwing things around the studio and suddenly right in the middle of all of it I would clear my throat, lower my voice in a sincere tone and say something like: " I am not certain how long I can do this. Not sure how long we can be here together at WXYZ. Joel Sebastian wants me out of here and he carries a lot of influence with the owners. It could happen any day. If it does you now know who's responsible. Anyway as long as you know this you won't be surprised when I am gone. So, for now, on we go with our little musical show".

Baker called me in his office. "The switchboard girls are complaining. They're getting hundreds of wild phone calls. Some are just calling in and saying a name and hanging up". "JOEL", said one caller, then hung-up. "LEE", said another then hung up.

"What's going on here Lee? You guys got a big problem with each other or what? Look, if you can't get along personally that's one thing, but around here and on the air, especially on the air forget it. Just drop it. I won't have it and that's final!

Bob Baker had been in radio since the Mayflower and even he believed it. Fell for the whole act and thought we were serious.

I just looked at him and said: "Bob, listen: Jack Benny and Fred Allen and their......" He didn't let me finish.

"FEUD!", he said.

"You guys are doing this on purpose!" Bob broke out in a loud laugh and buried his head on the desk.

"Lee, get out of my office…I love it".

Now Baker understood and the feud continued.

Chapter 33
CLUB 182

Friday night.

My first Friday night on the air at WXYZ.

After recording the last two hours of Friday night's show in the afternoon, there I was sitting in the lobby of UAW Hall 182 known to thousands of teenagers as Club 182 promoted and run by, you guessed it, three Policemen from Redford Township. Same ones who took a little $500 discount from me at Riverside Arena with a gun. You remember them right? Lovely gentlemen. Great examples of our law enforcement community. The same ones from Chapter eighteen who tried to see that I wasn't hired at WXYZ. Well, here I was ready to go on the air from their Club 182. I was in the lobby; Joel Sebastian was inside hosting the dance. Our friendly policemen were expecting the worst from me; they got my very best.

Friday and Saturday nights were big nights for music promotion people and radio personalities. Except for an elite few, radio personalities in the 60s were like sports figures, we didn't make much money so outside shows and personal appearances made up the difference between poverty and decent money. Friday and

Saturday there were high school sock hops, independent record dances, and shows for teenagers all around town. Detroit was important to recording artists and when they had something new that needed airplay the record companies always included Detroit on their in person promotional tour. LA, Dallas, Chicago, Detroit, Cleveland, Philly, Pittsburgh, New York. Get your record played in those markets and the rest will care of themselves.

Detroit was a personality radio town, Motown was starting to happen, Disc Jockeys were playing new music and new records played in Detroit could start a new artist on the way up. This was just a hot, happening town. If you were in the promotion business you had artists in town on Friday and Saturday and you were running from one dance or show to the next. Exposure, exposure, exposure! All the DJs wanted those artists at his event and promoted it on the air like:

"Don't forget now, I'll be at Notre Dame high Saturday night and my guest will be Brenda Lee, in person." DJs promoted the artists; played their records to promote their appearances and artists came to their events.

Gene Silverman was the music promotion man for Decca records and this night he was running with Brenda Lee.

Brenda Mae Tarpley was born in 1944 in Lithonia, Georgia. At five she was already on the radio in Conyers ,Georgia and signed with Decca Records in 1956. She was only 9 years old.. She appeared on television shows in the 50's on the big shows, Perry Como, Steve Allen, and yes The Ed Sullivan Show too. And then came "SWEET NOTHINS"

Brenda Lee sang with a voice that bigger than she was. She couldn't have been more that two inches short of 5 feet tall in those days. As Mickey Shorr would say: "She was two under a finsky". So, here is this pretty and petite breath of a shy, smiling little girl singing:

"My Baby whispers in mah eahh. Ahh SWEET NOTHINS"!

Every radio station in America was on the record like white on rice. In January of 1960 that's all you heard:

"MY BABY WHISPERS IN MY EAR...OOHH SWEEEETTT NOTHINS."

We all played it. After that Decca took a chance and released little Brenda singing a slooowww ballad.

"I'M SORRY – SO SORRY – FOR BEING SUCH A FOOL"

Decca had to get her out on the road to promote. LA, Dallas, Chicago, that night Club 182 in Plymouth, Michigan and 7 other dances in town. I was there in the lobby doing my air show and here came Gene Silverman with Brenda Lee in tow. She was 17 years old.

Gene introduced me, the record on the air ended and we were all on the air. I said something like: "Little Miss Dynamite is here, Brenda great to have you here at Club 182". And then, from that tiny bit of humanity came: "HI LEE, THANK YOU. GREAT TO BE HERE IN DETROIT." Her voice was nearly as low as mine! And big.

Now believe this or not it was exactly 8:30 when she walked in. 8:30! The exact time I had promoted all week that I was going to say something very personal about Joel Sebastian. To tell the truth, I had said that for the sake of continuing the suspense and interest of The Feud and didn't have a clue as to what I was going to say.

As if it had all been planned I said: "It is now exactly 8:30 in this big ole town and I promised I would say something very personal about Joel Sebastian at this time. So for those of you who have taken time to wait and tune in, this is what I have to say".

Before I could open my mouth Brenda Lee said: "Lee I heard you just started here a few nights ago and Joel doesn't want you here and nobody thinks that's fair of him, but you still like him and just wish him all the best!"

Gulp!

I was speechless. Did she say all that? How did that happen? Here is Brenda Lee, this little ball of energy with a booming voice, on the air with me saying that Joel Sebastian doesn't like me. That was more than anything else I could have said as my Friday night 8:30 announcement. I let it go at that. Nuff said.

SHE is helping me with the feud!

To this day I don't know if she believed it or if her promo guy prompted her. It worked though. I would see Brenda Lee three more times in the next year. The next time she had changed. I wonder if she remembers?

I promoted that dance as if there was never going to be another one. Club 182 sounded like the biggest, best, most star filled dance in town. I gave them extra commercial time. Brenda Lee was here, she'd be singing Sweet Nothin's, I'm Sorry, etc. I went on that Joel was here, even though he didn't like me for taking his job (had to get some of the feud in here), I was here, the music was here; everything was here! I refused to give the promoters even the smallest reason to complain. They had a great crowd. They knew it. Everybody knew it.

Oh yes there was something I knew too. I knew that John Gilbert, Bob Baker, Bob Baldricka the national sales manager, Bob Koch the local sales manager, and the rest of broadcast house were all listening to see if I could handle working for these guys who'd cheated me months before.

Next day I passed Mr. Gilbert in the hall. He just looked at me and gave me thumbs up. Club 182 had a record crowd and everyone was happy.

That wouldn't last long.

Tom Greenwood

'Horn' trumpets praise of radio's 'Lone Ranger'

Recently I penned a column about some childhood heroes, including **Clayton Moore** (TV's Lone Ranger) and former WXYZ Radio disc jockey Lee Alan. I said how I'd always had this secret dream that some day I'd grow up and be the Lone Ranger. I also said I'd spent many an evening cruising Woodward in the '60s, listening to **"Brother" Joel Sebastian** and **Lee "The Horn" Alan** and his "fine tone ashtray."

I must have stirred up a lot of memories, because readers wrote and called to say they admired the very same people. In the batch was a note from **Lee Alan Reicheld,** founder of the Reicheld Corp. ad agency. Drop the last name and you'll know who wrote it:

"Dear Tom: My childhood hero was also the Lone Ranger, but before Clayton Moore. As a boy growing up in Detroit I listened to *The Lone Ranger* as it was done live from WXYZ on the radio. My Lone Ranger in those days was **Brace Beemer.** His deep, resonant voice created a vivid mental picture of my hero. In 1965, I shared an office at WXYZ with my dear and recently deceased friend, Joel Sebastian. I heard a voice from the hallway. And there he stood ... 60 plus years of age — looking just like I always thought he would. I nervously introduced myself. He shook my hand, and with the other ... he gave me a silver bullet. Five days later he died.

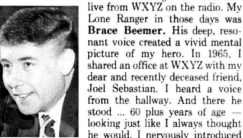

Lee Alan

"LAST YEAR at the national convention of the Friends of Old Time Radio, the *Lone Ranger* radio program was recreated by the original cast. They asked me to go and play Brace Beemer's part. For 30 minutes I was surrounded by all the thundering hoofbeats from out of the past and realized my boyhood dream. I *was* the Lone Ranger. ..."

Shortly thereafter, I received a call from "The Horn" himself, and let me tell all you "Wixie Pixies" out there that the man sounds exactly the same. "I retired from radio and opened my ad agency about 16 years ago," said Alan. "The horn and ashtray are locked up in a vault, along with photos and film clips from my radio days. But nothing means more to me than that silver bullet. That and the fact that I actually became the Lone Ranger ... if only for a little while."

Just a couple more followups. **Bob Beemer,** 61, son of radio's "masked man" and host of the Detroit Press Club since last June, reports that Oxford has really taken the Lone Ranger to its heart. "That was our hometown," said Beemer. "Now the city limit signs read 'Home of Brace Beemer — Radio's Lone Ranger.' They've also dedicated a park to my father. We're now raising funds for a nearly life-sized statue showing the Lone Ranger atop his famous horse Silver." Beemer said fund-raising efforts also include selling miniature versions of the statue — designed by Esquire magazine artist **Frank Varga** — for $4.95 each. Those buying a statue or making a contribution will have their names added to a plate on the statue. Write to Arnold Simmons, c/o the Oxford Twin Cinema, Oxford, MI 48051.

Brace Beemer

Clayton Moore — my Lone Ranger — still makes personal appearances dressed as TV's *"kimo sabe"* and recently celebrated his 72nd birthday. If you'd like to send a belated card, address it to Clayton Moore, 4720 Parkolivio, Calabasas, CA 91302. Think of it as a payback for all those memories.

Brace Beemer, Radio's & My Lone Ranger

Bottom Row: Far left, Fern Robinson, head of Cooley music selected me to narrate the Christmas Story. 4th and 5th from left, Al (Lee) & Ann, Pres & Sec of the Cooley Choir

From the Cooley High Yearbook 1953:

Left to Right:
Jim Scoggin (Pres)
Ann Hutchison (Sec)
Barbara Lilje (Vice-Pres)
Jim Hellwarth (Treas)

Cooley High School in the mid 50s.
My first public speaking part.
I still remember it.

"And it came to pass . . ."

```
                    Theresa & Fran Striker, Jr.
                         165 Singley Avenue
                        Runnemede, NJ 08078

October 22, 1985

Lee Alan Reicheld
31410 Northwestern Hwy Suite E
Farmington Hills, MI 48018

Dear Lee;

One of the first things that I wanted to do (when I returned home from the
Newark convention) was to drop you and Sharon a note— thanking you for
attending the Newark affair and for the excellence of your performance. As
is so often the case, priorities become changed and things go undone as time
marches on. At any rate-- a belated thanks.

Theresa and I enjoyed meeting and chatting with you both, our only regret is
that the meeting was so brief.

I must emphasize the outstanding performance you gave, Lee. I'm sure that
you couldn't see the expressions of shock which ran through the audience
when the redramatization began. Your rendering of their Lone Ranger was
truly exceptional.

Interestingly, last year when Dick Osgood asked me for some suggestions on
an appropriate script for this years reenactment, I had a concern for the
strong recognition factor of the Ranger's voice. I suggested a script from
what is known as the "transition series." (The transition series was
written to overcome the problems of voice recognition when introducing Brace
Beemer as the Lone Ranger after Earl Graser's death— the Ranger was
seriously wounded and had a limited role. He spoke only in a very weak
voice which gradually grew stronger as he recovered from his wounds.) The
WIXIE folks (Fred Flowerday) wanted a more typical, action packed, script
for this years reenactment and your fantastic contribution enabled a
genuine, "Return........ to those thrilling days of yesteryear......" for
all assembled.

Thanks also for your kind letter, Lee. I have never been a Ranger freak
either, but, having lived with a degree of name recognition (Dad's) all my
life I've been drawn into the old-time radio crowd. Many of the fans are a
bit weird, as I'm sure you noticed, but they are genuine and good people.
While I cannot share their degree of enthusiasm, I do appreciate it-- and am
quite humbled by their dedication to my Dad's fictional characterizations.

Enclosed is a copy of the book I put together a few years ago. It may offer
you some interesting insight to my Dad and provide some unusual anecdotes of
the the Lone Ranger.

Warmest regards,

Fran Striker, Jr.
```

His Typewriter Grew Spurs.....

A biography of Fran Striker-- writer.

Documenting the Lone Ranger's ride on the radiowaves of the world.

by Fran Striker, Jr.

Above: Fran Striker Jr.
His Letter of Thanks to Lee.

Top Right: Fran Striker Sr. Originator, Writer of The Lone Ranger

Left:
Brace Beemer,
Radio's Lone Ranger,
Died 1965

Right
Yours Truly
Lee Alan Sans Horn.
Honored to play
The Lone Ranger in 1985

LETTERS TO LEE ......

Hi Lee,

    I wrote to you on the website the other day and want to thank you for the really nice answer back. I 'inherited' a book my mom had. It's about Detroit, Wixie Wonderland, by Dick Osgood. It contains a very nice section all about you and some great pictures of you.

    I'm sure you are very familiar with this book and the fact that it covers the first 50 years of WXYZ. Reading it brings back so many memories! Where has the time gone?!

    I can imagine you are very busy now compiling all the information you are receiving and attending the many events you are being invited to. What fun!

    We are having our 40th Class Reunion in a few weeks so of course I'm really looking forward to getting together with my old friends. I had so much fun all during high school, and even had 4 years perfect attendance only because I didn't want to miss a day! Isn't that crazy? I lived for the nights I could go to Club 182 and Walled Lake Casino. Remember how the dance floor literally vibrated with the pounding feet at WLC, and the floor of Club 182 got so wet from all the sweat? Those memories are so vivid today for me. All the local bands that appeared and were given the opportunity to do their stuff and be heard was just too cool.

    I just feel very fortunate to have had the opportunity to be a part of all that. I can definitely say "BEEN THERE DONE THAT"! You, Joel, Dave, all made all that a reality for us teens and gave us the places to have good fun and make some of the best memories possible. I was very lucky to have grown up during the 60's. (I can't help feeling that WLC and Club 182 would not be possible today in the social environment that now exists. For one thing drugs are just too much of a factor in today's young society). Even the drive-in theaters can't exist anymore because today's youth can't just go there and watch a movie or two and make out in their cars. They have to get totally wasted, drunk, use it as a place to party. I miss those drive-ins.

    Well, I'm getting carried away here, I know. I swear I could talk to you for hours, and I'm not alone for sure.

    You take care and I wish you the best of luck, Lee! Thanks for everything.

Love,
Lauren Myers(Holmes), Clarenceville High Class of '63

Seven Swingin' Guys

Here we are. The line up as of May 23, 1966 and the music in Motown
(Courtesy Jim Hampton (lower left) now of Greenhouse Marketing Group, Los Angeles)

WXYZ DETROIT SOUND SURVEY
WXYZ'S OFFICIAL PLAY LIST
Monday, May 23, 1966

#	Title – Artist	Label	(Last)
1.	PAINT IT BLACK – Rolling Stones	London	(1)
2.	WHEN A MAN LOVES A WOMAN – Percy Sledge	Atlantic	(8)
3.	STRANGERS IN THE NIGHT – Frank Sinatra	Reprise	(7)
4.	I AM A ROCK – Simon and Garfunkle	Columbia	(3)
5.	MAMA – B. J. Thomas	Scepter	(17)
6.	THE MORE I SEE YOU – Chris Montez	A & M	(2)
7.	LITTLE GIRL – The Syndicate of Sound	Bell	(25)
8.	FARMER JOHN – The Tidal Waves	S.V.R.	(14)
9.	BAREFOOTIN' – Robert Parker	Nola	(15)
10.	SWEET TALKIN' GUY – Chiffons	Laurie	(4)
11.	IT'S A MAN'S MAN'S MAN'S WORLD – James Brown	King	(6)
12.	A GROOVY KIND OF LOVE – Mindbenders	Fontana	(9)
13.	My Little Red Book – Love	Elecktra	(5)
14.	Ain't Too Proud To Beg – The Temptations	Gordy	(18)
15.	Friends and Lovers Forever – Nancy Ames	Epic	(23)
16.	Come On and See Me – Tammi Terrell	Motown	(29)
17.	Green Grass – Gary Lewis	Liberty	(10)
18.	Opus 17 – Four Seasons	Phillips	(19)
19.	Did You Ever Have To Make Up Your Mind? Lovin' Spoonful	KaSu	(20)
20.	Cheryl Ann – Tim Tam & the Turnons	Palmer	(HP)
21.	Dirty Water – Standells	Tower	(28)
22.	Take This Heart of Mine – Marvin Gaye	Tamla	(31)
23.	Oh Yeah – Shadows of Knight	Dunwich	(55)
24.	Monday, Monday – The Mamas & The Papas	Dunhill	(11)
25.	Sunny – Bob Hebb	Phillips	(HP)
26.	Crying – J & The Americans	United Artists	(HP)
27.	You Don't Have To Say You Love Me – Dusty Springfield	Phillips	(30)
28.	Hey Joe – The Leaves	Mira	(HP)
29.	Paperback Writer/Rain – The Beatles	Capitol	(HP)
30.	Truly Yours – The Spinners	Motown	(–)
31.	Just A Little Misunderstanding – The Contours	Gordy	(32)
32.	Come Let's Go – The McCoys	Bang	(35)
33.	Break Out – Mitch Ryder & The Detroit Wheels	New Voice	(33)
34.	We Gotta Go – Shy Guys	Panik	(–)
35.	Double Shot – The Swingin' Medallions	Smash	(34)

Spotlight Sound of the Week
HE – Righteous Brothers – Verve

1270 ON YOUR DIAL

Listen. . . It's All Happening Again
The Music – The Sounds – The People

Scene From ABC TV's Club 1270.
L to R: Lee Alan, The Pixies Three, Al Valenti, Brother Joel Sebastian

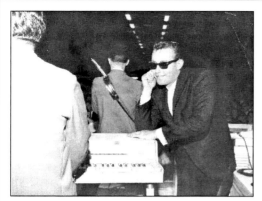
On stage at Walled Lake Casino

L to R: Lee Alan, Dave Prince, Marc Avery, Danny Taylor

Walled Lake Casino and Amusement Park

Dick Osgood doing news from Lee's WXYZ Studio.

LEE ALAN

PERSONALITY PROFILE

MONDAY - SATURDAY: 7:15 - 12 MIDNIGHT

LEE ALAN — is most commonly known as "The Horn" since his creative mind thought up the use of a "genuine imported Pakistani taxi horn." On the air Alan has captured top nighttime audiences in Detroit and is the undisputed leader of the personality pack. He has performed at more benefit functions and in-person celebrity appearances than perhaps anyone else in modern Detroit radio (at Walled Lake dances he hosted 75,000 young adults in 1963 alone). His recording, "Set Me Free," was sold to thousands of listeners—all proceeds going to the YMCA Summer Camp Fund. Our "young man with a horn" has a rapport with listeners unlike anyone else we know—when he says he'll do something — like offer a product to his listeners via a commercial—they respond en masse.

MARKET FACTS

Total Population	7,659,600
Radio Homes	1,627,940
Total Spendable Income	12,096,430,000
Autos with Radio	2,686,154

(Monday - Friday 7 - 12 MIDNIGHT)

85% of the cars are radio equipped.
Traffic Audit Bureau, RAB, SRDS, 2/1/64

BLAIR GROUP PLAN MEMBER

WXYZ 1270 RADIO DETROIT

❝ AN ABC OWNED RADIO STATION ❞

Richard E. Osgood
32575 NOTTINGHAM KNOLL
FARMINGTON HILLS, MICHIGAN 48018

313-626-7986

March 2, 1984

Mr. William E. Thomas

Dear Mr. Thomas:

I want to thank you for the interesting and flattering letter received from you yesterday. Much more satisfaction has come to me through messages such as yours and friendships made because of the book across the country than from skimpy royalty checks received, believe me.

You will be pleased to learn that Lee Alan is enjoying the success that he has earned - a much more talented man than I realized when I wrote "Wyxie Wonderland." We hardly knew each other when we both worked at WXYZ. To me he was another of those strange young men of a new breed, and to him I had to be an aging relic of the past who should make way for youth. It was Dick Kernen's enthusiastic appreciation of him that led me finally to tape with Lee and I have to say that along with Jim Riddell, Allan Campbell and Hal Neal, Lee developed into one of my favorite characters.

And I want you to know he has become a terrific friend. When the book was being promoted in very icy weather, he took me here and there in his four-wheel drive, took this old man's arm crossing slippery spots, and allowed me to introduce him after speeches here and there as one of the characters from the book. His little speech always topped mine and made the appearances successful.

Today, he owns his own agency, writes his own commercials, composes music for them, produces them and appears on them. And he does many voices.

He is also a devoted husband and father, has a beautiful home with swimming pool and is a generous host. You picked the right guy to idolize; he more than lives up to your memory of him. I am sending him a xerox of your letter, for I know it will please him.

Cordially

Dick Osgood

Dick Osgood & Lee

Detroit News Article – Sunday August 9, 1964

Detroit's 'Swingin' Kind' Aims for Big-Time TV

By Frank Judge
Detroit News Television and Radio writer

Can a network quality, nationally syndicated weekly television show be produced in Detroit?

The answer is expected to be learned at 7 p.p. Wednesday when WXYZ-TV (Channel 7) Presents "The Swingin' Kind."

The half hour program, with WXYZ-Radio disc jockey Lee Alan as host, features popular Teen-appeal entertainers, including those identified with the Detroit sound of rhythm and blues

If it clicks well enough with the public, this show will done as a nationally syndicated Program produced by Channel 7. The station is having a rating company take a special survey to determine the popularity of Wednesday night's show.

If it meets with only moderate success, the show probably will be turned into a local program, the budget for which would be substantially below the amount spent for Wednesday's show.

"It wouldn't be possible to do this quality of show, with its high production values and top stars, every week unless we could syndicate it nationally and spread the costs," says John F. Pival, president of WXYZ Inc. and head of Channel 7.

The show is one of three taped on location around Detroit. Wednesday night's program was done entirely at Metropolitan Beach. The others were taped in and around the Michigan Consolidated Gas Co. Building on Woodward and Edgewater park.

Wednesday night's show stars singer Lesley Gore and Little Stevie Wonder, who accentuates his singing with blasts on the harmonica. Featured on the program are the Shangri-Las, The Coasters, the Sunliners, the Dis-Coquettes Dancers and the Choker Campbell band. Peter strand was the program supervisor for the show, which was produced and directed by Chuck Snead, with technical direction by Paul Jantke. Choreography was by Jack Barnes and Richard Dean.

Seen by this writer at a preview screening in the Channel 7 studios, the show is a fast moving, swinging program with network potential.

It remains to be seen if the public will help turn it into a Detroit-originated, nationally syndicated show.

Stevie and Lee on TV at Metropolitan Beach

LETTERS TO LEE ......

Hi Lee,
I have so many fond memories of listening to you on WXYZ and other stations!
Here are a few:

First, I believe you were the first person to host an "oldies but goodies" show on Detroit radio, correct? I remember the show you did on Sunday nights on WXYZ when you would read letters from girls whose boyfriends were over in Vietnam, and then you would play "their song." I think you sometimes would talk directly to the servicemen because you would tape your show and send it to American Forces Radio to be re-broadcast.

I remember Fred Wolf's last show on WXYZ. There was a contest to try and guess what time an alarm clock would go off in the studio that morning, and I was exactly one hour off – I think it went off at 7:43, and I had guessed 8:43!

I "discovered" Wixie Radio in the spring of 1965. Dave Prince was on the air at the time, and I was hooked! I absolutely loved the station and the DJ's. Wixie was the station I was listening to when I was first bitten by the rock & roll bug and I started going out and buying records – I was 11 years old at the time. 1965 and 1966 were my all-time favorite years for music and for radio, and WXYZ was MY STATION.

There was that unforgettable night in April of 1966 when I tuned to Wixie at 9 p.m. and heard the debut of the Joey Reynolds Show. The first three minutes of that show is my all-time favorite moment as a radio listener. As you will recall, Joey referred to his competition at the other stations by name, dismissed them as poppycock and asked listeners to swear their allegiance to WXYZ. For me, Joey, and Wixie ruled! I went out and bought my purple candle and became a regular listener to the Royal Order of the Night People.

Recently WKNR has been getting alot of attention due to the Keener website and the Dream Cruise broadcasts, and that's fine - I love hearing about any memories of growing up in Detroit in the 60s, but every time I see someone raving about Keener I want to scream - WIXIE WAS BETTER!!!!!!!! I felt back then, and still do that Keener and CKLW were slick, pseudo-hip and flashy, but with little real substance. The WXYZ jocks by contrast were REAL, down-to-earth, and relatable - Personality Plus as you used to bill yourselves.

I was so into Wixie that I still remember the first time I picked up a copy of the WXYZ Detroit Sound Survey with the pictures of the jocks on the back. I lived in Ann Arbor and since we were in a fringe area for WXYZ's signal, the surveys weren't sent out to the record stores there. But on Thursday May 26, 1966 I finally got a copy during a visit to Hudson's at the Westland Shopping Center. I had been so curious as to what the jocks looked like - I had seen you, Fred Wolf and Dave Prince on TV, but everyone else looked nothing like how I had pictured them!

I'll never forget the day in the spring of 1967 when I tuned to 1270 and heard "The Sound Of The Good Life" for the first time. I was devastated. In the 36 years since, I have never heard another radio station that hooked me the way that Wixie did.

I wanted the station to "come back" so bad, and the closest thing to that happening came in 1969 when you revived your night show on WHFI. I have some of your most memorable moments from that show on tape. I have the beginning of your first show; the day you called Joey Reynolds in Hartford; the time during the Paul McCartney death hoax when you exposed WKNR for the frauds that they were; and from your first week on the station, the day you read my letter to you on the air. Basically I was asking you whatever happened to some of the old WXYZ jocks.

Another great thrill for me was hearing "Back In The 60s" on CKLW-FM in the early 90s. Lee, you did such a great job of re-creating the sound of your old show! It was a masterpiece, and one of the highlights was the theme song you came up with- one of the catchiest tunes I have ever heard.

In closing, Lee I'd like to thank you for all of the wonderful entertainment that you have provided me and so many others over the years. In fact you and the other Wixie guys were so inspiring to me that I decided to pursue a career in radio, and this year I celebrated my 25th anniversary in the business. It's been a rocky road at times, but remembering the joy you brought me with your broadcasts motivates me to hopefully do the same for my listeners. I await your book and the Walled Lake reunion with great anticipation.

Sincerely,
Jim Heddle

'I Accepted Gratuities,' DJ Don McLeod Admits

By James Hart

The spin-dizzy world of disc jockeys reeled on its axis today … new resignations followed … investigations over payola.

Don McLeod, popular veteran … WJBK radio … today, latest of … employes … than a few days.

Dale Young … on Detroit Bandstand … record program on WJBK-TV … signed early Sunday … No. 1 disc jockey among … Detroit area teen-agers, was fired by the station Saturday night.

While insisting his resignation was voluntary, McLeod said he had made "a few mistakes" and had taken some gratuities.

JAC LE GOFF WAS fired as WJBK-TV news director last week for what the station termed "editorializing" on a newscast.

McLeod said "a difference in principle" caused his resignation, adding:

"There was no pressure at … this was not done under stress. It is something I have been mulling over for some time."

He said he enjoyed a good life during his 11 years at the station.

"BUT I'VE MADE a few mistakes," he said. "I took gratuities. Who in any business hasn't?

"I've even taken money. But I've paid it back. I have some very dear friends in the bu…

SHORR: DJ Fired by WXYZ

Continued from Page One

thing with Gorelick came up and Neal asked that I elaborate on the activities of Aussie Records Inc."

("The thing with Gorelick" is a lawsuit filed by a rock 'n' roll quartet, the Royal Tones, against Stuart L. Gorelick, 23, of 25615 Parkwood, over royalties from a record.

(Shorr's name was mentioned in the suit but both he and Gorelick said money Shorr received was in repayment of a loan to Gorelick.)

"MY ATTORNEY, Avern L. Cohn, and I conferred with Neal early this week," Shorr said.

"When Avern read the line in the affidavit which said that I entered the Aussie Records Inc., with the knowledge of Mr. Neal, Hal (Harold Neal) did a double take.

"Cohn asked Neal if he would like to have us delete that line, but I objected, saying: 'I don't want to delete the line. I refused to purge myself on my own behalf so let the reference stand.'"

Shorr said he also included a statement in the affidavit that "I owned stock in the ABC which in turn owned stock in record and publishing companies."

HE SAID HE had put in the order to sell the stock several … to take me in as a partner," Shorr said. "I may go back into the auto business.

"I don't think I want to work as a disc jockey under the conditions most disc jockeys are required to work now. There isn't any creativity left in it. None whatsoever."

Shorr said that when he was released from WJBK in 1956 "I had my heart and soul wrapped up in this business.

"After I had been out of work for three or four months, I thought I'd never get another job as a disc jockey. I was very depressed.

"And it was just about this time that I received a conference call from two record manufacturers who wanted to know if I had any prospects of getting back into radio.

"WHEN I TOLD them 'no,' these two fellows offered to buy a bar or restaurant for me or to back me in the manufacture of records.

"I told them I would think about it and let them know after they told me that if I decided to go into business for myself they would be happy to back me up to $15,000 or $20,000.

"I assumed that this was a gesture of appreciation for the fact that I had helped them when I was in a position to and hadn't asked for anything in return."

Tom Clay Is Out; Dale Young Goes

Don McLeod, WJBK disc jockey, resigned today in what Garry Lipson, manager of WJBK-Radio, described as a "spontaneous" and "voluntary" act. McLeod had been scheduled for a noon to 1 p.m. show and for another broadcast from 3 to 7 p.m. McLeod was not immediately available for comment.

By James Hart

Two of Detroit's top disc jockeys are off the air today — one fired, the other by resignation.

Tom Clay, of WJBK radio, rated the No. 1 disc jockey in the metropolitan area, was fired Saturday night because he admitted taking payola — an industry term for a payoff to plug records.

Dale Young, director of Detroit Bandstand, a … television dance show, resigned from WJBK-TV early Sunday while station brass extended their investigation into payoffs.

YOUNG ISSUED this statement in connection with his resignation:

"In an atmosphere of … and … I have resigned from the staff of WJBK-TV and … a possible move to another …

DJ Mickey Shorr Denies Payola in WXYZ Firing

By James Hart

Mickey Shorr, "Good Buddy Dick" to thousands of teenagers who followed his WXYZ record show, joined the ranks of unemployed disc jockeys today.

Shorr was fired by Harold Neal Jr., vice president of WXYZ Radio yesterday.

NEAL AND OTHER station officials refused to comment on the reason Shorr was released, but Neal later issued a statement which said only:

"WXYZ today (Friday) exercised its right to terminate the employment of Mr. Mickey Shorr."

Shorr emphatically denied payola had anything to do with his firing.

"I have not at any time accepted payola. I'm ready to take an oath to that effect," he told the Times in an exclusive interview last night.

"I OBJECTED to accepting payola because I didn't want to be put into a subservient position," he said.

Shorr, 33, became the fourth Detroit disc jockey fired or who resigned during the current payola furor.

Earlier, Tom Clay, WJBK disc jockey, was fired for taking "payola," which he told the Times yesterday amounted to closer to $5,400 than to the $…000 I originally estimated."

Dale Young, master of ceremonies on WJBK's Detroit Bandstand, and DJ Don McLeod, also of WJBK, resigned.

WJBK-TV newscaster Jac LeGoff was fired last week for editorializing on a newscast. He described his comments as his "strong personal feeling" about the "payola" situation.

SCHORR, MARRIED and the father of three, had been with WXYZ since the fall of 1956.

He told the Times he was fired because he refused to delete several lines from an affidavit he signed along with other disc jockeys employed by the American Broadcasting Co., of which WXYZ is an affiliate.

The standard affidavits were signed a week ago after Ed McKenzie, a former WXYZ disc jockey, wrote in an article in a national magazine payola is common among radio's platter people.

McKenzie said some jockeys … up to $50,000 a year.

After the article appeared Neal issued a statement saying:

"IN CONFORMANCE with American Broadcasting Co. policy, WXYZ has been investigating its music-selection practices.

"Information available to WXYZ affirms that no disc jockey, now performing on this station, no person who participates in the selection of music for broadcast over WXYZ, nor I, this WXYZ station manager, has either solicited or accepted any personal consideration, money or otherwise, to have any record played on WXYZ."

Shorr said that after he signed the affidavit, "in…

Continued on Page 2, Col.

'Did Wrong,' Says Ex-DJ Tom Clay

"Payola is wrong, very wrong."

This is the message Tom Clay, former WJBK Radio disc jockey, hopes to impress upon each of his many teen-age followers.

CLAY, FIRED from the station a week ago after he admitted taking payola, will stage his final "big dance" — a record hop — at the light guard armory tonight.

He hopes to realize a personal profit of about $200 to be used, he said, in an effort to buy TV time "to explain to the guys and gals why payola is wrong."

The 30-year-old record-spinner said he had received thousands of letters from his youthful fans.

"Most of the letters indicate the individual writer thinks that payola is all right. Some admit that they don't know whether it is right or wrong," Clay said.

"I'VE GOT to impress upon those kids that I was wrong … that what I did was not right. I can't have them believing that payola is right." … forgive me and love me and a… that for what I have done.

"I think if they really understand what payola stands for they would realize it is wrong. But, I don't think they really know what it means."

Clay said he didn't get the full impact of the meaning of payola himself until he read a letter from a girl teen-ager.

"IT'S WRONG because the little people have to pay for the very same thing the big people got for nothing."

CLAY SAID he had received letters from many parents as well as from his teen-age fans.

"One letter, from a little boy really broke me up," Clay said. He quoted the letter as saying:

"Dear Clay, I use to lisse… When my dog made noise I shushed him up. I'm sory. … am 9."

Clay said the reason he "broke up" over this letter was because "the little guy doesn't even know what payola is."

"IT'S ONLY because of him and others like him that I … I don't have to leave Detroit," he said.

Clay hasn't made an attempt to buy TV time as yet …

MICKEY SHORR

The One & Only Mickey Shorr - WXYZ

John Pival in an undated file photo: His creative genius quickly made Channel 7 the king of local programming. Among the eventual celebrities he brought to the station were:

Radio disc jockey
Johnny Slagle

World traveler
George Pierrot

Sportscaster
Don Wattrick

"Polka king"
Warren Michael Kelly

John F. Pival – Genius TV Pioneer and Staff

John Pival – President WXYZ, Inc

Charles Fritz VP & General Manager WXYZ Radio

Dick Kernan - Producer in the Booth at Walled Lake Casino

Radio-TV- Show Producer John Dew

LETTERS TO LEE ......

HI LEE,

WE WERE BACKING JOEY DEE, AND THE STARLIGHTERS, AT ONE OF YOUR WALLED LAKE BASHES. EVERYTHING WENT GREAT, DOING "PEPPERMINT TWIST", AND A FEW OTHERS. AT THE TIME WE DIDN'T REALIZE IT, BUT ONE OF HIS BACKGROUND SINGERS WAS TO BECOME QUITE FAMOUS.
BELIEVE IT OR NOT, IT WAS JOE PESCI, THE ACTOR!!

AT ONE OF THE MANY SHOWS AT THE CASINO THAT WE DID, WE HAD JUST FINISHED, AND WERE PACKING UP THE GEAR. I HAD MY CAR AND WAS BACKING UP TO LOAD OUT, WHEN I ACCIDENTLY BACKED INTO A NEW RIVIERA. I WENT INSIDE TO FIND OUT WHOSE CAR IT WAS. IT WAS DAVE PRINCE'S!!
ALL OF US WERE FREAKED OUT, THINKING THAT'S THE END OF OUR CAREER AT WALLED LAKE.
DAVE WAS VERY UNDERSTANDING, AND WE BREATHED EASIER. WE EXCHANGED INSURANCE INFO, AND I FOUND OUT HIS REAL NAME WAS DAVE PRINGLE. THE REST OF THE GUYS FOUND THIS EXTREMELY ENTERTAINING. OF COURSE, MY DAD DIDN'T SEE ANY HUMOR IN IT AT ALL.

GOOD LUCK WITH THE BOOK!! HOPEFULLY, WE'LL SEE YOU AT THE BIG BASH.
BEST,   RAY MONETTE

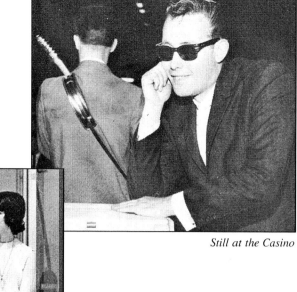
Still at the Casino

Swingin' Kind on ABC TV

Lee's Signature Photo

Love From Lee's Fans

WXYZ Stamp Drive

At the conclusion of the assembly, Ralph Perkins, in behalf of WWHS students, presented the WXYZ D.J.'s with 300 full books. Mr. Alan was speechless.

Sherri, Tom, Linda and Randy are only a few of the people that helped collect and paste the stamps.

Warren Woods High School
January 1966

After
Jan. 27

Edwin Star

Mr. Alan congratulates Mr. Soash and WWHS for a job well done.

WWHS's own talent.

"An Underdog"

"An Illusion"

Live Broadcast From Warren Woods High in Motown

Those Golden Oldie Guys

By PETER G. GAVRILOVICH
Free Press Staff Writer

What was it about Lee Alan that set us free? His horn? His silliness? His fine-toned ashtray?

The infamous Lee Alan fine-toned ashtray:

"Wait a minnnaatttttteeeee," Alan used to scream into the radio microphone. And then — and we can only guess — holding a metal ashtray on its side, he let it go:

ARRROOOONNN nnann
AHRROONN
ahronahronahron
nnnnannnn COOOOO-PHWHUMP!

"Hahahahaha," Alan would laugh in his high pitched voice, "You see that."

Actually though all those years of Lee Alan, 1962 to 1967 on WXYZ, we never really did see that ashtray; heard it a lot, yeah, and the low blat of his fine-toned Pakistani horn. The Horn. It was a measure of silliness that made

Continued on Page 32

Lee Alan, circa 1962

And The Hits Just Keep On Coming

L to R Poop Deck Paul, Milky The Clown, Toby David, Unknown, Johnny Ginger, Bozo The Clown

*Byron Macgregor,
Jo Jo Shutty Macgregor,
Lee Alan*

Lee & Crew ON The Air

*Lee Debuts
"Back In The 60s Again"
Live on Kiss-FM*

Lee and Dick Kernan at Walled Lake High 1965 Reunion

L-R: Kasey Kasem, Fred Wolf, Dick Osgood

GOLDEN OLDIES TALK RADIO

Casey Kasem, Fred Wolf (center) and Dick Osgood shared microphone memories at a Motor City radio reunion Saturday night at the Michigan In Kasem worked at WJBK and WJLB in the 1950s, and Osgood and Wolf (remember his Wacky Wandering Wigloo?) were WXYZ personalities.

Richard Lee/Detroit Free Press

LETTERS TO LEE ......

STEVEN GOLDSTEIN
Vice President
Group Program Director

May 28, 1985

Mr. Lee Reicheld
Reicheld Corporation
31410 Northwestern
Suite E
Farmington Hills, MI 48018

Dear Lee:

Thanks so much for being part of the WNIC "Reunion Weekend." I'm only sorry you couldn't have been here in person to share in the charismatic environment, however your program was excellent and the response was even better!

In fact, response to the entire weekend was overwhelming and it couldn't have happened without Lee Alan. As a small token of our appreciation, enclosed is a momento of WNIC's Reunion Weekend.

Again, thanks for being involved in a memorable radio event.

Sincerely,

Steve Goldstein
Vice President
Group Program Director

SG/crz

15001 Michigan Ave. • Dearborn, Michigan 48126 • (313) 846-8500

WXYZ
RADIO DETROIT

FROM: Toni Robinson
       444-1111 x 269
Date: 2.18.66

BRUCE STILL AND LEE ALAN PROMOTED

...Detroit....Charles D. Fritz, Vice President and General Manager of WXYZ RADIO announced today the appointment of BRUCE STILL to Operations Director and LEE ALAN to Program Director.

Mr. Still will supervise the activities of radio operations including traffic and promotions departments.
Still, came to WXYZ June 1, 1965 from WGR, Buffalo. He has held positions with KQV, Pittsburgh and WIL, St Louis.

Lee Alan, with his tremendous awareness of listener interests, program planning, and creative abilities, will handle all facets of on-the-air sound and the supervision of Air Personalities. He will continue his on-the-air work in the 7-10PM time period.

Lee Alan – Television Producer

Commercial Music - Lee Rehearses Singers

October 28, 1990

Notre Dame High School
A Marist Fathers Apostolate
20254 Kelly Road
Harper Woods, Mich. 48225-1287
313 371-8965

Dear Lee,

I was greatly honored by your appearance at our 35th anniversary sock hop on Saturday, Oct. 13th 1990.

I want to thank you for your kind words but most of all I was impressed how you held over 800 people in the palm of your hand; your rich voice capitalized the whole audience.

Yes, Lee Alan, you haven't lost your touch with humanity. I was so proud of you and greatly enjoyed your presence.

Your new project the "60's" and "70's" and 50's I hope will be successful. You're not a dreamer and with all your talents and experiences it is bound to be a success.

Before you came to N. Dame on Sat. Oct 13th I often wondered what you were doing. I knew that you had your own studio giving lessons in voice culture and radio expertise.

Continual success, Lee, and God bless you — I will always remember you when you were #1 with the teens.

Keep in touch.

Enclosed a few pictures of you taken at our anniversary sock-hop.

God bless you always.

Sincerely yours,
Father John W. Bryson S.M.

P.S. Keep me informed of your new ventures etc.

John

Letter from Father Bryson at Notre Dame High. His teen dances were famous.

Detroit sends a wave of patriotism over the air

■ **Cheers**: 375 stations will join three-day salute to freedom.

JIM McFARLIN

The phenomenal explosion of pro-America sentiment that accompanied Operation Desert Storm, Memorial Day and the ongoing International Freedom Festival should really hit an emotional peak on Independence Day Thursday. And American radio can tie a yellow ribbon around Detroit's Lee Alan Reicheld.

Reicheld, a Motor City radio legend who blew his "fine toned horn" in the 1960s under the air name Lee Alan, has operated a local audio-video commercial production company for the last 20 years. But he says he's never experienced a rush of acceptance to equal his three-hour holiday radio event called *The Americans.*

A patriotic celebration in words and music, the special has mushroomed from an idea into a phenomenon, airing this week on more than 375 stations from coast to coast — including two separately owned competitors in Metro Detroit.

Windsor's CKMR-FM (93.9) already ran the program once last weekend, and will repeat it at 4 p.m. July 4. On the AM dial, Detroit's newstalk WXYT (1270) will present it at 3 and 9 p.m. on the Fourth of July, and 6 p.m. Sunday.

Chrysler Corp. has underwritten the entire production as sole corporate sponsor, receiving at least 20,000 radio commercial messages in the process. In addition, *The Americans* will be carried on more than 400 stations in 123 countries over the Armed Forces Radio Network.

L. A. Reicheld

"It's absolutely unbelievable," says Reicheld. "If you're not an American now, you will be by the time this thing stops running. I'm happy for me, but I'm happy for everybody here. And I'm so darn proud of the fact that it's coming from Detroit."

The Americans, a long-form embellishment of Byron MacGregor's

National Publicity for Lee's "Americans" on 1,000 Radio Stations

Lee Alan The Actor as Abe Lincoln and Isaiah. Note Lincoln's wrist watch (It was a rehearsal)

LETTERS TO LEE ......

Lee,

I don't remember what I was looking for on the internet last week, but I came across a Detroit News On-Line article that reference your CDs "Back in the 60's." More searching brought me to your web site and WPON. Now I'm waiting for 2 of your CDs from 1967. I'll probably get the book soon.

I left Detroit in '73, now live near Seattle, but nostalgia has set in big time. I grew up near Grand River and Greenfield Rd at a time when Detroit was beautiful, and recall the rise of Elvis, the coming of the Beatles, through the change to FM like WABX. All my teen years and early twenties were accompanied to the tunes on WXYZ, WKNR, and CKLW. Very clear in my memory was your sign-off with "I Can't Get Started With You."

I have a closer connection, as well. It might have been 1963 when you were broadcasting one evening from Emmet Chevrolet on Grand River. I rode my bike down there, and you autographed my Pakistan horn, which I still have.

I don't know if that is of interest to you, but it sure has been great to listen to you after all these years. How bittersweet it is to think about Detroit, how nice it was, the wonderful memories, the girlfriends, the cars, the music. Hearing your voice makes me think I CAN go back, if only for a while, if only in my mind, and that's enough, that's all I can ask.

Thanks, Lee Alan, for still doing what you do and love the best.

Sincerely,
Bob Alescio

Lee & Martha Reeves without the Vandellas

Lee On The Air

Lee Alan & Temptation's Eddie Kendricks, Singer of My Girl and Scores of others.

Robin Seymor and his Swingin' Time TV Show in Motown

*Lee Alan MCs 30th Reunion
Walled Lake Class of 1965*

Lee shoots TV commercial for Kosins Clothes
  L to R: Bob Talbert, Jock Demers, Chuck Daly, Harry Kosins

Lee & Thee Horn Grand Marshall 2002 Woodward Cruise Motown

LETTERS TO LEE ......

STEREO 93.1

January 10, 1978

Mr. Lee Allen
Reicheld Corp.
24901 Northwestern Hwy.
Suite 413 D
Southfield, Michigan 48076

Dear Lee,

I hope this letter finds you and 1978 in harmony with success and happiness.

The response on your on-air New Year's Eve Party was again tremendous! It's the kind of radio event that reminds us what that "little box" with the speakers and knobs is really all about...communicating.

That word "communicate" tends to be over-used in our business. More often, and sadly enough it is also ignored. When WDRQ has the chance to exhibit that fine art of talking and entertaining people via you, not only does the listener benefit, but our own beliefs and ideals about radio are inspired and strengthened.

Thanks again for your involvement and also for reminding a young program director why he fell in love with this in the first place.

Jim Harper
Jim Harper

15933 W. 8 MILE
DETROIT, MI. 48235
(313) BR. 2-8000

Lee, The Advertising Guy

Son and TV Crew Chief Lee Alan Jr. with Chuck Daly.

The Little Guy From The Troy Post Office (See Chapter 72)

CAROL T's

Detroit News Sunday Magazine April 25, 1982

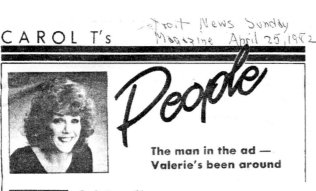

People

The man in the ad — Valerie's been around

Reader's Inquiring Minds

Q. Is it possible for me to see a picture of the man who does those Chrysler-Plymouth spots on WWJ-Radio? He comes on with such humor, he makes my day. Who is he?

Mary Groat
Lincoln Park

A. Funny guy who does the spots is **Lee Alan**, a top-rated personality on WXYZ-Radio during the 1960s. In 1969 he ended his gig as a jock to open his own broadcasting school in Detroit, which he later sold. After that he formed an advertising agency in Southfield called the Reicheld Corp., where he presides right now. Alan began doing the Chrysler-Plymouth spots in fall, 1980, and got an award last month from the National Automobile Dealers Association for having the "best ad campaign in broadcasting."

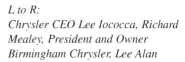

L to R:
Chrysler CEO Lee Iococca, Richard Mealey, President and Owner Birmingham Chrysler, Lee Alan

WALLED LAKE CASINO
Back In The 60s

Lee Alan briefs a band at Opening Night : 1961

Walled Lake Casino in Novi opened in 1928 and along with Walled Lake Amusement Park, made the area famous as a family entertainment center for the Midwest. When the big bands died, Walled Lake Casino closed. New owners opened again in 1961 Lee Alan brought the entire area back and put Novi and Walled Lake into the national spotlight.

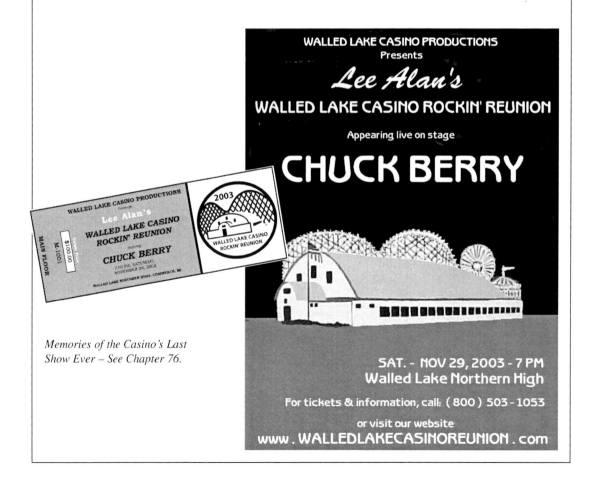

Memories of the Casino's Last Show Ever – See Chapter 76.

2003 L to R Lee Alan, Chuck Berry, Lee's Step Son Kenneth Daw

Nancy & Chuck Berry

2004 - Lee, Wife Nancy, Frank Sinatra Jr.
Lee MCd The Sinatra Show

Lee And Nancy arrive for the Sinatra Show in Motown

Nancy & Lee

L to R Nancy, Grandson Max, The Horn (Santa), Grandson Daniel

Listener's Winning Drawing of The Horn – 1965

Best Wishes & Happy Memories...

Chapter 34
WYXIE RANTS AND RAVES

WITHIN THE NEXT TWO WEEKS I MUST HAVE received 3,000 letters. 2,999 of them were about the feud. Seriously I did get that many letters, and so did Joel. They were all taking sides. Some were for Joel and against me and vice versa. Listeners believed there was a real feud and that either Joel or I would soon be gone. They were nearly right.

Meanwhile, back at the ranch. (oops, sorry wrong program). Things were getting wilder on the air. I mean I was getting wilder. The station had a format. A plan. A set of guidelines that we all had to adhere to. Certain music that had to be played from a printed and compiled list. The list was called the WXYZ Tunedex. (terrible name). We had to play the songs in a certain rotation, like one from the top ten, then one from the middle ten, then the top ten again, etc. We had to play the station jingles, give the time, temperature, weather, promote the other programs, etc. As long as we did all of those things we could also do other things. And that's where I kept getting wilder and wilder....

One night not long after I started I said on the air that we were going to have a contest, a battle of new records. I played a new record and gave the listeners 20 minutes to call the station and vote. If they liked it they'd call and say: MAKE IT, if not they'd say: BREAK IT! Later in the show I did the same using another record. The record that won was played the next night against another new song. That winner went to the next night and so on. Finally on Friday night the winner became the "Round One Of The Week" – (what a stupid name!) and would be played by everyone on the air all next week. People were calling, voting, driving the switchboard nuts. Some voted on records I never even played. Some didn't vote at all. It was a calling frenzy.

"MAKE IT OR BREAK IT" was born.

One night while I was trying to find commercials in the rack behind me I realized there was no way to do it and still sound like I was right on the microphone talking like a sane person and doing everything right, so I just turned around and away from the mike. I sounded like I was ten feet away and I was. In the process I accidentally knocked about a hundred records, The Horn, a large metal ashtray and everything else that was on the desk crashing to the floor. They didn't fall all at once though. They sort of went a few at a time. The crash seemed to take minutes. It reminded me of McGee's closet. Instead of going into a record and cutting off the avalanche I just sat there and waited with the microphone on for everything to stop. The last thing to go was that ashtray. When it hit the tile floor it spun like a top, around and around finally settling to the floor. Then after a second's silence, a cup fell off and broke into a million pieces. I didn't do anything or say anything for about 10 seconds. Like the famous Jack Benny pause there was only silence.

By now the engineers in master control were getting used to Horns and noises from me and weren't really paying attention. But when those ten seconds of silence happened they all panicked. One even woke up from his nap! Oh yes, those were great guys, but they could sleep through anything and usually did. The silence got to them though and everyone else. After the ten seconds from about 15 feet away with my face down on the floor I said in a loud voice:

"Did you hear that'? "Notice that ashtray down on the floor? Did you hear that ashtray? It has a wonderful tone. Ha Ha Ha!" And that's how Theee Lee Alan Fine Toned Ashtray was born!

Engineer on Speaker Intercom: "Hey what happened are you on the air?"

McGee's closet? Well here we go again back to the golden days of radio and a program called Fibber McGee and Molly. On the air McGee was a nice guy, but sort of like me, never organized. Anything cluttering the house got thrown into the front closet. Everything went into that closet. The closet was filled floor to ceiling and wall to wall with junk. On the show various visitors would come to their house and once in while make the mistake of:

McGee: "No...don't open that door!!!!"

But he always said it too late. The door would open and the crashing of junk coming from the closet would start. Sometimes it would last up to 30 seconds. 30 seconds is a long time. All you heard was the crashing, and then silence while the audience roared. Next time you're in the store look for some of these old radio shows. They are a hoot!

Yes, I told the engineer, we were on the air and I said: "Stand by, I liked that crash. Think we'll do that every night!" I used to love giving those guys fits.

Everything was getting wilder, funnier, more fun, and some of the things that came out of my mouth were really stupid. But they were all spontaneous.

"Now listen (I would say in a high voice at the top of my lungs) do not take offense at what I just said! Ha Ha Ha. If you take offense, how're you going to keep the dog in the yard?"

Or:

"You know what 's going to happen in exactly one minute from right now on this radio station WXYZ here in Detroit? (long pause, pound on the desk, throw the ashtray on the floor, wait for it to stop clanging)...Absolutely Nothing Friends!

Or:

"OK now we're going to give you a little color test. Here's your chance to adjust the color on your radio. Ready? OK. Stand by! You have to be prepared for this now. OK. Here's you test:" And then I would just say: RED (pause), GREEN (pause), - BLUE!!!

Yes, things were getting wilder. See, the thing was, I didn't know you weren't supposed to do these things on the radio. Crazy just came naturally to me; nobody from the front office was saying anything so I kept on doing these things. Ha!

One night I was trying to find one of those cut ins from a Jonathon Winters comedy LP when I ran across a selection called: "The Sail Cat". I listened to it and just fell on the floor laughing. It started out with Jonathon saying:

"Jesse...you know what a Sail Cat is?"

So without saying anything I played that phrase on the air:

"Jesse...you know what a Sail Cat is?"

All throughout the show, when I didn't have anything better to do I played that cut:

"Jesse...you know what a Sail Cat is?"

That phrase became part of the show. Letters started coming in asking. "What is a sail Cat"? First just a few, then lots of letters. "Hey Lee, don't keep us in suspense,

WHAT IS A SAILCAT!?"

I played that stupid sounding cut for the next four months. Never commenting on it. Just playing it after records, before the news, during jingles, over the intro to records:

"Jesse...you know what a Sail Cat is?"

The feud was still going on and getting hotter. Now the other air guys were talking about it. Actually they were saying they were all sick of it and they wished Joel and Lee would stuff it already. Dick Kernan, Paul Winter's producer, and John Dew, everybody's producer and a good friend of Joel's were saying that on the weekends, at the shows, dances, and sock hops, the biggest question was about Lee and Joel and why can't they get along. The other DJs on the station were not happy. Even they believed it was real. Besides they were sick and tired of hearing my name and Joel's name at THEIR events.

A call came to my home from Mr. Gilbert's office asking me to be there at 1PM on Monday morning. When I arrived, Joel was there waiting. Neither of us knew the other had been called in.

There was no smile on John Gilbert's face now. "Listen and listen good", he said. "No more shooting at each other on the air. If you guys can't get along then don't; but I don't want it to show on the air on my station. The whole town's talking about you. I can't go into a restaurant, my barber shop, even my own home without hearing about Lee and Joel and this…this…" "Feud", I interrupted. "Right, this feud", Gilbert said. "Enough or else!", he said.

Joel couldn't hold it any longer. He was laughing so hard it made me laugh. At first Gilbert was furious at this. He'd just delivered an ultimatum and we were on the floor. Laughing to the point of tears. We couldn't stop. After a minute or two his fury turned to a quizzical look and then he starting laughing too. He didn't even know what he was laughing about and finally said something like: "This is ridiculous, what are we laughing about?" And that brought on the second wave. By now we were knee slapping, pounding on the desk, and laughing so loud that the secretary poked her head in to see if we were alright.

Finally we explained that the whole thing was a put on. That we had to find some way to get the town talking about us and we did. We told him that after the payola firings and all the personalities who left the station we were sure the ratings would plummet unless we did something drastic. It worked! At least the town was talking. No ratings to look at yet, but they were talking. We told Mr. Gilbert about the famous Fred Allen-jack Benny Feud and what it did for their ratings in the 40s.

As we talked he backed up slowly, cocked his head, dropped his jaw, and sank into his big, high backed, cushy chair. It was a look of unbelief.

"This is all an act?" he said. "Why didn't someone tell me?" We told him that Baker was on to it so we thought he knew. John Gilbert's famous smile returned to his face. Still wiping tears of laughter he just said: "OK...Ok get out of here you guys. But I'll see you back here when the numbers come in." The numbers were the ratings. The ratings were our jobs. We all waited for the ratings.

We all liked our jobs —

Chapter 35
THE PHONE CALL

WHILE ALL THIS WAS FUN AND I WAS BECOMING KNOWN AS the wild man at night on WXYZ I was not doing well financially. Everyone else could MC shows and dances. I was on the air at night and couldn't do anything.

The call came one afternoon in the summer. "Is this Lee?", the caller said. After I assured him that it was he said he was a partner of Red and Cleo Kraemer the new owners of Walled Lake Casino and the Kramers were wondering if I'd be interested in MCing a dance out there. I told him to thank them but because I was on the air at night I would be able to do it. He thanked me and the conversation ended.

When Walled Lake Casino closed the doors in the late 50s, no one ever expected it to open again. The big bands were no longer popular, no one would come to see them on a regular basis, and the dance halls that hired them closed.

The Kraemers bought Walled Lake Casino sometime in early 1960. They tried to revive it. Tried to bring the Big Bands Back. It didn't work. Then they hired Disk Jockeys to do sock hops, record dances. That didn't work either. Depending on what part of Detroit you were coming from Walled Lake was 20 to 40 miles away. Who was going to drive that distance when there were dances going on in every neighborhood?

After a few days I had to face reality. I had a wife and daughter to support, a house to make payments on, a car, and more. I couldn't go to the station for more money. Not yet anyway. I had an idea and decided to call the Kraemers.

"Red Kraemer here", said the voice on the other end of the phone. I introduced myself and explained that nothing had changed. I still couldn't do anything at night but I said: "Mr. Kraemer, what are you doing out there on Sunday afternoons?" "Nothing Lee", he said. "We're closed". I gave him my idea.

It was summertime. There they were right on the lake with this big dance hall and they were closed! Why not experiment and open up on Sunday afternoon?" "If we do will you come out?", he said. I said I would. "What do you want out of it?" I told him if he'd spend two or three hundred dollars for commercials on my radio show so I could talk about the Sunday dance, I'd charge him a hundred dollars. If more than 600 people came I wanted half the admission after that. There was a long silence on the other end of the phone. Finally Mr. Kraemer said: "Lee, let's do it."

Red Kraemer had nothing to lose. He'd never had 600 people there at all. If we got that kind of crowd it would be well worth it. I called Jim Christi, one of the sales guys and asked him to call the Kraemers. He did. Red bought the time and we were set to start.

John Dew, my friend and a producer from WXYZ went out to the Casino. It was in good shape but the sound wasn't the kind that would let us play records the way we wanted, fast paced and one after another. Red Kraemer said he would upgrade if we could get the crowds.

I talked about Walled lake Casino on the air. Sunday dances by the lake. Music, Rock Bands, etc. Same type of promotion I was doing for Club 182. We had no idea if anyone would show up for that first dance; but they did. A little over 600 people came to my first dance at Walled Lake Casino. Red decided to go another Sunday. The crowd tripled. After that nearly 4,000 people were there every Sunday.

Sunday afternoon dances.

After a near death experience, Walled Lake Casino was alive again and I was making more money than I had ever seen.

A few weeks later the Kraemers came to me and told me they wanted to add Friday and Saturday night dances. If they bought time for commercials on the station would I provide them with a producer and an MC and come out in time to do a stage show before they closed at 11:30?

Sticky! I was broadcasting from Club 182, Joel's dances on Friday and Saturday. I absolutely knew my friends the upstanding police who were the promoters would be thrilled to have Lee Alan sitting in their lobby doing one commercial that says: "Come out to Joel Sebastian's dance at Club 182 " and in the next saying: "Come to Walled Lake Casino cause in a couple of hours I (Lee Alan) will be out there to put on a terrific stage show." Strange? Confusing? A conflict?

My answer to the Kraemers was that I would have to clear anything like that with WXYZ management. And I did. John Gilbert and Bob Baker said if Walled Lake bought commercials on my show they could advertise their event like anyone else, and if they hired me to go there after 9:55 when the live portion of my show was over at Club 182, that would be between them and me.

And that's what happened. I wish I had tapes of those nights to play for you because it was wild. There I was back in the saddle, on the air live from Club 182 The Horn Blowing, music playing, callers voting on Make It Or Break, crazy, wild, the feud going and of course every 15 or 20 minutes:

"Jesse…you know what a Sail Cat is?"

In one commercial I promoted 182, ten minutes later I was promoting Walled lake and my appearance out there later that same night. At about 9:51 the producer back at the station started a record for me and I was out the door. When the record was done news at 9:55 cut in from the network, then my recorded show from that afternoon rolled on. By that time I was 10 miles on the road toward Walled Lake.

When I got to Walled Lake that first Friday night there were about 2500 people all applauding when I climbed on the stage. They'd been dancing to records on a brand new state of the art sound system since 7 o'clock. Now they were ready for a show. The bands were ready, artists were ready and so was I. It was exciting, loud, emotional, and an important step in my career.

Now I was doing three shows and dances a week at Walled Lake. Friday, Saturday and Sunday. The City of Walled Lake and Novi, Walled lake Casino, and Walled Lake Amusement Park directly across the street were all alive again crawling with people. Young people. Gulliver was awake. The coma was over. The music was playing again, the roller coaster was going, Click, Click, Click on the way up then silence, then the screams of people on the way down. The whole of Southeastern Michigan was becoming aware of a hot, "in" place on a Lake where big shows were happening, big names were appearing, young people were welcome, and big crowds were going. And that was only the beginning.

On the air:

"DID YOU SEE THAT"?
"DID YOU HEAR THE TONE OF
THEEE LEE ALAN FINE TONED HORN?"

"Jesse…you know what a Sail Cat is?"
Jonathon Winters: "Oh we have to sit here for this?"

Detroit was Rockin' at night and the Motown Sound was being born.

Chapter 36
ANOTHER CALL

IT WAS GETTING TO BE A HABIT. I mean calls from Mr. Gilbert's office. This time it sounded urgent. As I said before in those days there were no contracts for new people like me. My job on the radio was literally day-to-day. We didn't dare have an agent or a lawyer call the station or meet with management in our behalf. They would have taken that as a threat and no more job. So, every time there was a call from the front office, or any office for that matter, insecurity surfaced and subtle panic set in. We already had the "feud" problem cleared up. At least I thought we did. So what was the problem this time? The Horn, The Ashtray throwing, The Sail Cat? Now what.

  I walked into John Gilbert's waiting room and sat down as if I owned the place. Well, I'd been there enough in the last three months. I could usually tell if this was going to be good or bad based on the demeanor of the secretary. This time though she was expressionless and had little to say except: "Hi Lee. I hope this meeting goes OK for you." She hoped this meeting goes OK for me!? Why did she say that? Was there a problem? What's going on? She didn't answer. Just looked up at me and slowly shook her head from side to side. I was already in shock and hadn't even been in Gilbert's office yet.

Suddenly, with a click that sounded like a gunshot and a jerk his door burst open. I stood up at attention. Reminded me of the Army. When I did my notebook and two pens flew from my hand to the floor. It was Mr. Gilbert. No smile. Stern face. He looked at me, pointed his finger and moved it back and forth with a "come here" motion.

He went immediately to his desk and said with a loud, firm voice: "Lee, look at this. This is your fault. Look at this!" Oh no, what now I thought. I looked. It was the rating book. I'd been at the station for a little over three months and the numbers were out. The report card of the broadcast business. Just keep in mind that we had no contracts in those days. It was ultimate accountability. Lose the numbers and you could lose your job. My fault he said! Just as I was contemplating cleaning out my desk and before I could read anything, Gilbert broke into a smile that nearly shattered his cheekbones and said:

"Lee, you're number one! Absolutely number one in your time slot! Not only that, but you have a 54 share! A 54! And on Saturday it's a 60! You and that stupid Horn. You did it in one book! And look at Joel. He's also number one with a big share. Looks like all that silly stuff worked, including the feud. Congratulations Lee."

A 54 share meant that 54% of the people listening to the radio were listening to me and 60% on Saturday.

ON THE AIR:
Music: Ends
HORN: Blows
LEE: Have you ever heard Thee Lee Alan Fine Toned Note?

Aged four long years in wood to make it sound good

Like a fine toned note should?
OK, now you have to be prepared for this. Are you ready
(In a Loud High Voice) Are you ready?
THE NOTE: (Lee Takes a deep Breath and then in his own voice):
Hhaaaaaaaaaaaaaaaaaaaaaaaaaaaaaaaaaaaaaaaaaa
Aaaaaaaaaaaaaaaaaaaaaaaa(getting louder)aaaaaaaa
aaaaaaaaaaaaaaaaaaaaaaaaaaaaaaaaaaaaaaaaaa
aaaaaaaaaaaaaaaaaaaaaaaaaaaaaaaa
(very loud as it ends)aaaaaaaaaaaaAHH!
DID YOU HEAR THAT?????????????????

Jingle: W X YYYYYYYYYYYYYY ZEE. (shout)Detroit!

Chapter 37
CHECKMATE

SALES PEOPLE FOR RADIO STATIONS ARE generally working on commissions. They receive a percentage of what they sell. And what they sell is time. Commercial time. In the 60s that meant 10-15-30 or 60 second commercials. They also sold sponsorships. News sponsorships, program sponsorships, Sports, etc., and Remote Broadcasts.

The bigger the ratings on a show, the more they could charge for the time.

Jim Christie was a sales rep for WXYZ . When I started the Walled lake Casino Sundays and now Friday and Saturdays, Jim was the sales rep handling the account. His job was to see that the Kraemers who owned the Casino bought as much time as they could afford and also to help them with promoting the whole concept.

One of the other sales people at WXYZ, Johnny Lyons was the sales representative for Club 182. Like Jim it was his job to see that Club 182 bought and received the commercial time they needed and to promote Club 182.

In order to have the station broadcast from a sponsor's place of business the advertiser had to qualify for the remote. Spend a certain number of dollars and qualify for one remote a week, go to the next level of spending and qualify for two remotes etc. If the sponsor qualified and wanted a remote they had to pay all the costs of the remote for the engineer, the remote studio, telephone lines to carry the broadcast etc. It wasn't cheap and it wasn't simple.

Club 182 had two remotes a week for months. Every Friday and Saturday night there we were, live from the Club.

One afternoon Jim Christi came to my office on the second floor of Broadcast House. He looked from side to side like one of the three stooges, covered his mouth with his hand and whispered: "Lee", he said, don't spread this around but I just learned that the contract for remotes that those cops have that Club 182?" "Yeah?" I said.

"Lee", Jim went on talking out of one side of his mouth, hand covering the other. Now that I think of it there he was standing in my office with glass walls that anyone could see through making it absolutely obvious that he was trying to conceal something. "Those cops haven't renewed their remotes yet. I don't know why, but until they get wise the remotes are available to anyone that qualifies." He didn't have to say any more. Jim Christi was telling me that if the Kraemers who owned Walled Lake Casino wanted to make it the biggest show and dance in the country they could. It was a golden opportunity. If they bought the remotes, instead of me doing my shows from club 182 and setting speed records after 10PM driving to Walled Lake. I could now broadcast the whole thing directly from the Casino and Club 182 would be sucking wind!

I told Jim I was sure the Kraemers would go for it, but because of my past trouble with the 182 promoters I had to stay out of the negotiations. Jim drove to Walled Lake, and met with the Kraemers. Red and Cleo Kraemer called me from the meeting. What did I think, they asked. I told them the truth. Fifty four percent of everyone listening to the radio at night was listening to

WXYZ. If I had the chance to actually broadcast live from Walled Lake Casino it would be the biggest thing ever in Detroit nighttime radio and would bring tens of thousands of new faces out to the big dance on the lake. Red said that was good enough for him and they bought the deal.

Red Kraemer built a Plexiglas bubble for me to broadcast from on the left side of the stage and the radio station wired it. I had them install a loudspeaker in the booth that was on all the time playing the music and crowd noises that were being heard in the hall so when I turned on the microphone you could actually hear the live sounds, music, people, and excitement. On the radio it would always sound like big time action was going on at the Casino. Within two weeks I left Club 182 and was on the air at Walled Lake.

The first Friday night was a total sell out. For two weeks I had been saying that I was now going to be broadcasting the entire Walled Lake event every Friday and Saturday.

The first band ever to appear for me at Walled Lake Casino was a local group called the Coronados. They were all in their teens, starry eyed, organized, and one of the best I ever had perform out there. In the following years they were there many times, even backing up major New York and Hollywood acts. Long after it was all over out there I heard that one of their members made the ultimate sacrifice for his country in Vietnam.

The first solo act on the stage at Walled Lake to kick off the broadcasts was Jack Scott.

Born in Windsor, Ontario, Jack Scott (born Jack Scafone, Jr., January 28, 1936) moved to a town on the outskirts of Detroit, Michigan when he was ten years old. At the age of 18, he formed the Southern Drifters and after leading the band for three years, he signed with ABC as a solo artist. Late in 1959, he switched labels, signing with Top Rank. His first single for the label, "What In the World's Come Over You," became a number five hit early in 1960.

It was followed a few months later by another Top Ten hit, the number three single "Burning Bridges." The pair of singles were his last major hits.

When Jack went on that stage he absolutely killed 'em. It wasn't Motown, it wasn't even R & B, which was the "in" music then it was just slow twangy Country Jack Scott. The kids were hungry for what Walled Lake was about to do and Jack was an original. He was a nice guy who helped me by appearing when I needed the help. I hope to see him and work with him in the future. I can still hear him....

"The Way I Walk is Just the Way I Walk
The Way I Talk is Just the Way I Talk"

About two years later I was doing my show from the big Fred Wolf studio on the second floor of Broadcast house. No one could get into the building at night unless they worked there or had a pass. It was about 9 o'clock at night and the studio door was open.

There I was on the air with my producer Larry O'Brien. Larry was one of the guys who handled my shows when I was out on remote. Back at the studio I usually produced my own show. I wanted to have control over the production so I played my own records, commercials, jingles, Horns, Ashtrays, Fine Toned Notes, and all the other serious, quiet ingredients of The Lee Alan Show. Ha! This night though, Larry and I were working together.

Anyway there I was in the studio. The hallways were semi dark, all was quiet when suddenly I looked up and there standing in the doorway was an absolutely drop dead gorgeous brunette about 28 years old, hands on hips, short skirt, and blouse unbuttoned! She slipped her hands down to the bottom of the skirt and raised it. She had nothing else on but a big smile.

Larry couldn't see this sight. He was in another part of the room behind the open door with headphones blasting and looking for the next records. She looked at me and said "Hi Lee, Jack Scott asked me to drop in and see you". The music was playing, Larry was busy and I was looking at a woman who, if she leaned over by sheer weight, would definitely fall over forwards. This woman looked like a brunette, topless Dolly Parton. Before I could figure the scene out she was motioning for me to come into the hallway out of the producer's sight and the spoke again: "Jack said I should come out and see if there was anything you needed or anything I could do for you". I jumped up, knocking The Horn crashing to the floor, went into the hallway and quickly ordered her down the hall and the stairway to the first floor. Just as she disappeared through the door she turned, cupped her breasts in both hands and gave me a "you don't know what you're missing" look.

I knew what I was missing. I was missing being fired if the guard ever saw this action in Broadcast House. Sometimes when we had to go to the bathroom if the record ended the producer would play a commercial, a station jingle or promo and then go into another record. That's what Larry did. He never saw a thing and I never told him.

Believe it or not, a similar scenario happened live on the air to Soupy Sales on our television station during his Kiddies show "Lunch With Soupy".

Soupy was talking to the kids on camera giving them his "words of wisdom" when there was a knock on the door. Soupy mugged the camera as if to say: "I wonder who's at the door", turned around, opened the door and there standing on the other side was a beautiful blonde stark naked. The TV audience couldn't see her but Soupy could. I think she was also doing a very sexy dance and making some very sexy moves. Soupy was floored. In those days he couldn't even make mention of what he saw let alone show her on camera. It's a classic scene that was preserved on tape or film I don't know which. Sorry, the scene only shows what the TV audience saw. The naked lady remains anonymous.

Oh Jack Scott? I don't know if he sent this Centerfold material that night to my studio or not. I never asked him and he never mentioned it. So let's not implicate him here. And I never saw her again. It's not on tape or film, but It was a two minute picture I'll never forget.

No film at eleven!!!

Chapter 38
TELEVISION

By now my daughter Dawne was nearly three years old. I wanted more children, didn't deserve more children, but I wanted them. I was spending nearly 12 hours every day four days a week on my Radio Show and two more days on Radio and the shows at Walled Lake. From Monday through Saturday there was no time for anything else. I knew that if I didn't constantly keep at it I could lose it, and there were only about seven other stations in town who right now would just soon see me out of the market. I was their nemesis at night. I had their audiences with me. In those days stations weren't into hiring the competition. Their thinking was that if they hired you away from a competing station, every time the listener heard you it would only make the listener think of that station. They were wrong but if you were a threat, they just wanted you gone. Out of town.

Since I seek to remember the truth here I must say that there was trouble brewing in my family. If there was fault most of it was mine. I was never home. Everything was the career, my beautiful daughter had a dad who loved her but didn't know how to be a dad. We are taught everything else in school, we are licensed to drive, to practice law and medicine. Why are we allowed to bring children into this world with no clue how to be a good parent and no required learning on the subject?

My marriage was in trouble. I think I was the only one who felt it though. Patti and I rarely talked about it. I was still influenced by Ann from a few years ago and my relationship with Patti had started out to be a selfish replacement for a 5-year teenage relationship. I now realized that I had made a mistake and that Patti was paying the price. I was now exposed on a daily basis to the adoration and recognition of an entire city. A small time version of a national talent accepted by men and adored by women. It was about to get worse. Patti was still singing to bring in extra income, but she was never dedicated to it. She never really enjoyed it or had aspirations to record or go farther with her talent. Come to think of it I never suggested it. I began to notice that the only time Patti sang, or even hummed was when she was on stage. We had a piano, but she never sang at home.

I was in the local and national spotlight and totally self centered.

Once again, how I wish I could go back and talk to that young Disc Jockey. Change some of his choices. Point him in a different direction. But none of us can do that. Our choices have a cumulative effect on our lives and everyone we touch. Mine did. And although I was well known and popular on the outside, I was unhappy on the inside and with all my success like the old Peggy Lee song I was wondering:

"Is That All there is?"

It wasn't. In a few short years I was destined to make another personal mistake that would affect the lives of everyone around me and even those yet to be born. More as we go.

"Lee, this is Bill Hendricks, could you come down to my office"? Bill Hendricks a television sales rep for Channel 7. He was also the brother in law of John Pival, the president of WXYZ, Inc. and General Manager of Channel 7, ABC Television in Detroit. Everybody feared Mr. Pival. He was the unorthodox leader of creative television in Detroit, an original thinker who was willing to take a chance on his ideas. He made television history with his innovations and use of talent. Much has been written about him so I won't waste you time or pages except to say that he discovered and named Soupy Sales and was the first to do almost everything that other stations tried to imitate. He was also gruff, a hard drinker, impulsive, outrageous, and when he was drinking he was a good guy to stay away from if you didn't want to be the subject of his wrath. Nearly everybody kept their distance from Mr. Pival who underneath was just a nice guy that needed friends.

Hendricks was short and to the point. "Lee, Coke and Better Made Potato Chips want to sponsor a television show for New Years Eve. They want you and Joel to host it and John Pival has given it his blessing. Want to do it?

Can anybody guess my answer?

Walled Lake was getting bigger, ratings were stronger, more and more bit artists were in town making appearances, and now television. In 1960 Detroit or Motown as the world was beginning to call it had only 6 TV stations, and two of them were UHF that practically no one could watch. How hard was it to get ratings? I mean if you were on TV and could move your little finger you had a chance. This was a golden opportunity for Joel and me.

WXYZ TV, Channel 7 was the Detroit outlet for Dick Clark and American Bandstand, but there was nothing from them on New Years Eve. None of the stations had any relevant programming for New Years. So here we were with another innovation of John Pival's ready to attack the audience.

Broadcast house had giant studios with overhead doors that you could drive cars and trucks through, high ceilings, floors that could be painted, permanent cyclotron draperies hanging from tracks around the perimeter that could be pulled into place and made to help form any kind of room or atmosphere. There were large rooms with mammoth shelves that held every type of room component you could imagine. Full walls, half walls, doors, window walls, and props of every kind. It was like a small version of a Hollywood movie company. Everything was new at Broadcast House.

For New Years Eve John Pival ordered the set to be built to look like a nightclub.

There were tables covered with table cloths surrounding a large dance floor. A stage at one end set up with a concert grand piano and band instruments, the draperies were pulled to form the room and lit to glow and show depth. Everything in sight said COCA COLA and BETTER MADE POTATO CHIPS.

There were two or three separate mini sets for Joel and me and also for interviews and commercials. About two hundred teenagers were recruited from Walled Lake Casino and other dance venues around town to be part of the show, occupy the tables, and just have fun dancing and yes applauding the acts that would be appearing.

For weeks before the show Joel and I taped various acts that were in town but wouldn't be there for New Years. They were interviewed and they performed in smaller parts of the set and in close up shots so the TV audience couldn't see that the room was void of the audience for the tapings.

11PM

New Year's Eve, 1961-62.

"Lee Alan & Joel Sebastian's New Years Eve Party" was on the air.

I had selected the opening theme. It came from the same LP as the American Bandstand theme. Very big and very up, it was called The Varsity Drag. The music started. The opening titles were running on the screen over a cover shot of the "nightclub" and two hundred teenagers from Motown dancing.

Off camera an announcer said:

"And Now, Live From Broadcast House in Detroit. Coca Cola and Better Made Potato Chips Present Lee & Joel's New Years Eve Party with The Everly Brothers, Jackie Wilson, Brenda Lee, The Ventures, Chubby Checker, Bobby Vee, Connie Francis and the Fendermen".

We had worked on this show for a month or two, but the second that it hit the air it was real. Electric. Live. The lights were brilliant, the kids were beautiful with impeccable make up, everything was pumped, and so exciting it was nearly heart attack time for me, a kid from Cooley High who just a few years before only dreamed of being in something like this let alone a co-host in a staring role with Joel Sebastian. The music finished, and while the kids were cheering and applauding the announcer went on:

"And Now Ladies and Gentlemen, from WXYZ Radio, Joel Sebastian". There was thunderous applause and cheering for Joel. For his occupation and position Joel was a fairly shy guy. I don't think he was expecting this much of an intro and showing from the audience. His smile was larger than his face and his face was beat red! Joel was a great looking guy of about 31 years old who looked about 25. He was dressed in an immaculate, shiny mohair suit that looked like it was molded to his body. Joel was dressed for New Years and if a man can be called beautiful, Joel looked beautiful. The applause and cheering continued as the announcer went on:

"And here he is the guy with The Fine Toned Horn, Lee Alan". This was the only time I have ever been nervous in my entire career. I was frozen like a statue. Couldn't move. Joel was standing smiling and now applauding in the living room setting with chairs, sofa; pictures of the two of us on radio on the walls with photos of Elvis, Frankie Avalon and others. The whole crowd was standing in front of him cheering when finally one of the stage hands literally pushed me through the curtains and out into the set.

The cheering and applauding continued, but now was joined with loud shrieks, screams, and hilarious laughter. Joel's back was to me. When he turned to greet me he was a picture of shock. Here I was my first time ever on television in Detroit with everyone in town watching and I was dressed like the New Year with a large banner across my chest bearing the year 1962.

I was wearing a stupid look on my face and a diaper! A diaper!

Nothing else!!! No shoes, no shirt, nothing.

We were live. The cheering turned to laughter and crowd talking and snickering. Joel was laughing so hard he couldn't speak. I said something like: "Here we are (pointing at Joel) the old year (and then at myself) and the new. Welcome ladies and gentlemen and while brother Joel and I recover from all this, let the party begin". The Ventures were on stage playing Walk, Don't Run. The kids were dancing and we were under way with innovation from the genius-programming mind of John Pival.

Jackie Wilson came on and blew everyone away

I don't remember much else about that show except it was fun and went too fast. I was there on New Year's Eve, not home, and once again I was not with Patti or my family. The strain on our marriage was becoming more intense.

Chapter 39
MONSTER

I had been on Detroit radio in some capacity or another for about nine years. As Lee Alan for about four years; but that one two-hour television show catapulted me into another sphere. Before the New Years Eve Party on channel 7 in Detroit I could still walk the earth with some degree of anonymity. Although I had appeared before many thousands in person most people didn't know me by sight. Only the voice. But those days were now over.

The ratings for the New Years Eve Party showed that over 80 percent of the television audience was watching Joel and me. 80 Percent! I felt it right away. Wherever I went. The drug store, gas station, shopping, and other public places. Everybody knew me now and it was scary.

Television was a monster. One show and my life changed totally. I can only imagine what it must be like for a film star and worldwide recognition.

Bill Hendricks was now in Television Heaven. The idea for a New Years Eve Party was successful beyond anyone's dream. The sponsors, Coke & Better Made Potato Chips, were ecstatic. John Pival was basking in another ratings winner born of his original mind. In later years ABC would peg Dick Clark to do a New Year's Eve Party on coast-to-coast television. Was it based on John Pival's intuitive ingenuity? We will never know.

What I can tell you is that selling an idea for a television show can reap terrific rewards or it can spell disaster for careers. If your idea works you're a genius. If it doesn't well, just forget about it! This one really worked and long before Bill Hendricks showed up at my office door with the next idea I knew all about it. Milton DeLoach told me!

Milton DeLoach worked for WXYZ Television, but nobody ever knew what his job really was. The late Dick Osgood, in his book WYXIE Wonderland, describes Milton this way:

> "Milton was a black man who held a unique position. He replaced light fixtures, drove VIPs to and from the airport, provided female companions for visitors who desired them, and often took John Pival home and put him to bed. He was powerfully built, like Pival, and the two of them were quite close".

Fact is Milton did everything at Broadcast House except show up on the air and now and then we even had him do that! He was a man who was always smiling, laughing, and talking. Milton was the only person I have ever known who could look at you, talk to you, speak absolutely plain English, and when he was finished you had no clue to what he said. The words were there; but they didn't say anything! And no one ever dared tell Milton that they didn't understand him. You just didn't do that. Not to Milton. He was a bear of a man who was wired to all the ABC brass. Milton's miscommunication was totally on purpose. When he wanted you to understand, he could be crystal clear.

The door to my office burst open and the loud laugh signaled that Milton wanted to talk. Milton liked me. I will never know why, but he did. "Crystal clear" and under his breath he said: "Pival wants you to do a regular TV show. You and Joel. The New Year's Eve Show was so big that he wants to keep it going". Before I could ask a question, Patty Robertson, a secretary came into the room with some paperwork and as if someone threw a switch Milton's language turned to loud, joyful, gibberish that no one could understand. Patty laughed and looked at me as if to say: "That's Milton". They both left.

Milton was never wrong. Ten days later Bill Hendricks told me what I already knew. Joel and I were going to start a regular weekly television Dance Party show following Dick Clark every Saturday. Mr. Pival was calling it "Club 12-7-O". The "1270" was WXYZ's spot on the radio dial.

Radio six nights a week from 7 to Midnight. Three shows a week at Walled Lake Casino, and now Television every Saturday or Sunday if the network pre-empted us. Along with Joel Sebastian and one or two others on rival stations I was the most well known air personality in Southeastern Michigan. I couldn't go anywhere without being recognized.

My family was paying the price!

Chapter 40
RADIO NIGHTMARE

I CAN'T GIVE YOU THE EXACT DATE OF THIS ONE, but it doesn't matter. What happened on that sunny cool Saturday in the Fall of 1962 caused a minor explosion in the black community and heads rolled because of it.

As I remember him, Fred Weiss was a silver haired, well groomed, soft spoken gentleman who loved radio and television, but hated being a disc jockey. He was a nice man who never uttered a four letter word and rolled with the corporate punches, played music he despised, and made his audience think he loved it all.

On the air almost all day on Saturday and Sunday, Fred was the weekend man, and the one who filled in for everyone else when they were sick or on vacation. His voice was slick, had a constant smile in it and pronunciation perfect. In other words Fred Weiss was relegated to being everyone's replacement.

One of the biggest local advertisers was a car dealer, Merollis Chevrolet. The dealership would later become famous for employing "The World's Greatest Salesman", Joe Girard. Who he was and what he did could fill another book. Actually, it has. On this Saturday Fred Weiss was on the air from Merollis Chevrolet in the

WXYZ remote trailer.

Now, I know I'm repeating here but, to understand how this whole thing happened I should review the setup. Fred was live on the air from the mobile home that had been converted into a luxurious remote studio and was parked in the median next to the sidewalk facing oncoming traffic. The engineer sat unseen in the back room while the DJ, Fred sat at a desk in front of a large window wall facing outside. It looked like a gigantic television set. All the records and commercials were played by the producer from a studio back at Broadcast House. Fred controlled his own mike and nothing else. There were problems with this setup. Either the speakers or the earphones weren't loud enough.

When a mike is turned on in a radio studio, the speakers are always cut off. The air personality can hear everything loud in the earphones, but there are no speakers. When the mike is off the speakers come back on. That's how we always knew that the mikes were really on. Speakers on meant mikes were off. Speakers off meant mikes were on. That simple. Problem in the remote studio was that the speakers were so low sometimes you couldn't tell if they were on or off and the engineering department refused to give the earphones any real volume. So, when the mike was on and the speakers were off no one could tell and the headphones were so low that if you were on the air with a live mike your own voice would drown out what you were hearing in the phones. Bottom line was that unless you paid close attention to a red light that lit when the mike was on you had no clue that it was on.

Fred had one earphone with the program in it. The other one carried the voice of the producer back at the studio. It was about one in the afternoon. I was driving to Broadcast House to record the 10 to midnight segment of my show so I could broadcast from Walled lake Casino that night. Fred was playing a song by Esther Phillips called: Please Release Me when the unthinkable happened.

Remember I said earlier that the station had a device that when a sudden loud sound happened it would compress everything else allowing the loud sound to be heard but not damage the equipment? As I listened I realized that Fred Weiss was talking, but not to the audience. The record was playing but the mike was still on and Fred didn't know it. He was talking to the producer back at the studio. His voice was loud and whenever he talked the music was compressed into the background. Everything he said was loud and clear.

Larry Obrien was the producer at Broadcast House. His studio speakers turned way down and his earphone wasn't loud enough either. As Larry and Fred talked neither knew that what Fred was saying was on the air.

Fred was talking about the success of Motown and black rhythm and blues music. How it had literally taken over the airwaves. And as the Esther Phillips record played: "Please release me let me go...."

Fred Weiss loud voice pushed the music into the background as he said to the producer:

"Those dammed niggers are getting pretty smart."

And the whole thing went on the air!

I heard it. I couldn't believe it. I was about two miles from the station and nearly drove off the road. Fred Weiss never even *thought* words like that let alone said them...and never on the air! Fred didn't know he was on the air and neither did Larry.

When I got to the station I ran through the parking lot, went into the back entrance and up the stairs to the studios two steps at a time. I burst into the studio and there was Larry O'Brien loading the cartridge machines, cueing up the next record, and laughing and talking with Fred on the headset. They still didn't know what happened.

The telephone next to Larry was lit. All 6 lines were flashing. When I told him what I heard his face changed to chalk. He quickly told Fred and grabbed the phone. It was the switchboard operator. She knew what happened. Before the end of the day a few thousand people told her what happened. I recorded my show and left for Walled Lake Casino. All I heard about that night was what Fred said on the air.

Monday morning the black newspaper, The Michigan Chronicle, printed the whole story and demanded that Fred Weiss be dismissed. John Gilbert complied. What he said was out of character, but Fred was fired before the end of the day.

Fred Weiss was gone for good. He landed a job in Washington DC. I haven't seen him since.

Those were different days. Radio couldn't even think off color words, four letter words; say them or even imply them. Today is different. Radio stations and on the air people have turned many radio stations into a cesspool. They think the more you can get away with the better the ratings.

I think of the hundreds of examples of powerful radio and television entertainers who not only never resorted to shock or filth, but couldn't. Back to Jack Benny, Milton Berle, Bob Hope, Fred Allen, Abbott and Costello, hundreds more. The Disc Jockeys and talk hosts from every city. The Real Don Steele, Dick Biondi, Arnie Ginsberg, Casey Kasem, Joel Sebastian, Joey Reynolds and yes even Rush Limbaugh.

I believe Howard Stern, the leader of Dirty Rotten Radio and Television is one of the most talented people I have ever heard; but he has no confidence in his ability. He uses foul words and sex as a crutch. What a legacy to be remembered for.

If Howard Stern were brave enough I would love to have faced off with him in a neutral environment and issue him a challenge. I would have challenged him to clean up his act for six months. Cold turkey. Just six months. To use his brains, his originality, humor, and all his reach and resources, but to lay off Rotten Radio. No nude women, no body parts, no drunks, nothing that you wouldn't want a nine year old child to hear, see, or learn from his program. I believe his ratings and advertising revenue would increase dramatically.

Howard was the first to lead all the parrots in this country to Raunchy Radio. He could lead them the other way and show the world that radio could be itself again. He would make the entire country talk and tens of thousands of new people would tune in just to hear how he was going to pull it off, or if he could stick to it. Problem is Howard will never do it. It takes confidence and some degree of guts. Think of it, Howard Stern would have to depend on his own talent.

It would have worked Howard.

Chapter 41
SANGOO...

THE WHOLE WORLD WANTED TO WORK AT WXYZ, the number one radio station in the number one music market in the United States, arguably the world, just 25 minutes from the Motown music phenomenon where million selling hits were being turned out daily by groups of musical geniuses both trained and untrained.

1962. Motown was just waking up. Marilyn Monroe was dead; the first man was killed climbing the Berlin Wall, the Cuban Missile Crises brought the world to the brink of war, The Beatles, known only in England, were rejected by Decca records.

The whole world was discovering a sound like none other and I was in the epicenter of all of it. I was on the radio, I was producing stage shows and dances at Walled Lake Casino, on television every week, and I knew everybody at Motown on a first name basis. They were all smiling, cordial, appreciative. They were writing, producing and recording hit after hit. Marvin Gaye, Mary Wells, The Marvellettes, Smoky Robinson, Diana Ross, Florence Ballard, Mary Wilson, Shorty Long, Little Stevie Wonder, the Temptations, Four Tops, Eddie and Brian Holland and Lamont Dozier, and dozens more.

The musicians in the studio who played behind the singers were all very cool and very accomplished. Everyone from untrained and play by ear back street jammers to Detroit Symphony and strings, to the genius guitar of Joe Mesina and flute virtuosity of Dr. Beans Boles. The sound was Berry Gordy Jr.'s dream. It was funky, driving, infectious, invasive, melodic, and the words were poetry.

That's what Smoky Robinson said. Smoky was a poet. Berry Gordy's kind of Poet. And the words just kept on coming. And the hits too.

Detroit, Michigan was becoming known for more than cars. The Detroit Sound, The Motown Sound, the sound everybody wanted to hear. We had it. We played it on the air, danced to it. We loved it and we did it all first! Before the rest of the country ever knew about it. Detroit first, and a musical bell weather for the world of popular music. And all the Motown singers and musicians were appearing all over town all the time. Having the Supremes, the Temps, and maybe Marvin Gay appear at a high school dance or Walled lake Casino all in one night was not an every weekend occurrence but it happened, and fairly often. This MO-TOWN was alive again and everyone knew it. Music born on our back streets because a young man dreamed that it could be done. Singers, artists, writers, musicians, choreographers, show people. Most from the slums. The projects. Most could never have done it without the dream. Berry Gordy's dream. Most would have ended up like the rest in the hoods. The Motown phenomenon changed all that for them, for us, and for me.

As I said, the world wanted to work for WXYZ, a storied station, and number one in the eye of the Motown storm. Fred Weiss was gone and the audition tapes poured in. There were hundreds of them from all over the country. The music people had spread the word and everyone wanted that job.

I went to Bob Baker and recommended someone. When

WKMH hired him from an Ann Arbor radio station, David Pringle was young, affable, ambitious, and good on the air but not relaxed and very straight and stiff in his approach. WKMH had moved me to afternoon drive time, a step up for most. Not for me though. Afternoon on that small station was out of the spotlight. Dave was hired for the 7 to midnight show I was leaving.

One night after a week or so I suggested to him that he loosen up a little. "Like Dave", I think I said, "Next time you turn on the mike why not just pick up that trashcan over there and throw it against the wall"? He did it. And he did it again. Then he made it sound on the air like he was going down inside the trash can. You could hear all the echoes of his voice down in there. I must say it was funny and the audience did react.

On another night I suggested that he invent a word. Some word that no one ever heard before. I grabbed some records and listened to the B sides. The B side or flip side is what's on the other side of a hit. I listened to the B side of "the Lion Sleeps Tonight" by the Tokens and there it was!
The tokens were singing: "T i n a S a n g o o" and then more of a song. I told Dave I thought he ought to make something out of the word: SANGOO. Like, "Do you know what a SANGOO is"? "SANGOOS are everywhere. Crawling on the turntables, on the ceiling, the floor, in your pockets, everywhere. Problem is you can't see them. They're invisible." And on and on. Well, Dave keyed on that and actually made a big thing about it. Later, he became known as SANGOO. The station got rid of the name Pringle, changed it to Prince and he became known as Dave "Sangoo" Prince.

Dave did well on 'KMH and after the Fred Weiss incident I recommended him for the job. Baker hired him and Dave moved to weekends at WXYZ. He also became everyone's substitute. That was the beginning of trouble.

Chapter 42
CLUB 1270

CLUB 1270 WAS A TYPICAL TEEN DANCE PARTY ON TELEVISION, except there were two hosts. Joel Sebastian and me. It was a cabaret setting. There were tables surrounding a dance floor with a stage at one end. Joel and I were usually behind a sort of counter top with pictures behind us, a place to announce the music and interview artists and do commercials.

Television has killed the careers of more than one radio personality. Great voices who did well on radio, but when they showed up on television they just weren't the same. They didn't look anything like the audience envisioned them, didn't carry their radio personality over to television, or just weren't comfortable in front of a camera. Most times radio people belonged on radio.

Mickey Shorr was one of them. As I explained in an earlier chapter Mickey was one of the best there ever was on radio. When he went on television though there was a problem. The major part of the audience had never really seen him. Mickey didn't look like he sounded. He weighed over 300 pounds and the camera never takes weight off. To the contrary, the television camera usually make you look heavier. When they saw Mickey the audience was shocked. There are scores of others who were terrific on radio, but the probing eye of television killed them.

When Joel and I teamed up to do that first New Year's Eve Party though there was an instant magic. The combination worked. For whatever reason the audience like it, and us.

Joel was handsome, smiling, serious, courteous, and everyone's friend. I decided that if I was going to do well on television I had to stay the same as I was on radio. Nothing different. Wild, crazy, and whatever else I had to translate the radio personality into something visual for television. I have never been comfortable staying in one place or even dwelling on one thought for too long so when Club 1270 hit the air I was all over the place, running all over the studio, poking my nose into the acts while they were performing, mugging the camera, blowing my horn. I was playing the fool and loving it. Because I was so outrageous and stupid most of the time, whenever there was something serious to do or say the audience paid more attention. It was out of character so they listened. Someone once said that a Disc Jockey is nothing but an actor with a bad part. I think that's close.

First off we were live! All live! No way to correct mistakes and whatever happened just happened. We usually followed the network's Dick Clark American Bandstand on Saturday afternoon. I wanted the opening of our show to be similar to his, to carry through the same feel. Dick Clark's opening theme was "Bandstand Boogie" from a Les Elgart LP called "Band Of The Year". My opening radio theme, "Zing Went The Strings Of My Heart" was from this LP and I went right back there to find our TV theme. It was the Les Elgart version of "The Varsity Drag". The same one we used for the New Years Eve show. Perfect for the opening of the show. Everyone liked it, except Joel. He didn't say anything, but he didn't have to.

Detroit was important to the music business then and because of it recording artists were in town every weekend and available to do the TV show. We had them all too. So with major recording artists, regular teen-age dancers, Joel and his terrific personality, it started to look like the same old "dance party" show.

Coke was a big sponsor on the show. Coke's local agency account representative, a woman by the name of Judy Anderson, didn't like me much so she always had Joel do the commercials. On the very first show Joel was standing in front of a three way set with huge pictures of people having fun at the beach. He held a coke bottle in his hand and was reading the commercial from a cue card. With no warning and especially with no permission I walked into the setting, looked back into the camera as I passed it, smiled broadly and while Joel was reading the commercial handed him two more coke bottles. He had no choice but to accept them and continue with the spot. After all, this was live TV!

He was ticked! It didn't show though, at least to the audience. I left the set, picked up four more cokes rushed back past the camera and handed them to Joel. Now he had six coke bottles. Within seconds I piled six more and so on. The kids in the studio were hysterical. The crew was laughing. No one could hear Joel whose face was now beat red. It was all on the air. All live. I heard about it from the public for weeks. And it was all positive. I don't think the agency ever realized that after that more people talked about Coke and Joel than they ever would have if the whole thing hadn't happened. What a hoot!

When Club 1270 hit the air it was an instant success. Here we were the only local Detroit music television show smack in the middle of the Motown music explosion. Every nationally known recording artist with anything to promote knew that Detroit was the place to "break" their records wide open for the rest of the country. A promotion tour was nothing unless included a stop in Detroit and doing a television show with a few hundred thousand viewers was a must. We had the only show and they all came.

Now here's the kicker. The artist's appearances were all free. Big names, small names - no charge. Because of the union contract ABC had to pay them minimum scale to do the TV show, something like a hundred dollars, but Walled Lake Casino and all the other personal appearances were absolutely free of charge.

The Kraemers who owned the Casino were the winners. Every Saturday or Sunday Joel and I would go on live television with the some of the biggest recording artists in the country. I'd tell the whole town that they would be appearing live that night at Walled Lake Casino and they did, drawing thousands of people. What a promotion! What a gift! There's never been anything like it. Free television publicity, free name talent, radio broadcasts from the Casino stage on the number one station in the Midwest. Walled Lake Casino was setting records and the best was yet to come.

Chapter 43
CHUCK BERRY

"IF YOU TRIED TO GIVE ROCK AND ROLL ANOTHER NAME, YOU MIGHT CALL IT 'CHUCK BERRY'." - John Lennon

The Rolling Stones' first single was a cover of Chuck Berry's 'Come On.'

As late as 1962 I had never heard of Chuck Berry! The father of Rock 'N Roll and I had never heard of him! Oh, I knew his name but I had never heard his music. In the late 50s when Chuck was becoming an icon I was no fan of rock music. I was in college, working at small radio stations and had never been exposed to the music of this genius that the music world would eventually copy almost note for note and thought for thought.

When I really got into radio and made it to the larger stations there was no new Chuck Berry music. The reason? Read on.

Here's a little background:

Charles Edward Anderson Berry was born on Goode Avenue October 18, 1926 in St. Louis, MO. There were six children. He was the third. He grew up in The Ville, north of downtown St. Louis. There were only a few areas where in the city where Blacks could own property. The Ville was one of them. Chuck went to Simmons Grade School and Sumner High School which was the first black high school west of the Mississippi river. Arthur Ashe went there as well as Dick Gregory and Tina Turner among others.

When he was 22 Chuck was married and from then until he was 29 he had all kinds of jobs. He trained to be a hairdresser at the Poro School, worked at the Fisher Body plant, assisted his father, and even freelanced as a photographer.

Although he was working at becoming a musician Chuck Berry was never paid for a performance until he was 26 years old and didn't record anything until three years later when, after taking the advice of the great blues man Muddy Waters Chuck went to Chicago and met Leonard Chess of Chess Records.

Chess immediately liked this long tall drink of water, was impressed by his savvy and simple approach to words and music, and especially by a tune Chuck played for them called "Ida Red", a sort of fast moving country sounding piece with a street smart set of lyrics. Willy Dixon, Chess house producer convinced Leonard to record the song and on May 21, 1955 with Chuck playing and singing and Willy on Bass they did just that with one small change.

They renamed it.

IDA RED became MAYBELLENE!

Leonard Chess gave the new record to influential disc Jockey Alan Freed who proceeded to play the record; not just once, or now and then. Alan Freed played the record for two straight hours on his show on WINS in New York. The song sold over a million copies and went all the way to #1 on some national charts.

Why did Alan Freed play the song so much? Well you might say it goes back to my discussion of Payola a few chapters back. If you ever see the record, or even a CD of the song look at the names of the writers. Along with Chuck Berry's you'll find the name Alan Freed. Writers or copyright owners get paid royalties every time a song is played. So, why did Alan Freed play the song so much? Duh!

Chuck was learning that stories of hangers on who had access to recording artist's money were mostly true. His road manager was pocketing money from his road shows, others were taking royalties by grabbing publishing credits, and sometimes local promoters would pay him short or charge expenses not agreed to in advance. He was being cheated and he knew it. Chuck realized that if he was going to survive in this business he would have to manage his own affairs or at least find ways to prevent others from scamming him. That was the start of his reputation of not only being difficult to deal with, but eccentric and strange in the way he approached the whole business of personal appearances and shows.

I'm not going to write "The Chuck Berry Story" here,. although he left out some of the problem parts of his life, Chuck has already done that. It's called, "Chuck Berry, The Autobiography". Out of print now but you can find copies on the Internet.

Chuck found that the 1955 release of Maybellene was hard to follow. Everybody knew Maybellene then and everybody knows it now, decades later. Next was Roll Over Beethoven in 1956, and then a string of them. "Thirty Days", "No Money Down", "Too Much Monkey Business", and on and on.

There was "School Days", "Sweet Little Sixteen", "Johnny B. Goode", "Almost Grown", "Back In The USA", all setting new standards for Rock music, all of them literally blowing other recording artists away. Everywhere in the country established artists were doing the Chuck Berry sound and that Chuck Berry guitar intro. That classic intro. Every kid in the country with a guitar wanted to learn it.

Chuck appeared in movies too, Alan Freed produced movies. Who knows what Freed was getting out of that. Movies like Rock Rock Rock, Mr. Rock and Roll, Go Johnny Go, and others.

By the time I joined WXYZ radio in Detroit, in Motown, Chuck Berry's music was already known to millions around the world.

Unbelievable as it may seem, I never heard any of it. Because of that a series of events were set in motion that would change my life and affect thousands of others even to this day.

Chapter 44
REELIN' AND ROCKIN

AT ONE TIME THE RECORD LIBRARY AT WXYZ WAS WELL KEPT. Thousands of records, both 45s and 12 inch LPs. If I wanted to play anything that was not currently on the station play list I had to search the library. One day in dearly 1962 I was back there bumbling around looking for some oldies when a half dozen 45s fell out of one of the shelves onto the floor. As I replaced them I noticed one of them on the CHESS label. Earlier that same month I had met one of the label's owners, Phil Chess at a party in Detroit. I was curious.

While I was looking for more records I put the CHESS record on the audition turntable. I couldn't believe my ears.

It was Chuck Berry. It was Maybellene. It was three years old and I was hearing it for the first time. Ever hear something like that? Something that makes such a first impression that you just keep playing it over and over? That's what I did. Played it about ten times.

To this day I am well known for playing things loud. The louder the better. When I hear music I want to be IN the music, not away from it. I had Maybellene going full blast. You could hear it for blocks. I was loving it. Finally Bob Baker came flying into the room yelling, "What the hell Is going on back there? Is that record stuck? How many times you gonna play it? And Lee that bloody speaker is so loud we don't NEED a radio station, the whole town can hear it. TURN THAT SPEAKER DOWN"!!

I spent the rest of the time I had that day finding Check Berry records and listening. I was mesmerized not only by the simple music but the words. Simple story telling words.

> *"Deep down in Louisiana close to New Orleans*
> *Back up in the woods among the evergreens*
> *There stood a log cabin made of earth and wood*
> *Where lived a country boy named Johnny B. Goode. . .*

You know the rest of it. I was struck by all of it. I got on the phone, called the local Chess Record distributor and told them I wanted everything they had in stock by Chuck Berry and I wanted it now. Next morning when I arrived at the station there was a large box on my desk. All Chuck Berry. And that was the beginning.

Station policy allowed me to play two or three oldies an hour. Guess what all of mine were? You got it. I was playing Chuck Berry music like it was all brand new. And it was! At least to my audience it was. There were a few generations that had never heard it, and definitely not the way I was playing it.

Start the record, recite the lyrics over the intro, sing with it, let it finish, cue it up again somewhere in the middle and play it again. Or play "Johnny B. Goode" and follow it with "Let It Rock", a song that Chuck wrote and sang that was also about trains; then follow that with Bye Bye Johnny. The Chuck Berry Music rocked and rolled for weeks, months.

Wherever I went people were now asking for more Chuck! I had to try and get him in for a weekend at Walled Lake Casino. I called Leonard Chess in Chicago and asked for a meeting. He agreed and I was on a plane. Actually, two of us were flying that day. Some months earlier I realized that I needed help at the Casino and had asked Dave Prince to do the dances with me. It meant that I had to give up some money, but it was worth it. The crowds were too big, the place was too successful to just have records playing while I was on the air. Dave Prince became a regular at the Casino and I was glad for it.

Leonard Chess was the reason behind the success of Chuck Berry. Oh, Chuck's talent would have found a way, but it was Chess who recognized it, recorded it, and hooked up with Alan Freed to force the hits. Let's just say that Freed was continually compensated and Chess was in control.

He couldn't have been happier to see us. He was cordial, cooperative, and there were dollar signs in his eyes. After all here was Lee Alan, the guy from Detroit who was playing old Chuck Berry music like it was new. And all of Michigan and surrounding states were buying it like it was new. Chess was pressing LPs and single 45s of old music and shipping to stores by the truckloads, all because I was playing Chuck Berry and listeners couldn't get enough of it. Chuck Berry was now an idol all over again, only bigger and more so.

"Leonard", I said, "I've got to have Chuck at Walled Lake and that's all there is to it. Send him in for a weekend. He'll do two nights at Walled Lake and the TV show on Saturday. Trust me, it will be standing room only" It was then that Leonard Chess told me why he couldn't send him and also why all of Chuck's music was no newer than almost three years ago.

He would not be coming to Detroit anytime soon, Chess told us.

Chuck Berry, the father of Rock And Roll was in prison!

These are the articles that were printed in the St. Louis Post Dispatch two and a half years earlier:

Warrant Issued For "Chuck" Berry

St. Louis Post-Dispatch January 1960 - A warrant charging Charles (Chuck) Berry, rock and roll singer, with transporting a 14-year-old Indian girl from El Paso, Texas, to St. Louis for immoral purposes was issued yesterday by United States Commissioner Irvin H. Gamble.

The girl, whose home is in Arizona, told Assistant United States Attorney Frederick H. Mayer that she and Berry left El Paso December 1 and arrived here about December 10, 1959. She said she lived at the home of Berry's secretary and worked briefly as a hat check attendant at Berry's tavern, 814 North Grand boulevard. She was turned over to juvenile authorities. Berry, 30, admitted to detectives and Mayer that he brought the girl to St. Louis. He has a number of popular recordings and appeared in night clubs throughout the country. His bond was set at $5000.

"Chuck" Berry indicted on felony charges -

St. Louis Post-Dispatch January 26 / 1960 -Charles E. (Chuck) Berry, rock'n'roll singer and guitar player, was indicted by the federal grand jury yesterday. The singer was charged with transporting a woman across the state lines for immoral purposes. Berry, who operates a tavern at 813 North Grand boulevard, has stated he lives at 3137 Whittier street.

Chuck Berry convicted of Mann Act violation

St. Louis Post-Dispatch -March 6 / 1960 - Charles E. (Chuck) Berry, rock'n'roll singer, was convicted by a jury in United States District Court late Friday, Mars 4, of transporting a 14-year-old Indian girl from El Paso, Texas, to St. Louis for immoral purposes.

Judge George H. Moore deferred sentencing until March 18 and declined to allow bond for Berry. The singer faces a maximum *of five years in prison and a $5000 fine for violation of the Mann Act. The Girl's home is in Arizona.*

She told Assistant United States Attorney Frederick H. Mayer that she and Berry left El Paso on December 1 and arrived in St. Louis December 10. Mayer said investigation showed his income had been as high as $115,000 a year.

Chuck Berry gets five years and $5000 fine
St. Louis Post-Dispatch - March 12 / 1960-Charles E. (Chuck) Berry, a rock and roll singer and guitarist, was sentenced to five years in prison and fined $5000 Yesterday by United States District Judge George H Moore. Berry was convicted in Judge Moore's court here March 4 of transporting a 14-year-old Indian Girl from El Paso, Texas, to St. Louis for Immoral purposes. Berry, operates a tavern at 813 North Grand boulevard.

Well, that was that. We left Leonard's office and made our way back to the airport. No Chuck Berry at the Casino. Not now anyway.

Understand that except for a few, by now I had met almost everyone in the entertainment world that I wanted to. But just when you least expect it, bizarre things happen. Here we were sitting in Chicago's O'Hare airport waiting for the plane. I was just sort of staring off into space not focusing on anyone in particular when my eyes came back into focus on the man I must have been staring at for five minutes. And now it registered. He was just reading a book. At first I thought, "No…I am not seeing who I think I am seeing". But I was! There sitting three feet from me was one the finest performers ever in the history of show business. He looked up, noticed me staring at him and broke out in the becoming smile that millions knew him for. I gave him a sort of "Sorry, I didn't mean to stare" look. He just smiled bigger, put out his hand and with a chuckle quietly said Hello, my name's Nat King Cole! It was a total thrill. Meeting Nat Cole for me was something very special. I'll never forget it. Three years later he died of lung cancer athe age of only 47! Every time I hear his daughter Natalie Cole or especially when I see the video of her singing "Unforgettable" and others with the old films of her father I think of that day. No, we didn't get Chuck Berry on that trip, but if you had told me I could meet Nat Cole just by flying to Chicago and sitting in the airport I would have done it. Today, nearly 40 years later the world is still a little less for the loss of this man.

It was late 1962. Our television show was getting bigger and the ratings were exceeding 50 percent of the audience. WXYZ radio was rocking, ratings were bigger than ever and Walled Lake Casino? Forget about it!! As Sinatra would say: The Casino was the oooonly place to be Buster! Big crowds, big talent, big everything. Coupled with Berry Gordy's Motown explosion, we were all at the center of the universe. We thought!

My daughter Dawne was four. She needed her dad and I wasn't spending the time with her. It was all work. All spotlight - all career. Patti and I weren't getting along either. It was my fault. Mind was always on the next show - the next promotion. Problem with that was that I had no plan for the future. There was no one there to tell me that what was happening was my 15 minutes of fame and I had better save money and protect my family. No one was there to beat that into my head. My home was suffering. I wasn't bright enough to know it. I was working seven days a week and was recognized wherever I went – by everyone. Everywhere! It was cool - for a while. I was the so-called "big guy" in Detroit now, making a big noise in Motown. And that's all that was important. Wrong! I was riding high! I would soon learn that the higher you ride, the bigger the slide when the bottom falls out.

Trouble was coming. Big time.

Chapter 45
THE BLIND GENIUS

EVERY WEEK THE CASINO JUST EXPLODED BIGGER. It was a ball. Ha! Bad pun. Really, it was more fun every time we went out there. And the people who came by the thousands came from everywhere. Going to the Casino was thee thing to do on the weekends and the recording artists wanted to be there. Hey, all the music industry knew that if they took their artist to Walled Lake they would perform the records for the crowd sure; but more importantly they would be privileged to hear The Fine Tone of Thee Lee Alan Horn which was made in Pakistan by a….ok I know I know.. sorry just got a little carried away that's all.

Anyway the recording artists also knew if they went to the Casino to perform, their appearance could make the papers and there was a good chance their music would be played on the air too.

Let me say right here that this was not payola! It was a commercial. Plain and simple. The Casino was the biggest thing in the Midwest period. But, nothing's easy. Every week producers for the Casino show and dance had to be in touch with music people to line up the acts for the weekend, big names as well as not so.. Local bands were dying to play there. If a major name wasn't coming from out of town, national artists I mean, we would just place a call down to West Grand Boulevard. Motown headquarters. They always had someone who could come to Walled Lake. One week they didn't!

"Nobody's in town", John Dew my producer told me. "They're all traveling, booked out of town. Everybody's on the same show at the Apollo in New York".

We were in trouble. A whole weekend's shows and no big name. We were spoiled. "Only one person in the whole place down there at Motown", John said. "They said it's a kid. Little kid using the studio for practice. We can go and look, but that's all they've got".

It was Monday morning. We had nothing to lose so we jumped in the car and headed for Motown. I don't know how you picture the Motown studios, the dynasty that was grinding out the biggest hits in the world back then, but it was no Capital Towers! It was a house. A small house located about two miles from General Motors World Headquarters on west Grand Boulevard in Detroit.. A very old, very small house that Berry Gordy converted into a studio. And that's where everything happened. That's where all the 60s Motown hits were born. You could stand and look through a glass window in the control room and watch everything in the studio. Compared to today, or any day you are reading this, the recording equipment in the 60s was primitive. The engineers sort of invented things as they went. They must have done something right. The sound that came from that dilapidated old house captured the ears of the world.

"He's 12 years old", the Motown promotion man told us. "Had one record that didn't sell. It was called: "I Call It Pretty Music, But The Old Folks Call It the Blues". I was looking through the glass. He was a thin, tiny, short kid wearing sunglasses ...inside!

This little guy was obviously blind!

When I first saw Little Stevie Wonder he was sitting at the grand piano keyboard. He didn't know we were watching. The mikes in the studio were on. He was playing flawlessly. Some kind of blues. Major chords, followed by sevenths, and minors with a rolling bass in the left hand that sounded like a combination of Motown and Gospel. His right hand moved like lightening over the keys. Never hitting the cracks. He was smiling, head moving back and forth. He was in a world of his own. The music he played came from somewhere deep in his young soul. It was music that had never been written. His music. His feel. The emotions of a seasoned, grown, experienced adult coming from a child's heart and fingers.

Suddenly he stopped, stood up, felt his way around the front of the piano and found the drums. If music can come from drums, he made the music. It was a rhythm I had never heard. First delicate, then violent, then controlled. A melody for drums, and this thirteen year old was inventing it and playing it at the same time. All spontaneous as he went.

The musical tour of instruments continued, and then we were riveted on what happened when Stevie started on the harmonica. He made it sound like a whole band. No 12 year old could play like that. Except he was! And all the time he was smiling. He had no idea anyone was watching and he was smiling. He was in his own world. A world where seeing wasn't necessary.

Steveland Hardaway Judkins was born in Saginaw, Michigan, on May 13, 1950. When his mother married he changed his name to Steveland Morris. He was born premature. In an incubator; he needed oxygen. They gave him too much of it. There was also a condition known as retinopathy of prematurity. They think the excess oxygen blinded him.

Stevie's family moved to Detroit in 1954. At four years old he was already showing signs of extraordinary musical ability. He was singing in the church choir. And that's where he started to spread his wings learning the piano, harmonica, and drums. There he blossomed into a genuine prodigy, learning all the instruments, one by one. By the age of ten he was considered to be accomplished on all of them.

Ronnie White, one of the Miracles heard Stevie and told Berry Gordy at Motown about him. Gordy listened and signed Stevie on the spot. Berry introduced him to Clarence Paul a producer/songwriter. That's when his name became Little Stevie Wonder and that's where I came in. He had already recorded a Jazz album that featured his ability on all the instruments. I hadn't heard it. I'd never heard of him. The album didn't sell. Didn't need to. Little Stevie Wonder was about to become known as "The 12 Year Old Blind Genius". I told the Motown people I wanted him at Walled Lake Casino and that's the way I would promote him, "The Blind Genius". They agreed. I only had five days to introduce Stevie to the world and promote the show.

Richard "Dick" Kernan was a talented producer at WXYZ radio and one of the reasons that Walled Lake Casino was a total success for me. His main job out there was to play the records that everyone danced to and especially to know what to play. He always did. He had the absolute knowledge not only of what was popular; but what those young people wanted to hear when they wanted to hear it. Dick did the same thing for us on the radio. He was one of the young geniuses that made us sound good and look good on the air. Others were John Dew and Larry O'Brien. They were always behind the scenes playing the records, station jingles, commercials, talking in our ears, and making our shows happen. Dick Kernan was especially fond of "The Casino" and to this day will talk about it.

Little Stevie Wonder was set to appear at the Casino on that coming Saturday night right after he appeared on club 1270 television that same afternoon. I was against having him on television.

No one had ever seen him yet and I didn't want him on television before the Casino. I wanted to talk about him, build the suspense, and describe him and what I had seen in the Motown studio earlier in the week. I didn't want anyone to see him first or spoil the anticipation. I finally won out and delayed his television appearance for a week.

From Dick Osgood's book WYXIE WONDERLAND here's what Dick Kernan had to say about Walled Lake Casino and how he describes what happened when Stevie Wonder made his first in person appearance there. I hope you'll forgive me printing all of Dick's words because they're a little self-serving, but these are his thoughts and his way of painting the picture:

"*Lee understood instinctively what was going on and knew how to use it.*

Knew what to say on the air, what records to play. He had a tremendous feeling for what was going on. Alan had showmanship and a flair for quality. He made the Kraemers (owners of the Casino) install the best possible sound equipment. He had 2 turntables installed, and a sound mixer. The operation had class. His manner of buildup on his broadcasts, and presentation in person at the Casino were made to coincide with the interests of the high schoolers and college crowd. He built up the success to 4 dances a week."

Kernan was all enthusiasm: "*It was just a very exciting thing. I remember a number of people that Lee brought out to the Casino that just drew crowds beyond belief. He brought in Fabian and I remember Lee and Red Kraemer and Cleo Kraemer (Red's wife) pacing up and down waiting for Fabian to get there and the crowd inside like 5,000 people going bah bah bah, where is he? And he finally showed up – just a super colossal event.*

Lee was instrumental in Stevie Wonder's success. Lee brought Stevie Wonder out to the Casino, promoted it, told the story about –you know—Stevie Wonder is a blind kid—staged it in such a way that Stevie Wonder at the Casino was probably one of the all-time entertainment events I have ever seen."

I did say that. And more! For one solid week on the air I told my listeners that I had seen something I would never see again as long as I live. A tiny person who could play and sing their music better than anyone I had ever heard, and I had seen and met them all. I told them what happened in the little Motown studio and that this little man was absolutely stone blind since birth, and that if they came to Walled Lake that coming Saturday they would be the first in America to see and actually be in the same room with a legend that would live and be remembered far beyond any of their lives. I also told them that they would be privileged to see and hear Thee Lee Alan Fine Toned Horn, made in Pakis…OK! OK! I know. Ha! Dick Kernan:

"It was not only that Stevie Wonder was good – obviously, you can't palm off a turkey—but the build up that Lee was able to do on the air and the presentation at the Casino, the suspense, the showmanship that he used in presenting Stevie Wonder was just unbelievable."

Kernan was right about one thing. When you build up an event that much the audience better see something spectacular or you'll lose them. Not only would the word of mouth be negative about that event, but all credibility would be gone for the future. They'll never believe you again and probably never come back.

I didn't want to just put him on the stage with a band and say, "Here he is." I wanted the instant I introduced him to the Casino audience to be something they'd remember. Every time they saw Stevie in the future, I wanted them to remember the first time they saw him as a boy at Walled Lake Casino.

The stage at the end of Casino opposite the entrance was big. It had to be. In earlier years it held the biggest bands in the world.

It was about four and a half feet higher than the dance floor complete with a theater curtain that could hide an act while they were getting ready to perform. The dance floor was about 140 – 150 feet long. At the other end there was another stage. It was about 10 feet in the air and we had never used it. It was about ten by twelve with a railing around it so the performers wouldn't do a nosedive. In the big band days the original owners built it so that when the featured band took a break another smaller group would take over on the small stage and the music would be continuous. They didn't want people to leave during intermission and get lost at the competing Walled Lake Amusement park across the street. I had never used that stage. It was always dark up there. No one ever even noticed it. Until now that is.

I convinced the Kraemers to go out and rent some large, powerful spotlights called Super Troopers. The kind that when turned on would bathe their target in so much brilliance that it would be like looking at the sun, nothing else could possibly be seen. I had them placed so that they were facing the small stage. There was one switch that would trigger them.

The night of Stevie's performance came. The routine always was that the Casino opened at 7PM. Dick Kernan, John Dew, or one of the other producers would start playing records from behind a curtain stage right (that's your left if you're facing the stage). The booth had a glass wall so the producer could see the dance floor if the curtain was open. If it was closed the booth was hidden backstage. I was on the air live from the glass bubble on the stage at 7:15. What I was broadcasting could only be heard on the radio, not in the hall. You'll remember I had the engineers install a speaker inside the booth that blasted what the producer was playing in the booth and anything else that was going through the Casino sound system so that when I opened up the mike the radio audience could hear what was happening in the Casino. Even if nothing was happening that speaker made it sound like the place was jumping, and it usually was.

I was on the air from 7:15 to midnight. My radio show was live from the Casino until ten o'clock. The last two hours were recorded earlier in the day and ten to midnight played from Broadcast House. Bands played on the stage anytime they were ready, but when there was a featured show like Stevie Wonder it would start after ten and run to closing at eleven thirty.

Stevie arrived with his companion, Clarence Paul at about 9:30. By that time 4,000 people were packed in there like sardines in a closed can. They were all dancing to the music and it looked like they were moving as one. So many people that I think if one moved the wrong way they all would have hit the floor. Before the Casino opened that night a small band had set up their instruments up on the small stage. No one noticed.

Clarence Paul helped Stevie up the winding staircase. The little stage was totally dark. Starting at about 8PM I was telling all of the Midwest on the radio not to come to Walled Lake. "You can't get in", I said, " Don't come. Everybody came to see this blind genius, Little Stevie Wonder and the place is full. No more room. Please don't try to come tonight." Well that didn't work. That was like telling them not to call the phone number. It just made everyone more curious and the traffic jam was something for the record books. They just kept on coming.

The only way I could possibly describe the atmosphere inside the Casino that night would be to say anticipation was boiling over. Everyone was expecting something electric, mind blowing, and nearly life altering to happen. I was hoping we had it right and that's the way it would come off.

A band was playing on the main stage at 10PM when I got off the air and the recorded segments started. I went out on the main stage and started my usual performance with the crowd. I have always had a way to talk with an audience and get them quiet. My secret is really no secret. I loved my listeners and my audiences and they could always sense it. Four thousand people were dead silent while I explained what happened that week. How we couldn't get anyone to appear, there was only one Motown person in town, we went to the Motown studio, etc. I told them all about Stevie, almost word for word what I have told you in these last few pages, except I didn't tell them about the surprise I had waiting at the other end of the Casino.

When I was finished and they knew what I wanted them to I introduced the "Twelve Year Old Blind Genius." When I said this the boys backstage started throwing switches. First the house lights. Everything in the Casino went totally black and stayed that way while I finished talking. It was still dead silent. Then, when I finally said "Little Stevie Wonder", there was about a 10 second pause (10 seconds is a long time. Look at your watch and count it off), and the Super Troopers blasted a shower of blazing light all at the body of 12 year old Little Stevie Wonder at the opposite end of the room 15 feet in the air. At exactly the same instant the band up there started to play and so did Stevie on his harmonica. Four thousand heads and bodies turned 180 degrees and looked up at this incredible picture.

Little Stevie Wonder was now a known entity. By now four thousand people have told that story to a hundreds friends, and still tell it. Do the math. A few million now know about the night when Little Stevie Wonder first appeared before a large audience in public at Walled lake Casino. And every time the story is told it gets a little better. That's how legends are born.

A few months later Stevie recorded Fingertips Pars 1 & 2. From that point on he belonged to the world. Even with all his fame though, he returned to the Casino many times in appreciation for the love he received that first night.

Years passed. I left the radio and ended up in the advertising business. One night in 1984 I was in Memphis, Tennessee recording commercial music I had written for a Chicago car dealer. I was alone and bored in the hotel room. The Memphis paper I was reading screamed:

STEVIE WONDER – TONIGHT – MASONIC AUDITORIUM.

I hadn't seen Stevie in nearly 22 years. It was only a ten-minute cab ride.

I sat in the back row because the place was a sellout and I almost couldn't get in at all. His show was electric and, like the Casino twenty-two years earlier, the crowd was totally into it. Stevie, now thirty-four years old looked the same to me. There he was playing a keyboard in front of him, blowing the harmonica, and singing all the songs that we know and have neatly deposited into our in our hearts and memories. I loved every minute of it. Pictures of that first night at Walled Lake rushed back into place and I could see it all again.

When the show was over I went to the front and started trying to convince the rent-a-cops that I knew Stevie and they should let me go backstage and see him. Ha! This was Memphis. Nobody knew me here and of course I was getting nowhere with security. I was about to give up when out from a backstage door came Clarence Paul, Stevie's longtime writer/producer and friend, the same one who brought him to the Casino that first night. Clarence looked at me, did a double take and said: "Lee Alan , what're you doing here?" I explained and he said: "Why are you standing out there come on back and see Stevie." The rent-a-cops who had been so impossible now parted like the Red Sea.

He was standing in the middle of a crowd of about 75 people. They were all talking. It was loud. You've been there right? Everybody talking and nobody listening? Then for no good reason there's a sudden silence. It's like everyone decides to take a breath all at the same time. At that instant I said in a loud voice: "STEVIE!". He cocked his head, turned toward the sound of my voice and said: "LEE, LEE!". Even though it was more than twenty-two years since we had "seen" each other, Stevie knew my voice in a blink. We had a few minutes to hug and talk, to remember, laugh, and promise to call each other. I've lost his number now and as I write it's been another 19 years. Will he remember me next time and remember you too? Absolutely!

I truly hope he and I can get together on the same stage once more before it's all over. I loved him from the first moment I saw him when he was a boy in that Motown studio. I love him now.

After Stevie Wonder's appearance at Walled Lake Casino word spread faster than greased lightening. The 12-year-old blind boy genius from Detroit with a cheerful, laughing, disarming personality who could play every instrument was on his way to international stardom. All he needed now was a hit record. We knew that would follow. Now he was in big demand for appearances in Detroit and soon the world. He would never be the only one left behind again when the Motown stars went on tour. Stevie would appear for me many times at Walled Lake Casino and on television. And in 1963 he even played the drums for me on one of my own records. Ha! What a hoot that was.

Chapter 46
SET ME FREE

BARNEY ALES (AY-LESS) WAS THE EXECUTIVE VICE PRESIDENT of the Motown corporation and Berry Gordy's secret weapon to getting his music played and sold to the white audience.

Barney and I graduated from the same class and year at Cooley High in Detroit. He joined Berry at the beginning. He was there on the ground floor of the Motown explosion. His timing was right, and his personality for sales of the Motown product was perfect. Barney laughed with everything but his eyes. His laugh was infectious, but his eyes always seemed to be probing and serious if not threatening. An interesting trait for a salesman. And that's what he was. A salesman. Have you ever known someone who would look at you, talk to you but his sentences are fast and sometimes missing some parts so you're not really sure what he actually said? That was Barney. And those eyes! When Barney Ales asked for the order, asked for the close, it was automatic. Just look into the eyes and you didn't dare say no.

We were not friends in high school. Didn't even know each other. Oh I had seen him in the hallways for four years, but only for a "Hey, how ya doing". Nothing more. We were into different things. Strangely enough I was the one who was into music, shows, entertainment. Barney wasn't! Not at all. Barney was tall, but way overweight for his stature, maybe 280 pounds, one of those guys who always wore the black leather jacket and hung out at "Zs". Zs was a little restaurant near the school where all the motorcycle riders and their girlfriends were. Where all the greasers gathered. There was always some kind of trouble at Zs. It always looked like a black leather jacket convention. In high school Barney was one of those.

Six years later while I was with WKMH I was approached by the music promoter from Warner Brothers Records, a six foot 2, slim, dark haired, good looking Adonis dressed in an immaculate mohair suit. As he was explaining that Warner brothers was not really into mainstream music and he really had nothing new to show me except for some Dixieland LPs I realized that I knew him from somewhere and looked at his business card. His name was Barney Ales. The leather jacket was gone and with it at least 120 pounds.

Barney told me that although he was making about 120 dollars a week with Warner Brothers, good money in those days, he had another offer for a third of the money from a young writer who needed help promoting his R & B music to the white community. Barney wanted my advice. It was a no brainer. The writer's name was Berry Gordy. His fledgling company was Motown.

Now, years later Barney Ales was the millionaire Executive Vice President of the Motown Corporation. This time I was sitting in his office looking for his advice. I had an idea for a record. The more I talked about it the more he said he liked it. Three days later I was in the Motown studio not as a disc jockey, but as a recording artist. Well I'm using the word artist here loosely as you'll soon see.

"Write it", he said. "Write it and I'll get you a producer and time in the studio. Let's see what happens." I wrote the song in about 20 minutes that night and delivered it to Barney's office the next morning. "What'd ya do, have this in the glove box the whole time?", he laughed. Minutes later Popcorn Wylie walked into Barney's office. "Let's put an arrangement to this." Barney said to him. "See if we can get it done later this week." Popcorn and I had met many times. He was one of an entire stable of producers who were responsible for taking the works of Motown writers and arranging them with instrumentation and style for the singers to sing. Without those arranger-producers there never would have been a Motown music explosion.

Two days later I was in the studio that today is a museum. People come from all over the world to see where the Detroit Sound of music was made. It was in a comparatively small room with sound equipment no one today would even use. But, like all early inventions it worked. Man did it ever!

About 15 people were in the studio. There was a short rehearsal and tape was rolling. Martha and The Vandellas were singing backup, Marvin Gaye was playing piano, "Little" Stevie Wonder was beating on a drum, Smokie Robinson was playing THEE HORN. And...Ahem..I Sang (if you can call it that). When you hear it sometime, listen closely to my voice breaking up...they gave me one afternoon to do this and I think I had the worst cold of my life!

LEE: *I GOT THIS HORN, JUST THE OTHER DAY*
FROM A MAN WHO CAME A LONG LONG WAY
HE SAID THIS HORN YOU UNDERSTAND HAS COME FROM PAKISTAN
AND WHEN YOU'RE ALL ALONE AND YOU HEAR THE FINE TONE
YOU JUST WAIT AND SEE ...THIS HORN....IT'S GONNA SET YOU FREE!

*I TOOK THIS HORN, I GOT FROM PAKISTAN. I TOOK IT
HOME. I MEAN I ALMOST RAN
AND WHEN I WAS ALL ALONE AND I HEARD THE FINE TONE
ALL MY WISHES CAME TRUE I MEAN MY DREAMS OF YOU
IT WAS SOMETHING FOR THE EYE TO SEE
THIS HORN.....IT LIKE TO SET ME FREE!*

SMOKEY: *BLOWS HORN*
VANDELLAS: *HEY LEE – THIS HORN IS GONNA SET YOU FREE*
SMOKEY: *BLOWS HORN*
VANDELLAS: *HEY LEE – THIS HORN IS GONNA SET YOU FREE*
*SO IF YOU'RE FEELING SAD. I MEAN YOU'RE FEELING
R   E   A   L
BAD
YOU DON'T KNOW WHAT TO DO. YOUR HONEY DON'T WANT
YOU.
JUST TURN ON THE RADIO WITH THE LIGHTS DOWN LOW
CLOSE YOUR EYES REAL TIGHT, THINK OF YOUR HONEY
TONIGHT
AND WHEN YOU HEAR THE HORN YOU'LL SEE
YOU'LL KNOW JUST WHAT HAPPENED TO ME
THIS HORN.....IT LIKE TO SET ME FREE*

The record was only available from the station (WXYZ). Cost was one dollar and all proceeds went to the WMCA. They said it sold in excess of 50,000 copies.

I looked on Ebay the other day. Someone sold two copies of "Set Me Free" for $500 each. Hmmmm!

Chapter 47
CHICAGO CALLING

THE EXACT DATE THE CALL CAME FROM CHICAGO HAS ESCAPED ME, but I remember everything that happened. Every detail. I just hope I can put all of it into words that will draw the picture it deserves.

As I said at the beginning of this rambling treatise I am writing all of it from memory, not researching dates, numbers, statistics. So far one event seems to recall another, each with its own impact. Some of it has been painful, especially the parts about my family.

Choices.

It was a Tuesday in late 1963. November I think! I was in the studio at WXYZ sitting in for Joel Sebastian on the air in the afternoon. I was never comfortable doing afternoon drive-time shows. It was the second biggest job in radio. Afternoons. Something about the time slot that was different and awkward to me. Not as intimate. I loved being on the air at night after seven. I might be wrong but I always pictured you, listeners, really listening. Hearing everything. Words…music…thoughts. The afternoon just seemed less friendly, too rushed, busy and impersonal. My friends were listening at night.

The phone call came during the Tom Mcintyre's 5-minute

local newscast. "Lee?" the caller said. "Lee, Leonard Chess in Chicago". Before I had the chance to reply he went on: "Chuck's out and you got him for this weekend". "Chuck's what?" I said. "Chuck Berry's out of jail and he'll be at Walled Lake Casino this weekend".

"No way" I told him. "It's Tuesday. I can't promote the show in three days. Leonard, that's not enough time to get the word out. There won't be a crowd."

"Sorry Lee", I remember him saying, "The parole board was told that Chuck's job was singing and recording and the one place he had to go to get the proper acoustics for a live recording was Walled Lake Casino in Michigan. Lee, Chuck Berry will be there Friday and Saturday this weekend. Can't stop it now".

"Oh and by the way", Leonard Chess added. "Chuck gets a thousand a night in cash." I started to tell him I couldn't authorize that and that the owners of the Casino would have to give the ok. "Leonard", I said. And he hung up.

And that's how it all started. Chuck Berry at Walled Lake Casino was on. I called Dave Prince, Dick Kernan, and John Dew, told them what happened and everything went into high gear.

John Dew, another of WXYZ's best young producers was a tall gentle giant who loved what he was doing and, like the others, really knew his music. John, as one of the original producers for me at Walled Lake Casino, worked with Joel and me on our television show, Club 1270 and was responsible for lining up the artists to perform for both venues.

"Chuck Berry? This weekend?" John said. "You've gotta be kidding." That's what everyone said. It was a panic. The father of modern Rock music was going to be here Friday afternoon for the entire weekend. We had to promote it and produce it in less than four days period. End of story.

John arranged for studio musicians at Motown to play for the two nights at Walled Lake as Chuck Berry's backup band. Television too. Back then we didn't know what we really had that weekend. No one else did either. More about that in a minute. A minute? There I go again. Sorry, thought I was on the radio....

Friday afternoon the call came from the Crestwood Motel on 8-mile road. The real 8-mile road. Same as Eminem's movie. Chuck Berry was there and waiting to be picked up.

He was tall. Very tall and skinny as anyone could be and still be alive. He was friendly and shook my hand till I thought it was going to fall off. We talked for a few minutes, loaded his guitar and amplified into my car and took off for the Walled Lake. It was 5:30 in the afternoon. I had to be on the air at 7:15. We had plenty of time. I thought!

From Dick Osgood's book WYXIE WONDERLAND:
"Late Friday afternoon, Alan drove to a motel to pick up Berry and take him to the Casino. He had never met Berry, was impressed by his height, and found him humble but suspicious."

"I'd like to see my thousand dollars," said Berry.

"Fine," Alan said. "The Kraemers will pay you when we get out to the Casino."

"No," the musician said. "I can't have a check."

Alan packed Chuck Berry, his guitar, an amplifier and himself into his little car and started out for Walled Lake.

"By the way," Berry said squirming around in the tightly packed little car, "I have to get a tube for my amplifier. Could we stop at a drug store? Even though Berry had been out of circulation for nearly two years the clerk in the store recognized him. By the time they got to the freeway leading to Walled Lake it was choked with traffic. It was almost 6 o'clock.

"What's goin on?" the recording star asked.

"I don't know. That afternoon rush from downtown should

be over."

I want to interrupt Osgood here to say traffic was more than choked. It was a total parking lot. Stopped as far as the eye could see. Most of the time not even crawling. Time was catching up with me. We were still a good seven miles from the Casino. 7:15 was looking more and more impossible. Finally, I saw a police car approaching on the shoulder, got out of my stopped car, and flagged him down. I asked how long it would be before the accident or whatever was holding up traffic would be cleared.

"No accident," he said. "Traffic's backed up all the way to the Novi exit. The one that goes to Walled Lake. All these people are trying to get to the Casino to see Chuck Berry!" I told him who was in my car and that I had to be there before 7:15. "Lee Alan?", he said. "Pull it out on the shoulder and follow me." So there I was with Chuck Berry following a state trooper with all his lights streaming and blinking and siren wailing…
Osgood continues:

"What did you do in Jail." Alan asked while following the police car.

"Oh, I wrote a lot of songs. I'm going to record one next week."

"What is it?"

Berry pulled an old crumpled envelope from his breast pocket. He said, "I don't have it done yet."

He had written the words but not the music."

No one tells this story better than my late friend Dick Osgood, but let me add that I may have been the first one in world to hear the words to Chuck Berry's new song. A few weeks after this he would record it. Every contemporary station in the world would be playing it. Here I was with a police escort, leading me past hundreds of cars stopped on Michigan's I-96 with Chuck Berry in my car trying to decipher the only copy of what would become a standard that dozens of other recording artists would eventually record, not to mention Chuck himself.

Osgood:
He read some of the lyrics:
>*"As I got on a city bus and found a vacant seat*
>*I thought I saw my future bride walking down the street.*
>*I shouted to the driver, hey conductor you must slow down*
>*I think I see her please let me off this bus.*
>*Nadine, Honey is that you?*
>*Oh Nadine Honey where are you.*
>*Seems like every time I catch up with you Darlin'*
>*You're up to something new*

"What're you gonna call it?"
"Nadine" said Berry.

When Chuck and I finally got to the Casino my show was already on the air. Larry O'Brien was back at Broadcast House handling things. At 7:15 he rolled the tape with my theme song: "Zing Went The Strings Of My Heart" that also had my voice on it with my own pre-recorded opening. The opening was 1:58 seconds long and a good producer could stretch the start of my show at least 7 minutes without anyone ever knowing that I wasn't even there yet. He'd play the opening theme, then the first record, then a station jungle, then another record. Hey, forget 7 minutes. He could stretch it to nine or ten if he knew what he was doing. And Larry did! Many nights I was still four or five miles away when the show started. Sometimes I wondered if management ever found out about this trick they might think of a way to cut costs and cut me. Ha! With my salary in those days they wouldn't have saved much on me…

The Casino was jumping. Roads for miles were jammed. Parking was not possible anywhere. People were lined up at the door. Hundreds, maybe thousands of them. Red Kraemer, the owner, had rigged a speaker outside and mixed with crowd and traffic noise it was sheer bedlam! Somehow the State Police squeezed us a place to park and ushered Chuck Berry and me inside through a back door.

As I said before, when I was out of the station on remote my radio show was always live until 10PM. At Walled Lake music was played from a fairly sophisticated sound booth equipped with a glass window so the operator could see the stage and the dance floor. That's where all the music came from until the stage show started. Dick Kernan was in the booth and tonight the Chuck Berry show was supposed to start at 9 instead of ten. We had about an hour and a half to get it together.

When we arrived I streaked to the glass booth in front of the curtain, grabbed the earphones, told Larry I was there, and Chuck went backstage where the Motown musicians were starting to assemble their instruments.

When I looked out on the crowd disbelief set in. We had capacity crowds before but this night there so many people out there on the dance floor it looked like that if one person fell over they'd all go. Talk about the domino effect. Dave Prince was on stage talking to the crowd between records and looking like he was expecting disaster any minute.

I was on the air now. My main job was to tell people not to come to Walled Lake Casino. Back stage Dick Kernan in the booth had another problem. Chuck Berry!

Chuck had gone directly to Kernan and politely told him he wasn't going on at all until he had his thousand dollars. In cash. I was on the air so Dick went to Dave and Dave went to Red Kraemer. That night the price of admission was two dollars. Red went to the ticket booth, got a thousand dollars, and gave it to Dave who delivered it in a paper sack to the booth. This took a while. It was now about twenty minutes to nine. Kernan took the brown sack containing one thousand one dollar bills and handed it to Chuck Berry who was sitting there with him…waiting.

To put in Kernan's words: "Out on the floor, four thousand folks were getting nuts!" Where was Chuck Berry? They wanted Chuck Berry and they wanted him now! But Chuck was oblivious to it. He was busy counting one-dollar bills and organizing them face up so that all was in order. One…two…three… Meanwhile they started to stomp. The floor was wood and when four thousand people started stomping on it the entire building shook like it was going into the lake any minute. It was deafening. Nobody was comfortable. Except Chuck Berry. 15…16…17.

Backstage the Motown musicians were ready and Dave Prince was getting ready to bring them on to play…while Chuck was back there in the booth.

27…28…29…

Who were those musicians? Well only 10 of the originals that played on Motown hits that's all. Let's see if you recognize the names.

    Benny Benjamin – Drums
    James Jamerson – Bass
    Beans Bowles – Sax & Flute
    Hank Cosby – Sax
    Joe Messina – Guitar
    And 5 others

Today we all know them as The Funk Brothers

So, while the room was literally Reelin' & Rockin', I was in the glass bubble pleading with the world not to come to Walled Lake, Kernan was in the booth playing records for a crowd that was stomping and yelling "Where is Chuck? Where is Chuck?", Dave Prince was running all over backstage getting ready to bring on the band to try and cool off the crowd, and Chuck Berry was in the booth with Kernan…175, 176, 177.

Dave introduced the band. They were terrific. Fantastic. But nobody heard them except for those of us who were on the stage. It was now 9:30. Chuck Berry was a half hour late getting on the stage when, according to Dick Kernan he finally finished counting. And then without missing a beat, he counted it all again.

Dave worked with the band. Introduced them individually. He played games with them. I stood offstage blowing my horn and playing the village idiot. It was ok for a while but soon the audience was having none of it. They wanted Chuck Berry and only Chuck Berry. Period.

Finally, nearly an hour late Chuck was satisfied with the money and I brought him on stage. The crowd went ballistic. Cheering. Yelling. Roaring.

And Chuck Berry?

Well, he was on. And he was terrible! Aweful!

Apparently they wouldn't let him have his guitar in jail and he just couldn't play. Besides, he forgot almost all the words. The kids in the audience knew more than he did and did a better job of singing. I'm sure they knew Chuck was not doing well, but they didn't seem to care. They loved him and they definitely loved his music. So, at least that night it didn't matter.

The night was over, Casino was still in one piece, but we all dreaded tomorrow.

And as usual Dave Prince was mad about something and left.

Chapter 48
CHUCK AGAIN

CLUB 1270 WAS LIVE ON CHANNEL 7, ABC IN DETROIT. Nothing on tape or film but some commercials and most of them were live too. Most of the time the recording artists would lip-synch their records though, but they themselves were live right along with us. Mistakes and goofs were part of it all and there were plenty of those. Joel Sebastian and I were on following Dick Clark and on this day, Chuck Berry would be live. After my experience the night before a live performance on television from him was going to be interesting to say the least.

We were all at Broadcast House very early in the morning. The Motown Band was there setting up to play live. About two hours before the show there was a call from the motel where Chuck was staying.

"Is this Lee Alan?", the voice on the phone asked. "Lee, do you have a Mister C. Berry registered here?" I answered yes, asked him if there was a problem and he said: "Well it seems that Mr. Berry has been up all night playing a very loud guitar. We've had numerous complaints. How long will he be staying?" I assured him it would only be another night and hung up.

Chuck Berry knew he was in trouble with that guitar and practiced all night. Now what?

Chuck is famous for not telling anyone what he's going to do or when. And that includes never rehearsing with the band. He expects them to know his music, play it, and just follow his lead. That Saturday was no exception. The show was live at 3PM. Chuck showed up at about 2:40 in time to talk with the director, Chuck Sneed, look at the set, tune his guitar, and that's all.

The rest is history. Before anyone ever called them the Funk Brothers, they became The Funk Brothers. They played like they had spent the day rehearsing. And Chuck Berry? He was amazing! It was the Chuck that I had listened to on records and played on the radio. He was upbeat, cute, clever, outrageous and played everything that nearly 45 minutes could take. The entire studio was mesmerized at his performance. They came from everywhere in the building to watch and listen. No one was disappointed. I announced on the show that Chuck would be at Walled Lake that night and suddenly it was 4 o'clock.

Before anyone could thank him Chuck disappeared.

A few days earlier I purchased a new Ampex tape machine. That Saturday night at the Casino Dick Kernan set it up for me and ran tape. The crowd was the same, but this time everyone had it together. Chuck was outstanding. Almost inspired. Saturday night was the antithesis of the night before. I have never been at a better performance before or since. He was electric and perfect. They sang with him. He duck-walked. He stopped his music and became a comedian. He read an imaginary letter from home.

Chuck: *My man called up on the telephone long distance to Chicago to borrow fifteen dollars from his friend.*
And his friend said: "What'd you say?
I said loan me fifteen dollars.

	He said...what'd you say again?
	I said loan me fifteen dollars. His friend said, there's something wrong I can't hear you.
	Then the operator broke in and said: Mister, the line is very clear I'm able to hear him.
	So the friend said well...you loan it to him then!!
Audience:	Scattered laughs
Chuck:	(rummaging through his pockets) *"I know I've got the letter here somewhere. I always have it with me. Oh shucks, it must be in my other suit. (Pause). No this IS my other suit!*
Audience:	*Scattered laughter*
Chuck:	(Finds the Letter)
	"Dear Ch... (spelling it out) C - H - U - M - P Huh! That's not the way you spell my name.
	(Continuing-reading letter) *Says we been havin' a little hardship down here lately.*
	Says the bathroom caught on fire, but we were lucky that the flames did not reach...the house.
Audience:	*Loud laughs*
Chuck:	Oh yeah that's right. They have that segregated deal down there..yeah......
Chuck:	Says: "Your sister slipped on a banana peal and she sued the police department.
	Says the accident occurred just as she was steppin' into a patrol wagon.
	Oh yeah. Your brother has a new 1963 Cadillac and only cost him 20 years!
Audience:	*Laughs*
Chuck:	Letter says: Oh by the way your mother in law died. Oh how my heart did yearn.

	I know she's up in heaven 'cause she's too darn tough to burn.
Audience:	*Applause...*
Chuck:	(Reading) *The little couple next door have a bouncing baby boy.*
	The child was born with calluses on his hands.
	He was trying to hold on until after the wedding ....
Audience:	*Loud laughter....*
Chuck:	*Oh yes. I would have sent you the fifteen dollars you asked me for, but I sealed the letter before I thought about it!!*
Audience:	*Laughing*
Chuck:	*Oh by the way. Uncle Benjamin married a 19-year-old girl. Three weeks later he died.*
Audience:	*Quiet subtle laughter.*
Chuck:	*Says it took the undertaker three weeks to get the smile off his face!!!*
Audience:	*Screams of surprise and roaring laughter*

He loved that audience and it was mutual.

Oh the tape? Just about a month before I started this book I ran across that tape. It is nearly 40 years old and sounds like it was yesterday. Quality is phenomenal. It is vintage Chuck Berry at his very best and with the band, many of them now gone it is a rare collector's item. I have called it The Lost Chuck Berry and hope to release it, with his permission.

Chuck's life and career have been punctuated with high highs and very low lows. Some of it caused by his way of doing business. Some of it by others, and some by his own carelessness.

There was a short prison term in 1979 for tax evasion, and in the early 1990's court battles with a number of women who accused Berry of videotaping them in compromising positions in Berry Park and his restaurant in Wentzville, Mo.

And so Chuck Berry has left his mark not only on the world, but personally with me and a few thousand others who now have memories of him good and bad, of his antics, and what happened when the father of Rock & Roll came to Michigan.

As my late friend Mickey Shorr would say:

Pavolia Chuck. Pavolia.

Oh, one more thing.

That Sail Cat? Remember that Sail Cat?

Well, finally one night after more than four months driving everyone crazy by playing that cut of Jonathon Winters saying:

> Jesse…you know what a Sail Cat is?

I played the answer:

Winters: Jesse…you know what a Sail Cat is?
Jesse: No, can't say as I do. Don't know what that is….
Winters: Well, one day out there on Route 35 a big old yeller Tom Cat comes out of a corn field and was a crossin' the road when a semi comes a truckin' by and flattens him. Kills him dead! Takes him down to about the size of a pancake. Then that poor ole cat lays out there on that road just a bakin' in the sun. Day after day all them semis just keep on runnin' by and that ole Tom, he keeps on gettin' flatter and flatter. Then Jesse, you remember old Billy Bob?
Jesse: Yeah I member him…Yeah I do….Ole Billy Bob….
Winters: Well, one hot afternoon along comes Billy Bob a walkin' down the side of the road out there on Route 35 and he spies that old Tom. He looks both ways, so as to make sure no semi's gonna come along and flatten him like that cat, then he slips out on the road, bends down, and pries the Tom off the road.
Sound: (Winters makes a loud prying sound)
Winters: Then ole Billy Bob reaches a way back…. and sails that Tom over the cornfield.

And brother…. THAT'S A SAIL CAT!!

Ha! Sorry.

Chapter 49
THE KEENER REVOLUTION

In 1963 the Detroit radio market was set in its ways and asleep with blinders on. It was an AM radio world. So like every other major city in America only a few stations controlled the radio listening. In Detroit there were nine.

WJR was an old line station playing some music, carrying the CBS Radio Network programs and even had a live house band complete with singers.

CKLW was playing the hits, but it was not a popular factor in the market.

WWJ was playing music, but it was a mixed up format and was an "also ran".

WCAR was the "Good Music" station

WXYZ was flat out number one.

WKMH was a mix of music, interviews, news, sports.

WCHB was all black and played rhythm and blues.

WJLB was ethnic and music

WJBK was playing the hits and was strong competition.

Every radio station was coasting. WXYZ and WJR were at the top of morning radio. At 10AM WXYZ died in the ratings. The one hour Breakfast Club from Chicago took care of that. It was an old outdated program that sounded old and had no place on a contemporary music station. From 12 noon until 6PM WXYZ was number one. Then another roadblock. WXYZ carried an hour and 20 minutes of news from 6PM till 7:15. A killer for a music station. So, when I started every night at 7:15 there were no listeners waiting. I had to build a whole new audience and hold them.

Everything was about to change.

Mike Joseph, a radio consultant who once worked for ABC Radio was hired by WKMH to make something happen. I've heard that Joseph surveyed the market, learned about the factory shifts, when they started and ended, schools, traffic, and anything else that affected radio listening.

All of us at WXYZ knew what was going to happen. Joel, Dave Prince, and I went to Chuck Fritz and warned him that unless we took immediate action WKMH was going to bury us. It fell on deaf ears. No one believed the WXYZ dynasty could be toppled.

"We're the New York Yankees, the Rock of Gibraltar", Chuck said. "Maybe WJR or WWJ could give us a run, but not WKMH. Not with their weak signal coverage. You can't even hear 'em on the east side at all".

I remind you again that everything I write is my own recollection. Except for quotes from other books and some conversation with a few people, all of this is from the memory of my own experience.

HALLOWEEN EVE – 1963

At the stroke of midnight from 1310 on the AM radio dial in Detroit these words broke through the weak, sometimes static signal and into the night:

"THIS IS WKNR – NEW RADIO THIRTEEN WHERE IN

EXACTLY TWENTY FOUR HOURS THE BATTLE OF THE GIANTS BEGINS".

And then the station played a recorded Halloween/Ghost story. When it finished the announcer broke in again saying something like:

"THIS IS WKNR – NEW RADIO THIRTEEN WHERE IN EXACTLY TWENTY THREE HOURS, 48 MINUTES AND 10 SECONDS THE BATTLE OF THE GIANTS BEGINS".

There were no commercials. There was no music, no jingles, no news or weather. There were no DJs either. There were just Halloween stories and those announcements heralding The Battle Of The Giants. WKMH had changed its call letters to WKNR.
WKMH Radio was dead, gone, and forever erased.

Keener Radio was born.

In 1963 Halloween was on a Friday. 19 hours after the midnight announcements on WKMH/WKNR began I went to Walled Lake Casino. The attack was on and had already started to take no prisoners. Teenagers were asking me if I had heard "that new radio station". My answer was that WKMH had just changed their call letters.

"Yeah, right", they said.

"But have you heard that new radio station, WKNR"?

I am not going into what else they did and how. Just let it be said that within 60 days, rotten signal or not, WKNR was on top in most dayparts.

Chapter 50
BEATLE MANIA

NOVEMBER 1963

Much like he accidentally found Surfin' Safari for me one night John Dew, my good friend and producer, hastily grabbed two records out of a stack in the studio for Make It Or Break It. I played them both. The audience voted. The winner for the rest of the week was entitled Please Please Me by a group called The Beatles from Liverpool, England. No one here had ever heard of them. The record was sort of throwaway from an overseas music distributor. I liked it and played it. Nothing happened. The stores didn't stock it and It didn't sell. After a few weeks it was off the air and back in the throwaway pile.

Over the next few months there was more music by the same group. Although the audience voted for the tunes, they didn't sell. Gradually though, others on the air in Detroit and the rest of the country started playing music by this unknown and mysterious group from across the pond. And then in February of 1964 Ed Sullivan, who had the most watched variety television program in the world "discovered" the Beatles and brought them to America.

There were two shows. The first on February 9, 1964, from

the Ed Sullivan theater in New York (today occupied by David Letterman) and the next week February 16, the second. This one from the Deauville Hotel in Miami, Florida.

On February 9 show, they sang five songs "She Loves You", "All My Loving", "Till There Was You", "I Saw Her Standing There", and "I Want to Hold Your Hand". There were other performers on Ed's show that night. They were Frank Gorshin, Acrobats Wells and the Four Fays, the Broadway cast of Oliver and others. No one cared about them though. The Beatles were the show.

The following Sunday night, February 16, they sang "This Boy", "From Me To You", "She Loves You", "All My Loving", "I Saw Her Standing There", and "I Want to Hold Your Hand". Other guests that night were, Allen & Rossi, Myron Cohen, acrobats the Nerveless Knocks, and Mitzi Gaynor. Nobody noticed them.

Back in November of '63 when I started playing Beatles music I realized that something was happening with these guys. My memory and a little history tells me that there have only been a few phenomena like this. Rudy Valee singing through a megaphone, Al Jolson, Glen Miller, Frank Sinatra, Elvis Presley, and then The Beatles. Because of television and other mass media the Beatles had the most powerful and immediate impact on the world.

When I saw the first Sullivan show on February 9, 1964 I knew I wanted the impossible. A personal interview with the Beatles. The next morning, Monday February 10, I went to to Chuck Fritz's office. Chuck was now the Vice President and General Manager of WXYZ radio replacing John Gilbert who had left for other pastures in New York. I told Chuck I wanted to fly to Miami and get the interview. His reaction was negative. His position was that the whole country wanted to interview these guys now. "You'll never get it." Chuck said. "You'll never even get close." I pleaded with him to let me go and offered a deal. "Let me go to

Miami. If I don't get the interview you don't have to pay me for the week and I'll pay for the trip. If I get it you pay me and the costs." He was reluctant, but Chuck agreed.

I needed help and asked John Dew to go with me, cleared it with chuck Fritz, and made one more call. My old friend and major singing star Del Shannon lived near Broadcast House. Del knew the Beatles. For months in England, Del was their opening act. They were friends. I asked Del to go with us. He had no bookings that week and unbelievably he said yes. So, within hours John Dew, Del Shannon, and I were on a plane bound for the Deauville Hotel on the Beach in Miami, Florida.

If we were successful in all this it would be the first personal interview with the Beatles by a local radio personality in America. Later when it was all over I wrote the whole story for the newspapers and a record release. What follows now is that original story as it was written then. The writing was a bit amateurish but it tells the story. I will comment on it at the end.

Chapter 51
A TRIP TO MIAMI

The day was Friday, February 7, 1964 and I was getting ready to go on the air. It was no different than any other day for the past two days except that tonight I would play one solid hour of Beatles records. Unheard of in Detroit Radio, but I always did the unheard of I guess. I had been promising this for a week and frankly, I was little doubtful about it. Detroit is the most competitive market in the United States. Too competitive to risk losing a lot of listeners by playing the records of just one artist; but I had committed myself and now, lose 'em or not, between nine and ten tonight I would keep my promise to a young public I loved. ONE SOLID HOUR OF BEATLES. Yeah, yeah, yeah, yeah, ……..

Saturday I had a lot to do. Record for radio in the morning, rehearse for and do a "live" one hour television show in the afternoon, put my radio show together later in the afternoon , and then drive like blazes to Walled Lake Casino so I could get to the remote broadcast by seven o'clock. At midnight my day would be over, all 19 hours of it.. It was one of my typical seven days a week.

Sunday was about the same. Then it happened.

It was Monday. It was noon. I walked into my office at the

radio station and I couldn't believe my eyes. There on my desk were what looked like hundreds of cards and letters. When that happens to a radio personality, many things run though his mind. " What did I say on the air? Did I slip and say something wrong? Maybe I insulted someone. All those letters. I must have really pulled one off this time. I wonder if the station knows. I wonder if I'll have to take the terrible trip down the hall to the General Manager's office butterflies in the stomach all the way. I had taken that trip many times before and it wasn't pleasant.

All these things were running though my mind as I eased over to my desk and peeked at one of the cards. I couldn't believe it. I looked at another one…and another. I opened a letter. They were all the same. Hundreds of pieces of mail all saying the same thing. Each one of them thanked me, simply and clearly, just for playing that one hour of Beatles. I was shocked. I knew the Beatles were big and popular; but certainly not that big, and certainly not this popular. But there was the proof. I had to sit down and think. If that many responded just because I had played an hour of Beatles……if that many people were interested…. and then it hit met like a bolt of lighting. It was an idea that would carry me thousands of miles in the next two days.

The Beatles were in Miami, Florida. They had just done the Sullivan show the day before. I, along with 73 million others had watched them... After getting permission from station management there was a lot to do.

John Dew, my friend and producer and I were meeting Del Shannon and he was going with me. I had called and talked with him on the phone. I asked him if he had ever met the Beatles while working in England and of course the answer was yes. What's more, he knew them and said there would be no problem for him to get in to see them. It was all set. We were going to interview the Beatles.

We drove into the airport parking lot, took the ticket that

popped out of the automatic machine, found a place to leave the car. I was thinking: "The next time I see this car I either will have seen and talked to THEM, or I'll swallow my pride and admit that the whole trip had been a waste. I locked the car, strapped the cameras over one shoulder, the recorders over the other, took my big brief case in one hand and started for the airport entrance. There weren't many people in the airport so I knew immediately that Del hadn't arrived yet.

Finally after about ten minutes, I saw my old friend amble in the far entrance, suitcase in hand. He had to hurry. We only had ten minutes to take off. We shook hands, cleared his tickets, checked the bags, and went through the Blue Concourse.

We boarded the plane, fastened our seatbelts, and taxied down the runway. The flight attendant checked to see that we were secure, and when she came to our seats she asked about the tape recorder. I told her what it was and what I planned to do with it while in flight. She explained that somehow that operation of the recorder affected navigation and I wouldn't be allowed to use it.

As I have said before, it was cold in Detroit. The temperature was somewhere around twenty-nine or thirty degrees and the sun was shining. We were flying above the clouds, and all we could see were their mountainous formations. Finally the haze broke and instead of ground all we could see were hundreds and hundreds of miles of what looked like sand.... Yellow sand. Then there was a voice on the loudspeaker: "Good afternoon ladies and gentlemen. We are approaching the Greater Miami Airport; however, there will be a slight delay. We will be circling at fifteen thousand feet while waiting landing instructions. The land below us is the EVER-GLADES" The great Florida Everglades. Men had entered that desolate swamp and never returned. It was full of alligators, snakes, wild boar, and a thousand other things. Finally through my thoughts I heard the captain saying that we'd been given the OK.. We were about to land. We were about to embark on our adventure..

We gathered up our paraphernalia, and stepped out of the plane onto the stairs leading to the ground. There we stood like dummies. We had cameras, recorders, briefcases, with our overcoats on. The temperature was eighty-two degrees and we had on our heavy suits and overcoats on.

Now we were in Miami. Making tapes of what we said and what we were planning as we walked, we headed straight for baggage pick-up. While Del was getting his suitcase, John and I hailed a cab. Del Shannon, John Dew, and Lee Alan all packed securely in a Miami taxi, the cabby said: "Where to". Del said "The Deauville Hotel", and we were off. The Deauville Hotel was the origination for their appearance on the Ed Sullivan Show. The cab driver was a man about fifty. He told us he'd been driving around Miami for thirty years. As a matter fact, he wouldn't stop telling us things. He talked so much about so many things that I reached over and turned on the tape machine. What he said was priceless. We asked if he knew anything about the Beatles. I think he knew more about them than we did. He told us that they arrived at the same airport we had just come from, and there was mass panic. He had never seen so many people turn out to greet anyone. There was so much traffic jammed up for so long that he and his cab made a small fortune. "It took me three times as long to drive anywhere, I collected double and triple fares." He told us that one of the local radio stations dressed up their disk jockeys to look like the Beatles, and just as the plane landed they all ran out from behind a big truck. The throngs thought for a moment that they were actually seeing the Beatles, and they were mobbed. Fortunately, he said, no one was hurt. To sum it all up, the Beatles caused pandemonium in Miami from the time they arrived until the time they left.

We were driving along the ocean and over the causeway, and before we knew it, The Deauville Hotel was in view. We had come thousands of miles in a matter of a few short hours. The last two hundred yards would prove longer and harder than anything I had ever encountered.

We pulled up in front of the hotel, thanked the cabby, grabbed our belongings and headed for the entrance. Police were everywhere. On the stairs, the entrance, and all around the building. As we entered the lobby there were more of them. .Miami policemen protecting the Beatles and the hotel.

The lobby was jammed. There were people everywhere. Old people, parents, children, teenagers, bellboys, police, and they were all talking. It looked more like a giant teen dance. I was trying to hide the tape recorder because it had the name of my radio station on it and I knew that if anyone saw it, even we would be mobbed. Del asked the man behind the desk for the room number of the Beatles' manager, Brian Epstein. He had met Brian on two occasions while in England. Brian had sent him an invitation to stop by and say hello if he happened to be near Miami during their visit to the U.S.A. We were stopping by to do more than say hello; but first we had to get the manager's permission. When we finally got his attention the man behind the desk barked: " I'm not allowed to give that information out."

We made our way through the crowd, past the desk to a long line of little booths. Each one of them contained a telephone. Del picked up the phone and asked for an outside line operator. When he reached the operator, he asked her to get him the Deauville Hotel. When the desk answered Del said: " Mr. Brian Epstein's room please." It turned out that the hotel operator asked him who was calling and of course he said, "Del Shannon." There was a slight delay, which seemed like an eternity. Finally, I could hear Del saying: " Hi Brian how're ya doing?" We had made a contact. Del was talking to the man who could say a simple yes or no to our request. Del was saying "Yeah, I'm here in the lobby…uh huh…well are the

Beatles in? They are."

That's the way the conversation went. Then the bubble exploded!!!! Del hung up the phone and motioned for me to come with him. We walked over to a part of the lobby that wasn't as crowded as the rest and sat down. He explained that the Beatles were in the hotel but would be giving no interviews, not to anyone.

They would be talking to no one. NOW WHAT? We had run up blind alley and it seemed that there was nothing that we could do.

Just then Del nudged me and said: "Don't look now but that guy walking toward us with the dark glasses is Brian Epstein." He walked over to where we were sitting and greeted Del with a big smile and a handshake. Del stood up and talked with him for a minute and then I was introduced. He wasn't quite as friendly with me as he was with Del. We were a lot better off than we had been a few minutes ago. Just then another man walked over and whispered something into Epstein's ear. This little gesture would turn out to be the key to our entire trip.

Brian Epstein was a tall, slightly built man in his early thirties. After listening to the whispered message, he turned and introduced his informant to Del and me as Mr. Jack Millman of Miami. We were to find out later that Mr. Jack Millman was the Capitol record representative for Miami. It was his job to see that the Beatles got from place to place all in one piece, and without being molested by the throngs that were to follow them wherever they went. Then, just as easily as if he were to tell the time of day, Epstein looked at Del and said in his Liverpool accent; " Del, I'm sure the "boys" would love to see you. Could you come back about five o'clock and have dinner with them in the room?"

Del had been invited to have dinner with the Beatles. This was great. All our troubles were over. I jumped in said: " That's great we'll be here at five."

It was 2:30 P.M. What were we going to do for two and a

half hours? I went to the reservations desk and asked if there was a room available. The man told me that in order to get a room there, I would have had to make reservations six months ago. As a matter of fact, he said there were no rooms available in any good hotels up and down the beach. He told me that if I just wanted a room didn't care what it was like, that I should call the dump down the street. He thought there was a possibility at least. So, off we went. Jack Millman, Del Shannon, John Dew, and I were on our way to see if there was a room at the "dump" down the street.

Well, I'll tell you one thing, the guy at the Deauville wasn't kidding. The place was definitely a dump with a capital "D"; but there was a room available. According to the proprietor it was "probably the last available room on the strip." So, there we were. We had our room at the dump and we were waiting for five o'clock to come so Del could go back to the Deauville and have dinner with the Beatles.

Jack Millman was a short, stocky gentleman with a genial manner about him, and I asked him if he would have dinner with John and me while Del went to the Deauville. He accepted the invitation and we began to talk. It turned out that he had been in the record business for a long time, and knew all about yours truly and our shows in Detroit. He even knew a lot of people I knew, and the conversation became long and involved. He told me had been assigned to take care of the Beatles while they were in Miami. He met them at the airport, and described the same scene we had heard earlier from the cab driver. His story was fascinating. He said the Beatles would be doing two shows on Sunday. One in the afternoon, which was a dress rehearsal and one at night, which was, of course their "live" appearance on the Ed Sullivan Show. "The week before they gave out about five thousand tickets for each show, and there were only two thousand seats… it was a mess." I was just listening … fascinated. "The kids couldn't even hear them singing. They were all screaming. The technicians for the TV show had trouble putting the mikes in the right place so the Beatles wouldn't be downed out for the millions who were watching at home." I asked Jack Millman, for his personal opinion of the Beatles. Without hesitation, he interrupted me... "Gentlemen... Complete Gentlemen... a credit to themselves, and a credit to their country." If you were listening when I broadcast the interviews on the radio, you heard Mr. Millman himself utter those very words. I was tape recording the whole conversation.

It was time for Del to leave for the Deauville and his dinner with the Beatles. He promised he would do all he could to convince them to talk with me and provide us with the interview. I wished him luck, and he was out the door and gone.

Jack, John, and I sat in the hotel. A couple of hours went by, and I knew that by this time Del had had dinner and was busily engaged in the business of trying to get them to consent to an interview. Finally there was a knock at the door. It was Del. "They're still the same." Del was so excited that I had a hard time trying to calm down. "What about it Del, do we get the interview or not?" "Well....(he hesitated) it doesn't look too good. They were happy to see me; but, no interviews. I leaped to the telephone and asked for long distance. I was calling a disc jockey I knew in New York. I was calling Marray Kaufman. He knew them. I asked him if he could exert any influence to get me in to see them. He said he would try. After that there was a series of calls going back and forth from New York, to the Deauvile, to the "dump", and back again. Meanwhile Jack Millman left to go back to the Deauville himself to see what he could do.

By now it was after midnight. Jack had been gone for two hours. Del was asleep. I was wide awake, staring at the wall waiting for the phone to ring or a knock at the door. By this time, the Beatles knew all about me and why I was here, and I hoped it all had done some good. I shook Del and woke him up. We decided to go out for a while, get some air. We left a message with the hotel, and grabbed a cab. We went to the Peppermint Lounge on the beach. We saw Hank Ballard and the Midnighters, and a group called the BG Ramblers, who months later were to appear on our TV show.

Now, it was nearly four in the morning. I felt like I hadn't slept for a week. We were just paying the check when the chair next to me moved, and a man sat down. It was so dark for a moment I didn't realize who it was.

"You got it", he said. It was Jack Millman.

"You got it", he said again and again.

"I got what?"

You got your interview with the Beatles". I couldn't believe it. I shook him by the shoulders. "Do you know what you're saying?" I said "Yeah, I know what I'm saying. Don't tear my suit!!!" I apologized. "All those calls from Marray Kaufman…they only made it tougher".

I asked him why. "Because they don't like him", he said. "You know what did it? "Simple. I finally convinced them that you had come all the way from Detroit just to get this interview, and that there were thousands of kids who would be disappointed if they wouldn't talk to you."

I couldn't say anything. I was still stunned. He went on: "It was Ringo".

Huh? I said brilliantly.

"It was Ringo. He finally said that he would consent to the interview if the others would. As soon as he said that it was all set. Eleven o'clock in the morning." Huh?, I said again. "Meet me at the Deauville tomorrow morning eleven o'clock and make sure that machine is working. We only have one shot at it."

You might have guessed by now there was no sleep for me. I was up the rest of the night making sure everything worked.

It was ten-thirty. Del, John and I started for the Deauville. The scene was the same. There were people everywhere. We climbed the stairs and entered the hotel. Sure enough, there was Jack Millman sitting on a sofa near the elevators. "Sit down", he said. "I'm going up to 1215 now. Be ready when I come down and we'll get started before somebody changes their mind." I asked him what 1215 was. "Their room number', he said, and he was gone.

The events of the past forty-eight hours were a blur in my mind. If I would have had to write this story then, I never could have done it. It all ran together. I had to think twice to remember what day it was. By this time there were about a dozen people around me. They didn't know who I was but somehow they sensed that I too would disappear into the elevator in a few minutes. They saw the tape recorder. They knew.

It was noon. I'd been waiting for an hour and a half, and still no Jack Millman. I was beginning to get worried. I waited another hour. Del had gone to make arrangements for our return flight. Just then the elevator opened. Jack stepped out and motioned to me and he said... "Let's go. Only you, Lee. Sorry John. And, oh yes, No cameras. Leave the camera here".

Now we were in the elevator. The operator said: "Floors please?" I said twelve please, and that's all there was to it. The doors opened on twelve and we walked out into the arms of a Miami policeman. "Your credentials please", he said. Jack showed him his papers, even though he had just come down, and we were directed to our left. We walked down a long dark hallway. When we got to the end, there were more police. Jack flashed his papers and we turned right. There were six rooms in that short hallway. In front of each room there was a Miami policeman. Six rooms. One each for Brian Sommerville, (the Beatles' publicity manager), Brian Epstein, John Lennon, George Harrison, Ringo Starr, and Paul McCartney. We walked to the last room on our left, and presented our credentials once again. The policeman tapped on the door. When it opened, a man stepped out. It was Brian Sommerville. He introduced himself and told us that he was in charge of all the Beatles' publicity. I asked him if I could talk to him on tape and he said he'd be glad to; but right now, if I didn't mind, the Beatles were ready to talk with me. He swung the door open, and there they were right in front of me like they had been waiting for me all the time. There were the Beatles from Liverpool, England.

Brain Sommerville introduced me to all four. I fumbled with the tape recorder. I was nervous; but I knew what I was going to say. The room was lined with boxes of mail. There was mail from all over the world. There were two beds in the room. John and Ringo sat on one, and George and Paul on the other. I sat on the chair between the beds, microphone in hand. Directly to my right was a huge picture window. I could see beautiful, blue ocean for as far as the eye could see. All four of the Beatles were dressed in their bathing suits. They were going to that private home immediately after the interview. We began to talk. All during the interview I was thinking how easy going these boys were, how natural and relaxed they were, I was thinking: "Here are four good natured English guys who have become more popular than any other four people in show business, in the world. They are talented, sharp witted, full of fun, and their success has not affected their ego…four regular guys."

I won't describe the interview, because if you haven't heard it, you will. When it was over, and after I had interviewed Brian Sommerville, we were on our way. Down the hall and into the elevator, through the lobby, onto the street and into the car. We only had thirty minutes to get to the airport. We drove back along the same route we had come. Along the ocean, over the causeway to the Miami Airport. After the plane took off, John, Del, and I relaxed for the first time in days. There were only three people on the flight and we were tired. I leaned my head back and closed my eyes. The events of the last few days we were still spinning in my mind. We had seen, met, and talked with the Beatles. We had been successful after all. It had been a long, hard, journey. Now, we were on our way back to cold, snowy Detroit.

So, that's how it happened. When I got back to Detroit the engineers and I edited the tape and got it on the air.

Every now and then, for years afterwards, I always received a card from the four of them on my birthday and sometimes just a phone call when they felt like it. Now archived and standard in every library, their music remains part of us.

Of course tragedy took John's life and now, as I write George is gone as well. I will remember them as four guys about my age who were having fun and absolutely overwhelmed by the magic of their instant success.

And Ringo, if you read this I want you to know that there's a guy in Michigan who'll never forget what you did for me and a few thousand listeners here in Detroit when I took that Trip To Miami.

Oh yes, the station paid for the trip and even the room charges at The Dump.

And then a few weeks later my life would take a dramatic and deadly turn.

John Dew remembers it differently. In a recent email he wrote:

I'll never forget the thrill of getting on a charter jet flight. Eastern Airlines "The Wings of Man" as I recall. There were just 3 of us on the entire plane going to Miami, you, Del Shannon and me. Somehow, you had convinced Chuck Fritz that you could land an exclusive interview with the Beatles. WABC in New York couldn't even swing enough clout to get an interview – but you could. Your "ace in the hole" was of course Del. Even so, there was no guarantee. They were the hottest commodities in the world, having taken

New York by storm via the Ed Sullivan Show. Now they were starting their US tour and every TV station and Radio station in the country wanted in on the action. I thought then that one thing you never lacked, Lee, was confidence – or at least, guts (we never used the term "balls" in those days.) It took Del, and every other string you could pull, push or yank. But you did it. Just you. I couldn't go (even though I was supposed to be your "engineer"). Del couldn't even go to their room. Just you. It was a fabulous coup.

Then we came back to earth. We checked into a cheap motel for the night and had to ride back like common folk on a commercial flight – coach class no less. But it all was worth it. You had a world exclusive for WXYZ. They sold it as I recall for a ton of advertising bucks and we eventually put out a 45-RPM recording of the trip and raised a lot of money for charity.

It would never happen today. TV would pay millions for exclusivity and radio would be an also ran. Thank God for the good old days.

John Dew
General Manager
WJZQ - 92.9 The Breeze
Traverse City, Michigan

Chapter 52
STORY UNTOLD

APRIL - 1964

The Corvette Stingray was all black. First one off the line at Chevrolet. It was powerful, different, prestigious, and definitely a signature for me. No automatic either. Four on the floor and a monster. I loved it!

Walled Lake Casino, personal appearances, opening the television show live on camera driving in the winding driveway at Broadcast House, all marked by my black 1964 Corvette Stingray.

I'd had it about four months and then came the dream. At least that's what I think it was. Specific memory seems to blur with time. When my late friend Dick Osgood interviewed me for his book "WYXIE WONDERLAND" (wyxie was the nickname for the station call letters. WXYZ = WYXIE) I told him it was a dream. That is what I have always told people. As I think back though it may not have been a dream after all. Sometimes when you tell a story often enough it changes in the telling and you start believing the changes.

Here's what I remember. Whether it was a dream, a premonition, or some sort of strange glimpse into the future I was terrified at what I thought I saw.

It was absolutely surreal, almost as if I was looking at a massive television screen in my mind. I could see myself driving in my black Corvette Stingray. It was night. I was going too fast. The radio was on. I was listening to Don Zee, the all night personality on WXYZ. I saw myself as I went through an intersection. There was a semi truck. We were both going too fast.

Dream or whatever, it was as if I was watching myself from another vantage point. Like some sort of out of body experience. I could see myself, the car, the situation, but had no control over what was happening.

The Corvette behind the semi. Both going over 60 miles an hour on that dark road. That's when it happened. Lights. Brakes. Noise. There was a ditch. The Stingray plunged head long into it, flipped end over end slicing a telephone pole in its path in two pieces, then rolling over and over finally settling upside down, the severed telephone pole and a dancing snake of sparks from a live wire on top of it.

I could see myself inside. When the gas tank exploded the Corvette was ignited. One huge blue and yellow flame. It was consumed in a matter of seconds. I actually saw it. It was real!

And there,. Trapped in my little Corvette on that cold night in 1964, I burned to death.

As I said, it was a dream. That's the way I remember it. But it stayed with me. Actually haunted me. Night after night. Same road. Same intersection. Same truck. Same ending.

I was convinced that sooner or later the entire episode would happen and my little Corvette was going to kill me. I never told anyone. Not even my wife Patti. Our relationship was strained enough as it was.

Two weeks later I went to Cloecy Pontiac on Grand River road in Detroit. When I told the general manager, Art Moran that I wanted to get rid of the Corvette he was blown away.

"Lee, this is a brand new 'Vette. You sure you want out of it"?

"Dead sure", I said. "And that's what I'm afraid of".

Art Moran had sold me cars in the past and was always a terrific guy. He asked no more questions and proceeded to show me the new Grand Prixs. So a few minutes later I traded my new black Corvette Stingray for a midnight blue 1964 Pontiac Grand Prix with white leather interior, a 440 engine, and four on the floor.

Now, although the dream persisted, the car in the dream was always the black Corvette. I was relieved and certain that it was all a stupid trick of the brain. Corvettes were made of fiberglass. There were newspaper articles about low ignition points and Corvettes burning. I was finally satisfied that my dream was just the result of information gathered and stored somewhere in my subconscious. That's how dreams happen, right?

It was midnight, one Friday night in early April when I finished my radio show, said my usuals to Don Zee and went to my office. Club 1270, our television show was on the air the next day and I needed to layout the music. About an hour and a half later I powered up the Grand Prix, made my way out the winding driveway at Broadcast House, turned left on 10 mile road and headed west. My home was about seven miles away.

The radio was blasting WXYZ. Don Zee was doing his usual show. Don was the best all night DJ I have ever heard. He was known as: "The Zombie", the leader of the Zee Zombies; all those who because of their jobs or insomnia stay up all night and needed a friend on the radio, a different group of people for sure. I knew about them from my days at WJLB.

News on WXYZ was always exactly at 55 minutes after the hour. The news was on now. It was exactly 1:55AM as I approached the intersection of 10 mile road and Lahser.

1964 was the first year I ever had a retractable seat belt in a car. As I barreled through the green light I was playing with it. Like a yo yo I was playing with the seat belt. I clicked it into place. I remember thinking it was so late I must be the only soul on the road when a few hundred yards ahead of me there appeared a large semi. A mile later I was on him.

I remember glancing at the speedometer and slowing down to 60 miles an hour to match the speed of the truck. We were both going too fast for conditions on that dark two-lane road.

It was then I realized I had seen all this before. The sudden flash of lights was all at once blinding and beautiful. Like Christmas lights that burst in a blur in front of me. Now everything seemed to go into slow motion. Although the road ahead was void of any traffic for some reason, unknown to me to this day, the monster truck had slammed on his brakes. The lights were his message that the brakes were on and locked.

What happened in the next few seconds seemed to take minutes, even longer. When the lights appeared I remember thinking that if I couldn't slow to his speed I would run right up under the bed of his truck. The top of the Grand Prix would be sheared off and my head with it. The only way to avoid this was to go around him.

I hit the brakes with all my strength and jerked the wheel to the left.

It worked.

I was now in the left lane. The oncoming traffic lane. The truck was moving forward again, lumbering on. I tried to straighten out. There was ice. I was still going too fast and the brakes wouldn't grab. Things seemed to move slower now. There seemed to be plenty of time to think. My God! This was my dream. Not the Corvette. The Grand Prix. The truck, the lights, it was all happening. This was my dream.

The ditch was next. The impact was so abrupt that the car

still couldn't stop. Instead the shear forward motion caused the rear end to keep going and to do a cartwheel. End over end. It was all happening in slow motion. Just the way I had dreamed.

The sounds were deafening and as if they were a tape recording playing at a slow speed. Slow crashing. Metal echoing. Scraping. Now the car was rolling over sideways. Over and over. Once, twice, three times.

Then, nothing!

The car was upside down.

Everything stopped.

The only sound was the radio. "This is Don Zee Reporting", and then: "Everybody Say Yeah….". Little Stevie Wonder was singing fingertips.

I couldn't move my body. I was hanging upside down and I was paralyzed! The I realized it was the seat belt. Seconds before I had fastened the seat belt and now it was holding me suspended. I released it and dropped to the roof of the upside down car. The first thing I did was reach out and turn the radio off. Silly, but that's what I did.

The driver's door was jammed. Couldn't open it. The passenger door was impossible to get to. That side of the car had been crushed like an accordion. There wasn't enough room between the roof and the seat for me to squeeze through. That's when I heard it. Whooooshhhh. It was the gas tank. The heat was indescribable. I thought: "I'm too young to burn to death".

The next thing I knew I was standing outside about 50 feet away from the car. I was in shock. That sight is imbedded in my memory. I remember thinking these exact words" "There's my new car on fire, upside down with a telephone pole on top of it. How am I ever going to get it fixed?" A stupid sentence, but that's what I was thinking.

The road was about 30 yards to my right. Instead of walking

that way I went to my left, walked all the way around the blazing wreck and then went to the road. Later the police told me that had I walked to my right and taken the shortest rout to the road I probably would have been electrocuted by the live power lines laying all over the ground.

It was about 1:15AM and I was standing by the side of the road trying to flag a passing car. None would stop. My chest was hurting some and blood was pouring from my mouth. Mouthfuls of blood. I was sure I had a rib through a lung. Finally a car stopped. I told him I knew he couldn't pick me up but asked him please to call somebody. He said ok and sped off.

I lay down in the ditch. Laying there I could hear cars passing and the sky was lit with the colors from the burning wreck a few yards away. Then the sirens. Police, fire, ambulance all seemed to arrive at once. Next thing I knew I was in Emergency at Beaumont Hospital. My personal doctor was there.

I won't bore you with all the gory details except to say that the bleeding was not from a rib lodged in my lungs. I had bitten my tongue most of the way through. There was a heart contusion, a few minor cuts, and three cracked vertebrae.

My dream had played out in real life, but it was wrong. The ending was wrong. I was alive. The Southfield, Michigan police told me that the driver's door was still locked, that it had been forced open and the hinges had burst by some great force from inside the car. They said I must have put my feet against the center floor with my back against the door. From there adrenaline took over. The doctors said that must have been how the vertebrae were crushed. Pushing with such force against the door that the hinges were literally split and the door opened. Back broken in the process.

Dick Osgood from his book WYXIE Wonderland:

"Fan letters were delivered to the hospital in sacks. While Lee was recuperating he did some hard thinking. Part of the

cause of the accident had been exhaustion. He had worked late at the station that night writing a script for a television show he was doing with (Joel) Sebastian. He was working 10 hours a day, 7 days a week. Too much. And since he had put his work first and his home second, his family was on the verge of breaking up."

I was in a brace for months. Had shirts made to fit over the brace. On television I looked like a stick man. Square shoulders and all.

I believe that Art Moran, now a world class Pontiac dealer and a dealer in other franchises as well, was instrumental in saving my life. He is a terrific guy and also a great salesman. He could have talked me out of trading the Corvette. If he had I am positive you would not be reading this.

I should have died there in that car. Knowing how foolish I was, careless with my life and loved ones, a habit that would continue regardless, it just wasn't my time. I believe that the hand of God saved me that night. He was with me in that car. He has been with me every step of the way. Most times I ignored Him. That night He saved me for some reason, for something. To this day I am still not sure why, or for what.

But God continues to watch over me and save me.

Chapter 53
CHANGE...

WXYZ Radio, its history, the people, and the formative years of the Motown music explosion were the most exciting years of my life and from what I can tell these days, for most everyone else who was in Detroit at the time. Listeners included.

My years were filled with success and, for a young man who thought he was headed somewhere, unbelievable consequences of unwise, no . . . just bad choices.

Choices.

By late 1964 my work load and my blindness to what it was doing to my family, was pushing me over the mental edge. The April accident served as a wake up call.

In about June of that year the owners of Walled Lake Casino came to me and asked me to take a cut in pay so they could do some remodeling of the building. That sounded reasonable and I agreed. Nothing else changed. The radio broadcasts continued, the dances kept going, and I was still on television with Joel Sebastian.

About two months later I went to Chuck Fritz, the VP and General Manager of WXYZ Radio on a Friday afternoon and told him that unless I could shorten my days and hours I was probably going to lose it completely. I told him my family was in jeopardy of a breakup and asked him to shorten my hours on the air from 7:15 to Midnight to 7:15 to 10. Taking two hours a night off my show would mean that I wouldn't have to go into the station at noon anymore to record the last two hours (10PM – Midnight) when I was on remote. It would give me time at home and get me out of the worsening atmosphere of the music business and their demands. Temptation was everywhere and I was beginning to think about giving in to it.

"What about the Casino? What about the dances and your extra money?" Chuck asked. I told him if he would give me 10PM to Midnight only, I would continue doing the remote broadcasts at Walled Lake, but not the stage shows. I would leave there at 10PM. Dave Prince could do the stage shows. He was already out there with me anyway. The Kraemers liked him. I would be on the air working for the station, but Dave would work for them. I would essentially quit the dances at the Casino and only do the remotes for the station. I would give up that money and just do radio and television.

Chuck was understanding, but wanted the weekend to think about it. I thought that was fair enough. I felt better already.

That night, after the show at the Casino I went to Red and Cleo Kraemer and told them what I had said to Chuck Fritz. Dave Prince was there in the meeting. I assured them that nothing would change really. I would still be there live on the station. Still be telling everyone to come out to the Casino. The only differences were that I would leave at 10 o'clock and not do the actual stage show, and they wouldn't have to pay me anymore. Dave would handle all that and I'd just be working for the station.

They seemed to accept it. I didn't perceive any problem and they didn't object. At least then they didn't object. I came back Saturday night as usual, did the show and left.

That was the last night I would ever see The Kraemers or Walled Lake Casino!

Chapter 54

BEGINNING OF THE END

THE CALL FROM BOB BAKER, THE PROGRAM DIRECTOR OF WXYZ, came Monday at 9AM. It was very short and right to the point. "Get your tail in here. Fritz wants to see you NOW!"

Something was very wrong. Couldn't be my Friday meeting with Fritz. He was too compassionate and understanding for my family situation, too agreeable to my proposal. Had to be connected with Walled Lake. Everything else was going too well, at least with my show.

Walled Lake. Had to be something to do with what I told the owners of Walled Lake about me not being involved with the stage shows out there. Dave Prince was in that meeting. He could corroborate anything that was said.

When Dave answered the phone I told him of the call and asked him to go to Broadcast House and wait for a call from Fritz's office in case I needed him. He agreed and I blew out the door. Broadcast house was only 20 minutes away. I was in Baker's office in 15. His face was red. Just the way it looked after a three-martini lunch at Polumbos, the favorite station hangout on eight-mile road. Yes, same one again. There was no smile and this time he wasn't talking fast. He wasn't talking at all. When he saw me he just extended the first finger of his right hand pumped it in a violent pointing motion in the direction of Chuck Fritz's office. I did an about face and went there.

Nancy Galagher, Chuck's secretary wasn't smiling either. None of this was good. She got up from her chair and opened the door to Fritz's inner sanctum. This was the same office where an excited and smiling John Gilbert hired me a few years before. There were no smiles now. The normally affable and friendly Chuck Fritz just motioned for me to sit down.

Charles D. Fritz was a nice guy. A radio salesman at heart. A millionaire at an early age from stock bonuses and his position as local head of a national sales rep firm, Chuck joined WXYZ when it was riding high and number one in the hottest radio market in the nation. His predecessor John O. Gilbert had left for greener pastures as general manager of WABC-TV in New York and in July of 1963 35 year old Chuck Fritz became the 7th general manager of WXYZ, one of the most storied radio stations in America. At first he didn't change anything. But this morning he was about to.

I had barely settled in the chair when a stern faced Chuck Fritz looked directly at me with his steel gray eyes and said:

"Lee I'm going to fire you this morning!"

After 40 years I can still hear the words. How they sounded. Still feel the hot bolt of fear and desperation that took over my brain and like a tidal wave spread over my entire body. I don't remember what I said. I was paralyzed. Actually paralyzed.

Most radio and television people I have known over the years are used to moments like this. Ratings drop, programs change, times change, people lose their shows, leave, get fired, go on to the next gig, in the next town. Getting fired was usually no big deal. Grab your mike and headphones and move on. But this was WXYZ. This was a dream for me and I was losing it.

I don't know how much time had passed, but I finally recovered enough to ask:

"Why.?"

"Lee", Chuck said, "After you left my office Friday afternoon you went out to Walled Lake and told the Kraemers that if they didn't double your money out there you'd see to it there would never be another remote broadcast and you wouldn't be there to do the radio shows."

"But Chuck, I." Chuck didn't stop.

"You pressured them and used the station as a lever to get more money. That's against all ABC policies and opens us up to lawsuits. You're fired Lee and that's final."

Stunned is not the word. Nothing like that was ever said. Nothing like that happened. I knew it. The Kraemers knew it. And my partner out there Dave Prince knew it.

"Chuck, none of that happened. None of it. WXYZ is the most important thing in my life. Not just a radio station. Not just a job. Chuck, I promise you, something is going on here that I don't know about. Call Dave Prince. Prince is here. He knows none of this ever happened.

He's in the building now Chuck. Please call him."

He spun his chair around and picked up the phone.

"Nancy, page Prince."

We waited in silence. Finally after about 5 minutes Chuck excused himself and entered the private bathroom that was part of his office. Nancy poked her head in and gave me a look that told me she couldn't find Dave Prince. When Chuck came back she told him there was no answer to the page.

"Prince isn't in the building."

He just looked at me and said:

"Lee, there's no more to say. It's over. Good luck." He sat back down and turned his chair back to me.

There's no way to describe how I felt and what was going through my mind. I got in my car, drove out that beautiful driveway. I went home. Stayed home. More than three months. No friends. No calls. That's when I learned about depression. Even now as I write this I feel it. I want to go back there, get everyone involved in the same room and say:

"Wait a minute. Let's fix this. Let's not have this happen."

I didn't want to see or talk with anyone. They recognized me everywhere. Now, I didn't even want to be seen.

Once again, when I should have been concerned with my family, nurturing them, loving them, and putting them first, I was only thinking of myself.

Choices

If only I could go back and talk to that fool, how different things might have turned out.

Chapter 55
PATTI & DAWNE

PATTI AND I HAD BEEN MARRIED FOR 7 YEARS. My beautiful daughter Dawne was 6 years old. She needed me. They needed me. I wasn't there for them. Oh the money was ok, but I wasn't. I was totally immersed in career and self.

I never thought about how all this was affecting them. How Dawne might be exposed to comments at school, or how Patti would be regarded by her friends and family.

My mother and father were 54 and 60 years of ages respectively. Dad, a major work clothes manufacturer in Detroit, had a stroke at age 59, was forced out of business by partners and had gone through his own bout of depression. After months of seclusion he bought a party store in my old neighborhood of northwest Detroit.

And there he was seven days and nights a week. Mom and dad working together at Toby's Party store. The whole area knew them. Everybody knew Al at the party store. And everybody knew Al's son was on the radio. He made sure you knew it.

He had my picture posted everywhere.

"That's Lee Alan," he would say. That's my son. If I was in

the store seeing him he would introduce me to everyone.

"Meet Lee Alan", my son.

He was proud of me. Mom, although less outspoken was proud too.

I never thought about that when I was fired by WXYZ or how it would affect them.

I was running out of money. Patti was singing as much as she could. She did it cheerfully. She loved me. She really loved me. Whatever she did, she did it for me and for Dawne. I was oblivious. I believe I was in what today would be diagnosed as clinical depression. Back then it was unheard of. So it went untreated. My depression found a target, the nearest one available. My own wife. I was indifferent. Distant. Outwardly unfeeling. I was starting to convince myself that my marriage was a mistake. And that was the beginning of the end for Patti and me.

The victims of my stupidity would be Patti & Dawne. And eventually many others.

Then one afternoon the doorbell rang. Patti answered it.

The car in the driveway said WXYZ – TV Channel 7.

Chapter 56
MILTON

THE MYSTERIOUS MAN FROM BROADCAST HOUSE was in the foyer talking to Patti. His laugh was unmistakable. Remember what I said about him earlier?

Milton DeLoche worked for WXYZ Television, but nobody ever knew what his job really was.

The late Dick Osgood, in his book WYXIE Wonderland, describes Milton this way:

"Milton was a black man who held a unique position. He replaced light fixtures, drove VIPs to and from the airport, provided female companions for visitors who desired them, and often took John Pival home and put him to bed. He was powerfully built, like Pival, and the two of them were quite close"

Fact is Milton did everything at Broadcast House except show up on the air and now and then we even had him do that! He was a man who was always smiling, laughing, and talking. Milton was the only person I have ever known who could look at you, talk to you, speak absolutely plain English, and when he was finished you had no clue to what he said. The words were there; but they didn't say anything! And no one ever dared tell Milton that they didn't understand him. You just didn't do that. Not to Milton. He was a bear of a man who was wired to all the ABC brass. Milton's miscommunication was totally on purpose. When he wanted you to understand, he could be crystal clear.

And now the pipeline to everything that was happening at Broadcast house was sitting my living room. He was John Pival's man. And Mr. Pival, president of WXYZ Incorporated was THE MAN.

I didn't want to see anyone, but Milton was different. When we were alone the smile disappeared from his face and he started to talk. Now was one of those times he wanted to be understood and he was crystal clear.

"Why aren't you on television?" Milton said as eloquently as James Earl Jones.

"Milton I was fired!" I said

"Who fired you?" said Milton

"Well, Chuck Fritz." I said

"Did Pival fire you?" Milton asked?

I asked Milton what he was getting at. He went on to explain that I made another big mistake. I was only fired from radio and that the very next Saturday I should have showed up for Club 1270 and continued on television. He said that John Pival was not consulted and was not part of whatever the plot was to get me out of the station. Now it was going to be tougher.

He was right. I was sick. The only management conversation I had was with Chuck Fritz and there was never a mention of television. Fritz had no control over Channel 7. It never occurred to me then. Club 1270 was a big show. Remember in 1964 there were only 4 television stations that anyone could see; not hundreds like today. Channels 2-4-7 & 9. Channels 50 and 56 were there, but not all TV sets could see them. A converter was needed. Bottom line is that the audiences were huge.

Milton looked at me and said, "Call Mr. Pival's office."

"What for?" I asked.

"His secretary has a message there for you. Call there at 9AM tomorrow."

At that Milton got up from his chair and started laughing and talking in circles. Patti was back in the room with something for him to drink, but he politely refused and was gone.

"Does anyone ever understand what that man is saying?" she said. "Only when he wants us to", I said. "Only when he wants us to."

I made the call

"Lee Mr. Pival wanted me to tell you that you can go back on the Club 1270 television show if Joel Sebastian agrees."

That was the message. I contacted John Dew, still the show's producer and my old friend from radio and Walled Lake. John sounded a bit apprehensive, but said he'd talk to Joel and get back to me.

Two days later John called and said that Joel was OK with doing the show on his own and that the answer was no. Joel Sebastian had refused.

Milton was back that afternoon.

"Call Pete Strand." Milton said.

Pete strand was the program director for WXYZ-TV. He was responsible for all the programming and hiring.

"What for?" I asked Milton.

"Just call him. And that comes from the highest authority. Just call him! And no matter what he asks just do it!"

Pete Strand asked me to come to Broadcast House the next night and take an audition. An audition! I had been on radio at that station for nearly four years and on television for a year and a half and he wants me to take an audition? I agreed.

Next night I drove to Broadcast House. I hadn't been near the station in three months and was self conscious about even being seen there. I know now that I was in a state of depression. I just didn't want to see anyone. Didn't want to talk about it. So, I actually snuck into the back door of the building under the cover of night.

From his book Wyxie Wonderland, here's how Dick Osgood describes what happened:

> "Only one person at WXYZ kept in touch with Lee Alan after he was fired, and that was Milton DeLoche. Deloche often called Lee while he was convalescing from the auto accident, and he continued to call occasionally after the firing. During one visit he said: "Lee, I want you to call Pete Strand. There's going to be an opening on the announcer's staff at Channel 7."
>
> "No Milt, Pete Strand won't talk with me. I've tried."
> "I want you to know from the highest authority," Deloche insisted. "You should call Pete Strand."
>
> Lee Alan was so embarrassed to return to the station that he entered the building as inconspicuously as possible through a door into master control hidden under the executives' carport. It was night. He went up the back stairs and auditioned. A week later he had a call from Pete Strand.
>
> "We'd like you to come back for another audition."
> "Don't give up," Milton Deloche advised him afterwards on the phone. "just don't give up."
>
> The station was testing his humility. He was called a third time and asked to read news on camera. More days went by before Pete Strand called him again.
>
> "We have a job for a staff booth announcer," he said. You would have to open up the station at 6 o'clock in the morning and you'd be through by 2 in the afternoon. Do you

want it?"

"I'll take it."

And so the super star of radio became a booth announcer in television."

The job was interesting. I wasn't on television anymore. I was an unseen voice coming from a soundproof booth with a glass that looked out into a massive control room much like you see today if you watch Dateline or CNN. Lots of equipment, video- tape machines, complicated control consoles. There were technicians operating all of this and in front of them were very large and long glass studio windows that looked down into the actual studios one floor below.

The booth announcer (that was me) had a loose-leaf book with commercials, station identifications, and other things that needed to be said. In the booth was a microphone, controls to operate it, headphones, and television monitors so the announcer could watch the programming and also see what he was describing.

There was usually at least a half hour between live announcements. And on some of the breaks there was nothing to do but a station break:

ANNC: THIS IS WXYZ TV CHANNEL SEVEN, DETROIT

I knew most of the directors either from doing my own shows or from the same classes at Wayne University when we were students. The job was easy. Watch them, or listen in the headphones for a cue, read the script, and wait for the next break. The hard part was getting up at 4AM to get there by 6AM. At 2pm another announcer came in and the shift was over. Some of my friends there at Channel seven did that routine their entire lifetime.

The Channel seven announcer's booth was on the second floor of Broadcast House about 50 yards, and just around the corner from the studios of WXYZ radio where I worked for so long. I never went that way. I came and left by way of the back stairs. Nobody in radio ever saw me and although they all knew that I was there, no one ever came over to television to see me. I was banned. Blackballed really, and I never saw them. I was a ghost, a voice that no one ever saw.

A very shrewd John Pival, the president of the company, had engineered my new position and nobody knew it.

Chapter 57
INVESTIGATION

Russ Knight, known as The Weird Beard, a Disc Jockey at KLIF, Dallas was a giant in that market. Now a member of the Texas Radio Hall of Fame, Russ was hired to replace me. They gave him a plane ticket and a big check. He started off with what I left him, a 28 share. That is to say that 28 percent of the audience was listening to me when I was fired. Knight was hired to keep those numbers and increase them. His new job depended on it.

Meanwhile, since Mr. Pival, the president of the company, apparently had some faith in me I was going to back it up and prove him right. Even though I was working for ABC again, it was television. The same company owned radio, but radio fired and blackballed me and I soon learned that no other station would touch a guy who was fired from ABC under questionable circumstances. Unless I got to the bottom of it my career was over just like those who were fired for payola.

I hired a private investigator.

His job was to find out why the Kraemers told the station I demanded double the money or WXYZ would never do another remote broadcast? For me to make that statement would be foolish.

I was only a paid Disc Jockey. For a mere DJ to dictate where the station would broadcast was not possible. Only management could make that decision.

Besides, when I really think about it now, some 40 years later, with the massive audience I had, a worthless threat like that would be a silly reason for a station to fire its number one air personality. But that's what happened. With that incident and the raid that KEENER had made on the market the entire radio station was in traumatic shock.

I told the detective that I wanted to know everything, the finances of the owners, the records of the corporation that owned the Casino, everything. Who were their business partners if any? Who were their vendors? What did they know about the business of Walled Lake Casino? Something was behind all this and I needed to know.

John Pival was known as a creative genius and for some reason he liked me. Maybe he felt sorry for me that I had been fired without good reason, but he liked me and helped me. Oh he kept himself at a distance, but behind the scenes it was obvious that he was working in my behalf. When Rita Bell, the morning movie host couldn't make it to the station because of a snowstorm Mr. Pival called and instructed the director to put me on live television to do news, weather, and traffic reports. No other booth announcer had ever done that. There were always extra things I was asked to do and for which I was paid. It was Mr. Pival working in the background.

One afternoon I was called to his office.

"Lee I'm going to produce some one hour television shows. If we get any decent ratings it could end up on the network. Chuck Snead will be the director and I want you to be the host. See Chuck and get started." That was it. I left his office in a daze. John Pival learned that Joel Sebastian refused to let me back on Club 1270 so he just made another show, called it The Swingin' Kind and ordered it done.

The first one was at Edgewater Amusement Park in northwest Detroit, the second at Metropolitan Beach on Lake St Clair, and the third in Downtown Detroit. These were high budget shows with professional dancers, choreography, massive production crews, and name stars. The Supremes with Diana Ross, Little Stevie Wonder, Marvin Gaye, Leslie Gore, The Coasters, Frankie Valli and The four Seasons, Smokey Robinson and the Miracles and more. And these acts were not appearing free like they did at the Casino. ABC Television was paying the tab and a healthy tab at that. I was the host…the "Dick Clark or Ed Sullivan".

The first show ran in October in that year, 1964. The ratings were crazy. Over 65% of the audience watched it. The next two were the same. Big, big ratings and totally sponsored. Ha! I was still a booth announcer and we were a hit.

Meanwhile there was a massacre in radio. Ratings were terrible. Joel Sebastian left for an offer in New York, Bob Baker, the program director was fired along with most of his staff. Chuck Fritz was reaching for anything to save the ship.

Then I got the call I was waiting for from the detective. He said he had the answer and wanted to meet with me. I couldn't believe what I heard, but there it was in black and white. I called Chuck Fritz and nicely, but firmly demanded a meeting. He agreed, but wanted it to take place away from the station.

The next day I met him at the Kingsley Inn in Bloomfield Hills, an upscale restaurant and watering hole where he knew we were not likely to be seen together. After the usual small talk I placed a folder containing the documentation given to me by the detective. Fritz was already into his second drink when I started the scenario.

According to the detective the Walled Lake Casino was purchased by the Kraemers at a very reasonable price. The big bands had died and the original owners wanted out. After trying a number of things like bringing big band dancing back, disc jockeys holding record hops without any noticeable advertising, and who knows what else the Kraemers and I stumbled on each other and the rest is history. The success was phenomenal. The crowds, the stars, the reputation, the publicity, the radio station, and of course me, Lee Alan. It was now all part of the Walled Lake Casino story.

That's when, without my knowledge, it was put up for sale! All of the ingredients were part of the asking price. Me included. Apparently when I walked into the Casino that night in May of 1964 and announced that I was quitting the stage shows there were already prospective buyers with large checks considering buying the Casino. It was my guess that the owners panicked and in an attempt to make me continue, they called the station and told them I had threatened to leave totally unless my money was doubled. They felt that the station would force me to stay on, producing the stage shows and erase any possibility of losing the remote broadcasts.

The problem was they underestimated Chuck Fritz and ABC radio. Never in their wildest dreams did they think the station would fire me and thereby kill everything. How could they have guessed that ABC would fire its number one air personality in Detroit in the name of integrity? But that's what happened. The Walled Lake Casino was being sold and me with it, but totally by accident I had scuttled their plans.

Chuck listened and then looked at the paperwork. He was a hard businessman, but underneath there was a good heart and he just looked at me and shook his head. We talked about it for more than an hour. By that time Chuck was well into his drinks and although he didn't offer anything I had the feeling that he would look into all of it and I would hear from him. And soon.

Chapter 58

BACK FROM THE DEAD

Monday, November 2, 1964

Russ Knight's Detroit broadcast career was short lived. WKNR, "KEENER" helped it along. On October 17, 1964, only a few months after he arrived and before he could even figure out the Detroit radio audience, Russ was sent packing back to Dallas.

Meanwhile, Dave Klemm, the new program director had been searching the country for a replacement even before. As an interim solution he hired an itinerant radio performer from England by the name of John Benson to do a two week shot on the air. The British invasion of music started by the Beatles a few months earlier was still hot. Dave thought a DJ with a British accent would make waves. He didn't. Not a ripple. At the same time he hired Pat "Madcap" Murphy, a very funny guy to replace Knight. But then there was a call from New York.

Hal Neal cut his teeth in Detroit starting out as a sound effects technician and announcer at WXYZ and ended up not only running the station, but became the President of the ABC owned and operated stations. Books have been written about him and how he built the modern day WXYZ radio empire in Detroit so I won't go into all that here. Let's just say this. Hal Neal, the president of the ABC owned and operated stations in New York called Chuck Fritz and said:

"Look, you're running all over the country looking for somebody and you've already got that somebody right there in the TV announce booth. Hire him"!

No one could tell the story better than Dick Osgood so once again from his book WYXIE Wonderland here's what happened:

> *One afternoon Lee Alan was standing by in the television announce booth for Don Karle, one of the other staff announcers who was out freelancing for extra income. The phone rang. It was David Klemm, the new program director of radio.*
>
> *"Hi Lee! Would you come over to my office, please?"*
>
> *As soon as he was relieved, Lee Alan visited the radio section of the building for the first time since he had been fired from it."*

I will insert here that before I was fired I knew Dave when he was Director of Promotion. I found him to be a bright and friendly guy with good ideas. Maybe not programming a radio station types of ideas, but for promotion he was terrific.

Osgood continues:

> *"How'd you like to come back to radio?"*
>
> *"What do you mean? Are you serious?"* Alan said.
>
> *"The night ratings are way down and the Weird Beard is no longer with us. Have you been listening?"*
>
> *"No Dave. I haven't."*
>
> *"Well, I've had a disc jockey from England for two weeks – 7 to 10 – as a stunt – until we could find a permanent replacement. And for 2 weeks, we've been announcing a big surprise tonight."*

His face wore an expression of mischief as he added, "And at this point nobody knows what that surprise is going to be, least of all myself or Chuck."

Klemm chuckled.

We've found a funny little man named Pat Murphy, Madcap Murphy, and we might put him on but – how'd you like to come back?

"Tonight?"

Klemm looked at the clock on his desk, smiling.

"In about an hour. Seven o'clock. Chuck wants to see you."

Fritz shook hands with him and his smile was friendly.

"Lee ….we'd like to have you back. Frankly, I'm not too sold on Madcap Murphy. We'd rather make you the surprise!"

"Well, I would be just fooling anybody to hedge," said Alan. "Pride is something I don't live with now. Of course! I'll be glad to be the surprise."

He accepted $100 less than he'd been paid in radio before.

"There is one thing I really have to do first," he said. "I have to go down the hall and talk with Mr. Pival."

"I'll wait here for you," said Klemm.

Lee found John Pival sitting at his desk. It was 6:30. When Alan told him what had happened, Pival extracted a bottle from the lower right-hand drawer of his desk, poured a drink into a glass and held it out to Alan.

"I don't think I'd better," said Alan.

Pival downed the liquor

"I wondered how long it would take 'em to get smart enough to hire you back," he said. "But I'll tell you some-

thing, Lee. You're not getting out of The Swingin' Kind and I'm not letting you out of my booth up there until we find a replacement."

John F. Pival was short, with little hair, a mustache and when he grinned he looked like the human version of a Cheshire cat. He was grinning now. As I stood there in front of him, the president of WXYZ, Incorporated and vice president of ABC I realized that this man was the sole reason that in a few minutes I was going to rise from the dead. No one had ever been fired from WXYZ and re-hired.

If there ever was an original thinker, he was one and constantly thought outside the box. Without him there never would have been a Soupy Sales. His original programs are legendary and have all been written about before by others. He was there at the very beginning of television. He was an inventor, an oracle, and without the enemies he had today he would be in every hall of fame.

"Thank you Mr. Pival", I said

"For What"? he said still grinning.

"Get out of here. And you better not be late for the TV booth in the morning".

"No Sir", I said as I sort of backed out of his office.

It was 7PM. Dave Klemm was waiting for me outside Mr. Pival's office. I was due on the air at 7:15.

"I want to wait about 12 minutes, then we'll go up", he said.

"What about my opening theme, the music and everything else I need'?

"It's all up there ready to go".

From day one my opening theme was "Zing Went The Strings of My Heart", by Les Elgart, cut #2 on an album called: "Band of the Year". Cut one was Bandstand Boogie, the original theme for Dick Clark's "American Bandstand" on television. I might as well complete the trilogy here and say that cut #3 was "The

Varsity Drag", the theme I picked for "Club 1270", the television show.

"Jim Hampton has the tape with your open, but it's not labeled. He has no idea what's on the tape. He's been told not to listen to it until he plays it on the air at exactly 7:15".

"Who knows I'm going back on the air", I asked.

"You, me, Chuck Fritz, John Pival, and Hal Neal will be listening on his direct line in New York. No one else, not even Pat Murphy who's up there right now thinking he's on at 7:15. This is a total surprise. A shocker".

A shocker! Ha! No one was more shocked that I was.

"It's time. Let's go", Dave said.

We walked the hall from Mr. Pival's office and up the stairs to the second floor of Broadcast House, four doors and a hundred feet down the hallway. The door on the right led to a short hall with glassed in studio windows on both sides and a large studio at the end, the same one where the Fred Weiss and "naked lady" incidents took place.

Dave entered the large studio first. As he did Jim Hampton pushed the button with the opening theme. The first sound was my voice.

"From now until midnight in Detroit WXYZ radio presents: LEE ALAN – ON THE HORN".

Then came the Elgart theme....

As it played loud on all the speakers in the studios I walked into the room I had spent hundreds of hours in but hadn't seen in six months.

Hearing the tape Jim Hampton was ashen. Before I could sit down people appeared from everywhere. Engineering, news people, even television people abandoned their posts. All wanted to see if what they were hearing could be true or just someone playing an old tape. It was just utter pandemonium. And the phones? Forget about it. Every line was lit and stayed that way. I learned later that at least two sales people who were driving along peacefully listening to the radio drove off the road. One wrecked his car.

Through it all, Dave Klemm stood there looking like the cat that swallowed the canary. He needed a big surprise, something that would set the town on its ear and start them talking.

Mission accomplished!

The rest of that night remains a blur to me. For the first time in my life I was nervous on the air. I was flying, loud, fast, and…I was home. They recorded that show. I still have that recording.

Ironically my new time period was 7:15 - 10PM. The very same I had asked chuck Fritz for months earlier four days before I was fired.

One more thing. Klemm was wrong about who else knew about this before it happened. There were three others. I called Patti and my two biggest fans, my mom and dad. I think that was one of Dad's happiest moments in life. His son was back on the air. How proud he always was.

"That's Lee Alan. That's his picture. That's my son!!

Chapter 59
REACTION

The next day I heard there were so many phone calls that the phone company registered complaints with the station and the operator on duty had nearly quit! No one told her anything and without warning the switchboard heated up and stayed that way the entire night.

My office was flooded with telegrams. Bobby Vinton, Frankie Valli, Stevie Wonder, Del Shannon, The Supremes, Marvin Gaye, even Chuck Berry and Elvis. All welcoming me back.

I think everyone in the building came in with congratulations. Well all except Dave Prince who refused to speak with me.

Joel Sebastian was leaving for a job in New York and Dave was to be the new Afternoon Drive time personality taking his place. He was also the new host of "Club 1270", and the dances at Walled Lake Casino. Dave wasn't talking to me. Not a word and everyone knew it.

I made it a point to say hello to him at every opportunity. Prince would glare and ignore. I never quite figured it out either; except that I had done something he didn't expect and that he definitely didn't want.

I came back!

It was as if I had died and was buried. Good Riddance. Over. Done with forever!

And then...not. Back from the dead. Dave's childish and vindictive silence was soon known all over town. It was embarrassing and uncomfortable for everyone at the station, affected the entire staff, and the strain could even be heard on the air.

Prince was simply not speaking to me, period. Not for just a day or a week; but for over seven months. His action became legend.

Dave Klemm was under pressure. KEENER was stomping everybody and Klemm's job was to stop it. He called everyone to a meeting.

"Shut up and play the music", he'd say.

"Read the station slogans, never talk for than 20 seconds unless it's a commercial. Play the jingles, the promos, be happy, be pumped up, and on and on".

Fred Wolf, harassed by Klemm and hating the music more and more couldn't take it. Now independently wealthy and the owner of a bowling establishment, Fred told Fritz it was either him or Klemm.

In July of 1965 Fred Wolf, a giant among giants just flat out quit. His last show was one long stream of people. Celebrities, office people, friends, there were all kinds of people. Hundreds of them. All with something to say and most bearing gifts.

Shortly before all this Dave Klemm himself resigned. The pressure and futility of it all destroyed his personality. Basically a nice guy the "dictator" description follows him to this day. He became strict, firm, and loudly threatening. Dave realized what this was doing to him as a person and chose to leave. I think he knew that his ride at WXYZ was over and there was nothing he or anyone could do about it.

This left Bruce Still in charge of programming at WXYZ.

Bruce was a quiet, laid back little man who was lost in his new position and without a clue. I was back on the air, but realizing that none of us would last if the ratings got any worse and I would be back on the street looking for a job.

I decided to go back to Chuck Fritz one more time. The entire station sound was old and scratchy. I convinced Chuck that I could brighten it all and make things happen. I recommended that Bruce Still be director of operations, but not be involved in programming. Chuck was in trouble too. He was the general manager of WXYZ on the way down. A distinction no other GM had ever had.

He listened. Chuck always listened. Then, he called a meeting of the whole station.

Everyone except the switchboard operator crammed into the boardroom. It reminded me of that first meeting there when I joined the station. Standing room only and three deep to the wall. I was at the table along with others of the air staff. When Chuck Fritz rose and unfolded his 6 foot 3 three inch frame to speak there was total silence. The whole station was there, sales traffic, accounting, promotion, air personalities. And no one knew what Chuck was going to say. We all sensed that something big was about to break but none of us knew.

"Effective immediately" he said, "I am appointing Bruce Still Director of Operations".

There was little reaction to this. A slight murmur, polite smiles and nods in his direction, but that's all. Everyone liked Bruce, but realized that if he continued as Klemm's replacement the station would never recover from its slide.

"Also", Chuck continued.

"Our station sound and approach to the strong competition needs some originality and leadership. We need to think outside traditional channels and bring something new to the table".

"Therefore today I am appointing a new Program Director of WXYZ who will be responsible for the entire on the air sound of this station. I am appointing Lee Alan".

An immediate shock wave went through the room. No one could have expected this, least of all me. I had only gone to Chuck with ideas that I thought should be adopted to save the station from certain doom. I didn't expect him to do this! It took everyone by total surprise. As Chuck stood there grinning the people closed in from all parts of the room to congratulate me. With few exceptions the reaction was favorable and exuberant.

The first hand to shoot across the table with a "Congratulations Lee" belonged to Dave Prince! And that caused a second shock wave. Larry O'Brien looked at me pointing a finger so Dave couldn't see it and mouthed: "hypocrite".

The weeks that followed were filled with excitement and promise. I met individually with everyone who had anything to do with the "on the air" sound of the station, DJs, Newspeople, engineers, producers, and Bruce Miller our newly acquired Production Director. I wanted their input. Needless to say the meeting with Prince was awkward.

I decided to build an image around the word "Personality" for the station. Music was the key, but what set us apart from the others was Personality.

The jingles were antiques. I wrote new ones and with Chuck's blessing went to Chicago and recorded them with producer Dick Marx and the Anita Kerr singers. They were bright, up beat, melodic and designed to permeate the station sound.

"Personality Plus. That's us
Double U X
The Detroit Sound
W-Z
Twelve seven Oh".

I told Chuck that we needed to be as different from the other stations as possible but still play the most popular music and more of it. We should be totally distinctive. No mistaking who we are. Easy to remember and a complete personality of our own. I convinced him that one of those differences should be putting a helicopter in the air over the freeways and start traffic reports from the sky during rush hour.

My old station, WJBK tried it in 1957, it was not successful. It was totally sponsor driven. The station had used the helicopter as something to attract advertisers for paid commercials and not as a bona fide traffic service. The pilot was Barney Stutesman, a friendly, smiling 33-year-old guy with a personality that could charm anyone and could have won any election. He was only the pilot though. The voice on the air was that of Bob Martin, the program director of the station.

I told Chuck he could increase his adult audience with the Traffic Copter and he bought it.

I called Barney Stutesman, the same pilot who had done it before. He now had his own company, Hi Lift Helicopters. We talked and to start off I hired him to do the traffic reports in the morning drive time with Marc Avery who had now replaced Fred Wolf.

Barney charged the station about $45 an hour for the service portal to portal plus a fee of $15 when the reports were sponsored. Cheap and worth it!

At WCFL in Chicago Dick Orkin and his crew had produced a series of hilarious two minute vignettes called Chickenman. It was all about a character who, Monday through Friday was a shoe salesman in a downtown department store, but on weekends he donned a feathered costume and mask to become the most fantastic crime fighter the world has ever known, "The Fantastic Feathered Winged

Warrior",

CHICKEN MAN – HE'S EVERYWHERE –
HE'S EVERYWHERE!!

So, within 60 days there was a totally new station sound. Helicopter reports, high quality station jingles, Chickenman and a staff re-positioned to handle a new bright on the air presentation.

Chapter 60
DOWNFALL

EVERYTHING WAS GOOD. The station sounded terrific, but we were still saddled with the hour of The Breakfast Club at 10AM and an hour and twenty minutes of news at 6PM. These shows were major interruptions to the music programming and something that Mike Joseph counted on when he planned the KEENER onslaught.

I begged and pleaded with Chuck to eliminate these programs. Even put them on FM instead of AM. He wouldn't budge, or couldn't budge that is. They were network programs, provided some revenue to the station and our company owned them and had to have a Detroit audience. They stayed and were killing us.

Marc Avery was a morning personality hired from WJBK radio to do the midday slot. He had replaced Fred Wolf in the morning rush hour and was doing an acceptable job, but Chuck Fritz and the brass in New York were not impressed. Even before Marc, they had been after a morning team in Cleveland. The team of Martin and Howard was number one in the morning there and Cleveland loved them. I was sent across the lake to hole up in a motel, listen to them, record them, and come back with an opinion and a report.

I did. I listened. One night while station surfing I stumbled on another personality. Joey Reynolds was the most talented, original, and outrageous person I had ever heard on the radio. Still is. On in Cleveland from 7 to Midnight he was a laughing, funny, fast and furious motor mouth with an irreverence no one in Detroit had ever heard who obviously understood radio and how to use it.

I couldn't turn him off.

I had heard of Joey Reynolds. His track record and background was legend. He was another innovation and a big noise that we needed at WXYZ to take the focus off of KEENER and I intended to hire him.

Back in the office of Chuck Fritz I reported that, in my opinion, Martin and Howard were ten years behind Detroit and that their humor was corny to the point of irritable. Ever hear joke so far out that you felt badly for the joke teller? That's the way Martin and Howard affected me. WXYZ was offering them a fat six figures and my vote was to let them stay put in Cleveland.

I predicted that if we hired them the money spent for them was so big that the station brass would want to soften the music in the morning. Kill the hits to be more "adult", and thus not play what the majority wanted to hear. Because of their humorous skits we would be letting them talk longer, they would play less music overall. And even then it would be the wrong music. That would mean that Martin and Howard would have to be the sole reason for listening.

No way I said. And further I told Chuck that it would be the start of changing the rest of the station to match the morning. And that, radio fans, along with the Breakfast Club and the boring news block at 6PM would be the end of any comeback period.

Chuck Fritz was not pleased with what I had to say, but he sounded OK with it. He thanked me and waived me out of the office.

"Chuck, there's one more thing", I said

"OK, make it quick. I've got another meeting".

By this time in 1965 I was up by four in the morning and at Broadcast House at 6AM to fly over the freeways in "The Whirleybird Watch" doing the traffic reports.

Barney Stutesman, the pilot and owner of Hi Lift Helicopters was the best in the business. We hadn't been able to find anyone who could either ride with him and voice the traffic reports, or was brave enough to go up there over the freeway every morning in a helicopter. So, I was it!

By 8:30 I was back on the ground and in my office with my Program Director's hat on. Soon The Whirleybird Watch was so popular and different that I added afternoons. So there I was back in the copter for the 3:30 to 5:30 reports and then 7:15 to 10pm on the air for my own show. A totally killer schedule. On top of it all I was still doing the TV show for Mr. Pival. Whew!

I told Chuck about Joey Reynolds. Played him tapes of Joey's Cleveland show and watched for his reaction. It was the same as mine. I explained that the pre-promotion and Joey's mere presence on the station would cause talk and strike a little fear into the competition including and specifically WKNR. Handled properly it could reverse the ratings drop and help bring us back to our rightful place in the market. And again I made it clear that the only thing that could hold us back were those ridiculous network commitments.

"Kill those programs. Forget Martin and Howard, let me find a powerful, young morning personality to match the new bright sound, if Avery continues to sound like an old man move him out or at least back to midday, add some contests, have fun with our listeners, get involved with the schools and the community and the station would be just like me:

Back from the dead.

But first, please let me hire Joey Reynolds!

He did!

He let me hire Joey Reynolds, that is; but not the rest of it. And that's what would bury us.

Chapter 61
JOEY

JOEY REYNOLDS HAD SOME PERSONAL PROBLEMS (don't we all?) that needed to be addressed before he could join the station. Once they were handled I was able to convince him to get on board. Joey is a highly talented guy and had been involved in recording and records. There was a very strict rule at ABC about that.

Ever since the payola purge in 1959 radio and television stations were very careful to make sure that no one on the air had anything to do with ownership in the music business. I never thought it made sense. We couldn't even own stock in a company that had anything to do with records or music.

Great rule for ABC Radio and Television!

Ever hear of ABC Records?

Right! The very parent company we worked for was massive in the music business. We could not own stock in our own company. At least we weren't supposed to.

Joey had been a producer of records and music and I had to specifically have an agreement with him that all that had to stop. He went along with it and he was hired.

There was a two or three week waiting period before he could start and what a waiting period it was!

We were promoting his new show the whole time. When the promos started we could almost feel the reaction. The whole town was hearing about Joey Reynolds and his Royal Order of the Night People – The Teenage Underground and combined with listener calls he provided to us, the promos were saturating the airwaves. I was running them twice an hour. Slamming the market with

Jooooey Reeeeynolds!

At the end of the three weeks I thought the whole town was going to blow up from anticipation and curiosity. Then, when Joey hit the air it was the most powerful kickoff I have ever heard before or since.

I was on the air from 7:15 to 9PM. Then Joey Reynolds. When his theme song rolled on that first night it was like an atomic bomb at ground zero. You could feel the ears listening. Not only the normal radio audience, but new listeners, not the least of which were the ears of the competition to just hear this radio phenom, Joey Reynolds. His theme was sung by Frankie Valli and the four Seasons to the soundtrack of "Big Girls Don't Cry".

So, instead of: BIG GIRLS DON'T CRY EYE EYE.
THEY DON'T CRY
BIG GIRLS DON'T CRY.
It was: JOOOOEY. JOEY REYNOLDS SHOW.
WHAT A SHOW.
JOEY REYNOLDS SHOW.

The music played, Joey was on live with it, and the first words out of his mouth were:

"Here we are again at another radio station. Ladies and gentlemen this is the new sound of WXYZ Radio and we're going to be doing a lot of things that have never been done before in Detroit Radio. Would like to formally dedicate our very first show to the fine people at CK Country (CKLW) and as we all know that is located in the province of Ontario and also everybody at the Keener Wiener. WKNR 13

on the dial in case you never heard of them and the 15 cent hamburger at night Scott Burger, 100% pure ham. I'd like to thank Duke Windsor for stealing my idea for the Teenage Underground. One of the fine things about the Teenage Underground is that it is maintained as a secret organization, so secret that tonight we're going to change the name of it and call it The Royal Order Of The Night People. I actually came to Detroit to find the KEENER WEENER, but couldn't hear it. I live on the East Side".

Joey Reynolds was on the air and the town would never be the same. He did exactly what I wanted him to do. Demoralize the competition and make everyone talk about us for a change. He was just as outrageous on the air as everyone expected and it worked. The problem was he was also outrageous off the air.

There were rumors and innuendos about Joey. All kinds. Without proof, I refused to listen to them. I heard that Joey was staying at the Detroit Athletic Club and that he caused some of the old folks down there some problems, including Fred Wolf who got him in there for a while. I had no first hand knowledge of any of it.

Joey was dynamite on the air. The whole town was talking about Jooooey…!

In his book "Let A Smile Be Your Umbrella But Don't Get A Mouth Full Of Rain" (Red Brick Press), Joey describes his wild ride at WXYZ.

Quoting Joey: *"I had the freedom to play whatever I wanted on the air. And if I played a record, it became a hit. I had a lot of freedom off the air. Too much freedom. I drank a lot of scotch and smoked a lot of pot and screwed a lot of girls. I wound up in strange beds in strange places, like boats on the Detroit River. I'd wake up in the morning and forget where I was and how I got there. It was the beginning of my alcohol addiction."*

From then on Joey Reynolds was the most talked about radio personality in Motown. He was a master of the unpredictable, the wild and the crazy. Joey was the weapon, the power punch WXYZ needed to recover from the ratings dive and frankly I didn't use him properly. He was buried at night.

Now, here for the first time I will say that I should have tried to convince the New York brass to forget Martin and Howard and instead, replace Marc Avery in the morning drive time WITH JOEY REYNOLDS!

Detroit mornings never would have been the same and I firmly believe that Joey would have returned us to number one in that time slot almost instantly and changed the face of Detroit radio.

Six months later after turning radio upside down in Detroit I called a meeting of all air personalities and producers. Joey didn't show. Patti Robertson, my administrative assistant made a few calls and found him at a recording studio downtown cutting some new records. ABC gave me no choice. I was forced to let him go. I have regretted it ever since. I should have ignored it. Forgot about it. Joey was a giant to a surprised Detroit audience with an unmatched wit and a way of absolutely capturing an audience.

Like him or not, everyone knew Joey Reynolds. He was the most exciting thing on Detroit radio since..well... Ahem!

Joey was just with the station for a matter of a few months, but to this day, decades later he is the only radio personality I know of who is still remembered after only being here for such a short time and so long ago.

Years later as I write this chapter Joey Reynolds has proven his genius. He is a very special talk show host on WOR in New York. Recently he and I spoke live on the air from New York. He was so complimentary and humble to me I was embarrassed. I should have defied ABC and kept him.

I love you Joey and trust me, I will take you up on that offer to see you and be on your show in the Big Apple.

Chapter 62
HOME

MEANWHILE MY MARRIAGE TO PATTI CAME TO AN END. I will admit here for the first time and for my children to see that bringing it to an end was my fault and my doing. It just had never worked for me. My total focus on career and lack of time and attention to Patti and especially my daughter Dawne who was now 8 years old was a main cause. It was my fault. I could have stayed. Should have stayed, but didn't. My leaving caused both of them pain for life that I could never take back or make up. I thought then it was the best thing to do. Give Patti a chance at a life with someone who would be better at it than I could or would. As for Dawne, I promised myself that I would never leave Detroit for a job anywhere else. I needed to be here and be some kind of a father, though apart during the week and only seeing her on weekends.

    I wanted more children. Patti was reluctant and under the circumstances wisely so. For me, a messed up local Radio/TV personality with a major ego, and constantly living with public adulation everything came to a head. I saw a lawyer, filed for divorce, and moved in with my disappointed parents. Patti was hurt and confused and I was the cause. As I have said before, I only wish I could go back and shake some sense into that idiot fool. I was that fool. Our little home was sold. Patti and Dawne moved into an apartment and so did I.

It is a common thought throughout my family that I left Patti for someone else. That is not true.

Yes, I left Patti and yes someone else came into the picture. But there was no cause and effect. The two were not related. To this day, and as I write and reflect I feel a lump in my throat when I think of Patti and the pain I caused her and my daughter. We could not continue our marriage, but Patti is an exemplary person who deserved better than I gave her. My beautiful daughter Dawne needn't have suffered the anguish that she must have. I've always wanted to talk with her about it, but never have. I didn't know where to start and she never asked.

So here, now, and publicly, I say to them;

To Patti and Dawne, this older, wiser, more mature man and father acknowledges the blind stupidity of his younger self. He constantly feels the very pain he inflicted upon you.

This is a part of my life and how I affected those who loved me I truly regret. I was the cause.

My career, my ego at the time, and my selfishness inflicted permanent pain on my wife Patti and molded a lifetime of anguish for my daughter.

The stupidity doesn't end here. Unfortunately there's more.

Choices.

Chapter 63
BEGINNING AGAIN

BELIEVE IT OR NOT THE MOST POPULAR NIGHTSPOT IN MOTOWN in the late 60s was the Club Gay Haven. It was not a Gay hangout. In those days the word "gay" meant happy and had no sexual meaning. The gay Haven was where all the entertainers, media people, and radio and TV celebrities gathered after their shows and gigs around town. Big names, small names, they were all there almost any night of the week. Unfortunately for me I was a frequent visitor on the weekends after the Walled Lake Casino shows and even after all that ended.

Hey, everybody knew me right?

Wrong!

One night at the Gay Haven I was sitting at a table with some people listening to Jamie Coe and the Gigolos, the house band at the time when a friend of mine grabbed me by the arm and dragged me to another table. Pointing to one of the women at the table my friend said:

"Sharon Cole, meet Lee Alan".

The little Redhead said:

"Lee Who"?

I was at once curious and a bit blown away that she didn't know who I was.

Sharon Cole was a short, slender redhead, 23 years old with a smile that could light up any room. Conversation revealed that she was recently divorced for reasons I believed then, but don't now.
I don't remember the rest of the conversation except that we did talk for a long time and I was smitten. From then on she was someone I wanted to know better. Much better.

I was killing myself trying to bring recovery to the fallen radio power of WXYZ in Detroit. At the same time I was an emotional wreck. My marriage of nine years was over, the divorce was in process, and with all my public popularity I was feeling utterly alone.

For me, Sharon came along at the wrong time. I was not capable of making sound personal decisions. In spite of it Sharon and I dated. Movies. Shows. Media events. It caused talk. Colleagues, friends. My mother and father and my sister Karen all thought I was in need of mental help. I thought I was in love and no one was going to talk me out of it.

Consider this.

I held the ideal job in my chosen career. I was the Program Manager of one of the most storied radio stations in the world. I was on my way up the ladder with ABC Radio. Although the ratings were suffering for all the reasons I have covered, I had totally free reign to create the sound, the approach, the music, and yes, even hire the people to make it happen. I was still on the air, well known, on television, and making a terrific salary. I was the center of attention and now personal controversy at the same time.

I was about to destroy it all. It was about to come crumbling down around me.

Choices.

Because of my personal life and new personal relationship, my reputation inside the hallowed halls of ABC Radio was suffering. And rightly so.

Choices.

Chapter 64
COOKIN'

BY NOW IN 1966 EVERYTHING WAS COOKING ON THE AIR. My goose was cooking too, except I didn't know it.

The station sounded terrific.
The Detroit Sound of Radio
Personality – Personality Plus

Barney Stutesman and the helicopter traffic reports.
Great News People:
    Joe Vaughn
    Porter Borne
    Tom McIntyre
    Ed Hardy
    Dick Osgood
Air Personality lineup:
6 - 10AM   Marc Avery
10 – 2PM   Pat Murphy
2 – 6PM   Dave Prince
7:15 – 9PM   Lee Alan

9 – Midnight Joey Reynolds
Mid – 6AM   Don Zee – Jimmy Hampton
Weekends: Danny Taylor & Steve Lundy

And the funniest of all:
> C – H – I – C- -K – E – N - - - M – A – AAAAAAN!
> He's Everywhere – He's Everywhere!!!!!!

The problem was that with all that we were still a loser in the rating battle with KEENER and especially in the morning against WJR's J.P. McCarthy.

We were still bleeding from the daily wound caused by the Breakfast Club and that nightly news block. Chuck Fritz blamed the ratings on the morning and Marc Avery, and still insisted on replacing him with Martin and Howard from Cleveland. The top brass handled that one. The team was signed, sealed, and the brass told me when they would be delivered and ordered me not to breathe a word to anyone until it was time. It was top secret for a lot of reasons. One was Harry Martin's wife who was looking for him and a piece of that fat new contract. Another was that Marc Avery was about to be either demoted or blown out of the station. No decision had been made on his fate.

Marc Avery loved being on the radio in the Morning Drive hours. He felt out of place in any other time slot. When Marc was assured that he would be replacing the retiring Fred Wolf he was in the exact spot he wanted to be. A dream job on a dream station.

Since I promised myself that I would tell only the truth here I have to say I never liked Marc Avery as an on the air personality. That's not to say that he didn't have the tools or the smarts to be a DJ, or even that he wasn't good at what he did, its only saying that Marc was just not a personality that I was confident could have an absolute number one rated show.

He knew the music, knew a lot of people, knew how to do all the things it takes to compete in a large radio market but like many of us, me included, Marc Avery was his own worst enemy.

Remember, these are my opinions only, but Marc was self centered, hotheaded, difficult to get along with, and it affected his whole being. It affected his on the air shows, his every breath seemed to be in constant in turmoil. He always seemed to be mad at someone or something.

Chapter 65
1966 – BATTLE FOR RATINGS

I HAVE TO SAY THAT IN SPITE OF CHUCK FRITZ and ABC's stubborn refusal to kill the old network programs and let us be the killer sound we needed to be to get back to the top we gave it everything we had and had a terrific time doing it.

In early 1966 the big craze was BATMAN. Adam West's Batman on television was the biggest thing on the network and we took advantage of it. America was insane for Batman.

I acquired a replica of the Batman Uniform from New York and dressed Danny Taylor in it. We announced on the air that Batman was in town and could pop up most anywhere in the BAT-MOBILE! And:

"If you see him, call WXYZ, tell us his location, and if you're right you win!" I don't remember what the prize was, but the whole town went berserk looking for BATMAN.

Our Batmobile was a brand new Oldsmobile Toronado. The first car of its kind ever seen in Detroit.

Danny was a terrific guy, but was not in love with being Batman. Ha! I don't blame him. He was doing it free…no charge. We did things like that in those days.

THE SUPREMES were the biggest female group in the world and Berry Gordy Jr., founder of Motown decided to have them perform at the Roostertail Supper Club on the Detroit River, a first class venue that looked like it belonged in Hollywood or New York.

I arranged for WXYZ to broadcast the event. It was a knockout Gala event. Every big name and politico was there. All the Motown stars too. Marvin Gaye, Little Stevie Wonder, Martha and the Vandellas, Mary Wells, Smokie Robinson, and dozens more including fabulous artists from New York and California.

WXYZ was at the epicenter of it all. The entire lineup of DJs was there, each positioned at a different location in the mammoth nightclub. Practically no music was played on the air. Everyone had a star to interview so the mike went from Marc to Danny to Pat to Lee etc. We were written up in the papers. The broadcast was perfect and the Supremes were powerful and glittering. Three girls from the back streets of Detroit who now belonged to the world. What a night. I still have the tape and someday will release it. Talk about a collector's item

THE WYXIE WARRIORS were a fearsome Basketball Team made up of all the air personalities on WXYZ. At least all the ones who could move, run, or breathe.

We challenged the teachers in all the high schools to play against this rag tag team and it was a huge success. Problem was, we always lost. No heart attacks though and once again the whole town knew about it.

With all of this excitement and happening I still had hope that ABC would kill the Breakfast Club and that "listener chasing" hour and twenty minute news block at 6 o'clock when Bill Drake came to town and did exactly what Joel Sebastian, Dave Prince, and I had pleaded with Chuck Fritz to do back in 1963. Bill Drake came here and turned CKLW into THE BIG 8. Bill Drake made The Big 8 happen. Did it against WKNR just the way we could have!

Now we had both CKLW and KEENER to contend with. Instead of staying in the battle Chuck Fritz and WXYZ were about to give up. About to surrender.

Martin and Howard were hired. $115,000 a year worth. Big, Big time money in those days.

The scene was set for the end and would unfold just as I had predicted.

Chapter 66
AGAIN

OVER A PERIOD OF MONTHS THINGS GREW SERIOUS between Sharon and me. She decided to take a vacation trip to Europe with two girlfriends. After a week or so there was a phone call from her from Switzerland. She told me she had met someone else there and would not be coming back. I was able to convince her to at least come back and talk with her parents about it and then make her decision. And that's what happened.

When she returned I talked her in to marrying me. It happened on November 26, 1966. There were about a hundred people at the reception including Chuck Fritz and many of the people I have mentioned in earlier pages. Including my friend and benefactor Milton DeLoche who carried the encouraging words of John Pival to me when I was down and out.

After the wedding we took three weeks and went to the Virgin Islands, among other places.

While we were away, back in Detroit Marc Avery received a phone call from a friend in Cleveland.

Quoting from Dick Osgood's Book WYXI Wonderland:

"What bad luck?" Avery asked

"Losing your morning show. Are they putting you in another spot?"

"Another Spot? What are you talking about?"

You mean to tell me you didn't know Martin & Howard from here are set to replace you in January?"

Five minutes after that call Marc Avery walked into the office of Charles D. Fritz.

"What's this about Martin & Howard?" he demanded.

"Who's Martin & Howard?" Chuck replied

"Chuck! Don't hand me that. Okay. Look. My father-in-law is very ill in Cincinnati. My wife and I are going down there today. You figure out what you owe me, and pay me. I am through here as of the show I just finished. To this day Fritz doesn't believe that bit about my father-in-law," Avery remembered. "But it was true. He died."

It was January of 1967.

Chuck Fritz started fulfilling my predictions. First, he hired Joe Bacarella from WCAR in Detroit. The same station where I played the Wabash Cannonball and went head to head with the owner's wife year's before. WCAR was what in those days we called "A Good Music Station". Not playing the hits. Just playing album music and standards and the occasional non rock hit.

I was an absolute non believer in Martin and Howard and knew that if they came to WXYZ the money they were being paid would end up controlling the station. All the music would change and the station would be totally out of the race to win.

I have never felt comfortable being number 4 or 5, but it was happening before my very eyes.

Joe had no experience with being on top. Although he had been on the air he had never been umber one himself and had never worked for a number one station.

Joe Bacarella and Lee Alan butted heads from the very start.

I wrote music for Martin & Howard and the station went nuts promoting them. The promotion was so heavy that no one could ever have lived up to it, let alone these guys from Cleveland and their humor and skits. Bacarella and Fritz changed the station to a strange mix of music and proceeded to bore the town to death with it.

I expressed my opinions and Joe didn't like it. Fritz wouldn't listen.

At one of the meetings we were all supposed to turn in some sort of a plan to make this work. I didn't turn anything in. I knew they were spending a fortune to fail and I wanted no part of it.

Bacarella asked me to leave and I was glad. I didn't want to be associated with the failure that was in process.

Fred Wolf, Paul Winter, Joel Sebastian, Don Zee were gone, Danny Taylor, Pat Murphy, and Steve Lundy were leaving. CKLW was kicking Keener's tail and FM radio was taking a foothold. WXYZ was a skeleton of its former self. No one who worked there ever believed it could be a factor in the market with listeners again. It was just a place to work and take ABC's money.

Eventually the helicopter traffic reports with Barney Stutesman were cancelled. Not an affordable program element they said. The copter was quickly considered by WJR and then hired by CKLW with Jo Jo Shutty at the mike. At the controls? Barney Stutesman.

I was out of a job and couldn't leave town to find another.

Chapter 67
DEAD AGAIN

So there I was, three months after being married, out of a job, flat broke, and no station in Detroit would take me because I had either worked there or because of my recent association and objection to WXYZ's "Good Music"

An idea had been lurking in the back of my mind for a long time. Thousands of people had asked me how to get started in radio and television. There was never a good answer. Preparation, practice, and education was the answer, but in the Midwest there was no where to go. No where to get the knowledge and training.

So, I decided to start a broadcasting school, to teach the subject of practical broadcasting. Not just how to be an air personality, but all of it, sales, programming, news, all aspects of radio broadcasting.

Not long before this there was a school of announcing in Detroit with a very bad reputation. It was closed one dark night when an outraged and jealous husband murdered the owner and two others. They were not announcing at the time. They were making pornographic movies inside the school. Because of this and the massive publicity no one thought starting a school of broadcasting was a good idea.

A full-fledged vocational school had to be licensed by the State Board Of Education. Courses had to be written, study materials prepared, applications submitted, and a zillion other red tape details had to be met. This was going to take time.

I called Chuck Fritz, told him of my plans and that I needed some kind of a job while I tackled this monster. Fritz lined me up with a dentist who owned a small station in St Ignace, a very small town in northern Michigan. The dentist needed help. I was hired to bail him out of some trouble with the FCC and program his station for about eight months while I made application for the school.

We packed everything up, moved north and there I was working at a radio station with about 6 other people and no listeners.

My career was dead and I felt that I was too. I longed to be back in the action, but there was no way. I finished the mound of paperwork, submitted it to the state and waited for the license.

The entire summer passed with no word.

A few months earlier I had been the voice of some political commercials for the Governor's race in Michigan. My side won and now out of desperation I called Lieutenant Governor William Milliken's office to ask for help. His aide promised to look into my license process and call back. Weeks went by. Then, one morning the call came. The aide asked me when I was going back to Detroit. I said I could go anytime. He said: "Lee, Lt. Governor Milliken asked me to tell you that whenever you go your license will be there ahead of you".

The Lee Alan School of Broadcast Arts was born. Classrooms were in rented space in a banquet hall in Redford Township, Michigan. Chuck Fritz arranged for me to conduct tours for students at WXYZ radio and television. Soon the school was doing well enough for me to buy a building and set up our own facilities.

WHFI, a Detroit FM radio station was making some noise with some of the personalities who were causalities of the radio wars. Don Zee, Marc Avery, and some others were there. I was asked to join them. Soon I was doing my night show again, this time by remote from the school studios.

The school was successful, but small. There were only a few students in each class. I turned down more than I accepted. I wanted good potential talent waiting to be trained. I never intended it to be anything else but a small boutique where I could teach the subject and turn out some terrific people who would then have a chance to make in radio.

After about two years I was bored. I didn't like the business. I didn't like trying to convince high school grads to come to a vocational school when in my heart I knew they should be getting a solid University education first.

"Go to college", I wanted to tell them.

"Put something between your ears first so when you open your mouth on the air something intelligent will come out". I did tell many of them that and lost a lot of students because of it.

Some great names and talents came out of that school. Many are still on the air today. They became Disc Jockeys, Radio News Journalists, Station Management people, even newspaper columnists and a few made it to television news anchors.

Names you might know. I still see them and hear them.

By late 1969 my days of owning a broadcast school were numbered.

Chapter 68
ADVERTISING...

BY THIS TIME THE MARTIN AND HOWARD MORNING SHOW on WXYZ had failed and ABC Radio did not renew their contract. Harry Martin and Specs Howard split up. Harry left town and Specs stayed here working some radio and looking for some sort of an opportunity.

WXYZ was failing too. "The Good Life" as they called it was not so good. The ratings were terrible in the morning and all day long. Strangely the management people who engineered the demise of this once great radio station stayed on while nearly everyone else was either let go or left in disgust.

Nearly three years earlier I predicted all this and when they didn't like what I said I had to leave.

Truth is that if ABC had simply allowed WXYZ to drop those old time network shows that killed the music consistency on the station it would have been a different story.

Three years after I created the Lee Alan School I decided to sell. I placed a blind box ad in the Wall Street Journal. There were 147 replies.

As it turned out I didn't need the Journal ads. Johnny

Randall, a terrific air personality and friend whom I had hired at WXYZ learned that I wanted to sell the school and passed the word to Specs Howard. That's all it took. On November 26, 1970 I sold an option to Specs Howard to buy The Lee Alan School Of Broadcast Arts, the buildings, equipment, everything.

The Michigan State Board of Education was very careful about awarding licenses to vocational schools. In order to transfer the license there had to be an investigation of the present school, its owner, and the new prospective owner.

I knew the process could take a couple of months, but was ready for it to move ahead and so was the Specs Howard group.

We just needed to make sure that there was nothing unusual that would delay or prevent the transfer of license.

I was ecstatic. Maybe now, I thought, I could concentrate on getting back on the air. The Horn was not rusty and looked like it had a few years left so I was anxious and ready.

That day turned out to be one of the personally worst, and most embarrassing days of my life. . . .

Chapter 69
THE FM REVOLUTION

EVERYTHING WAS A CONFUSED MESS. I was selling the school and I wanted to go to LA, New York, somewhere, anywhere to do what I did best. Just to try it. Make the rounds of the stations. Others had done it. Get on the air again on a major station. Get back in music, entertainment, and especially the competition. I was at a prime age and longed for it.

As I said earlier, in 1970 in addition to the school I was back on the air in a small way. Don Zee, Marc Avery, and other ex WXYZ personalities were all back on the air. All on the same station. Like me, all trying to recreate the past.

On FM.

WHFI – FM.

"STEREO - NINETY FOUR"

Back on the air. At night. Like before.

The Horn.

The Fine Toned Ash Tray.

The music.

Mr. Sinatra.

All of it.

But, like Rick Nelson's experience at Madison Square

Garden. Something was missing. It just wasn't the same. It was like nobody knew I was there.

Like Nelson says in the record. "They didn't recognize me". And because the old WXYZ station "sound" wasn't there the jingles, contests, format, discipline. "They didn't know my name."

It was my "Garden Party".

And the biggest reason? There just weren't enough FM radios, period!

In 1967, as program director of WXYZ, I created a new station when WXYZ-FM broke totally away from WXYZ-AM.

If you had an FM radio in those days the big thing was that you could now listen in stereo. Stereo FM. I hired a half dozen air personalities, wrote new jingles, and built the format around soft music. Standards. Tony Bennett, Sinatra, Andy Williams, Steve and Eydie, etc.

The air personalities were known only by their first names.
"MICHELLE"
"DONOVAN"
"MICHAEL"
So, for the few who had FM radios WXYZ-FM was born.
Stations all across America did the same.

There were now hundreds of new stations and all kinds of formats.

Free Form Formats - Underground Radio - Love Radio - California Radio

Protest Radio - Soul, In Stereo – Progressive Rock - Stereo Island.

And of course here in Motown the standard for radio chaos and weirdness in those days was WABX-FM. Radio had been forced to reinvent itself. FM delivered better frequency response. Everything sounded better. No static. Music had life. All in stereo. FM was new and AM Radio was about to suffer, and some said, even die.

So there I was in 1970 on WHFI-FM with a team of ex WXYZ personalities who were all trying to do what they did on AM years before. It wasn't working. It was old AM radio on new FM. The big AMs CKLW & WKNR were still hot.

I was not!

November 26, 1970

There I was in a small studio in the back of The Lee Alan School of Broadcast Arts doing my show for a much smaller audience than before.

The day I sold Specs Howard an option to buy the school was also our fourth wedding anniversary. By then Sharon and I had two sons. Bill, almost three and Lee, 18 months. My daughter Dawne lived with her mother on Detroit's east side and was with us every weekend. The classroom in the front of the building was dark. The studio had a separate back door entrance that led to a garage. The microphone was on and I was talking on the air when suddenly there was a loud crashing and pounding coming from the door. I started some music and opened it.

The man standing there was a stranger.

Before I could say anything like:

"Who are you and why are you pounding on this door", he laughed and said: "Hey...Are you Lee Alan"?

As I said yes and started to answer he extended his right hand. I started to do the same when his left hand hit mine with a large packet of papers.

He backed up and said:

"Sorry Lee, I'm a big fan and hated to do this to you".

With that he turned and hurried away leaving me standing in the doorway, music playing in the studio on the air and a handful of what obviously were some kind of court papers.

I called the station, told them to take over, sat down and started to read.

Divorce papers.

November 26, 1970.

Sharon was suing me for divorce.

As I write this I don't even remember why. There were reasons, financial, responsibilities, others but I don't remember them.

Never mind fault. My fault, her fault, our fault. No reason could've have been good enough. Not to end another family. I was already guilty of doing that when I divorced Dawne's mother Patti. And no reason would have been good enough to scuttle the sale of the school.

Choices.

Just as we were about to reap the rewards from selling the business and possibly were getting on to something really productive in my career and our lives the brakes were on. Financially and emotionally.

I panicked.

Specs Howard panicked. The station panicked.

Specs' potential new business was on hold as well as both our families. The investigation by the State Board of Education loomed.

The entire situation was in Sharon's hands.

We had not discussed divorce. It was a total surprise.

She had discussed it though. With friends, one in particular, and other family.

A few weeks, and a few thousand dollars paid to two lawyers later, Sharon withdrew the action and our life went on.

It was never the same.

A month or so after we nearly all lost everything because of the divorce action, the Michigan State Board Of Education approved the transfer of the school license to Specs Howard, and the sale was completed. Specs and his partners had big ideas and they immediately opened a school in Cleveland, Specs' hometown. It didn't work and sometime later it folded.

I had hoped to retain some contact with the school, possibly teach there. I believe that the divorce action soured him on any further contact with me, so that didn't happen.

The terms of the sale provided for a long-term payout to me in monthly installments of principal and interest. A nice annuity for us. But, because we bought a house, and because of the all money it cost for the divorce lawyers, I was forced to go to Specs and ask for a lump sum payment that would pay off what he owed. He agreed. The amount was a fraction of what the long term would have been.

The lawyers made money.

We lost big time, but I had to take it.

Choices.

I have not seen Specs Howard in person more than a few times since I sold the school to him in 1970. He has always been cordial, but I have never been inside his present school location. I have never been invited. As far as I can determine Specs has done a marvelous job of building a big business and running an exemplary broadcast school. For some reason though he always said that when he bought it from me it was very small. He was right. Small, as it was intended. Small and professional.

By this time I was again without a job. I was still on the air at WHFI-FM, but now I was on mid days. The station was foundering. None of us had any ratings and in a cost cutting move I was let go.

I always wondered when I might hear the next knock on the door, and be handed another set of papers.

Eleven years later.

The next "knock on the door" came eleven years later.

This time it was my fault.
So now the school was sold and I had no job.
Now What…..?

Chapter 70
THE AGENCY

FRANK IMBURG CALLED ME ALMOST EVERYDAY I was in the school business. I met Frank, a radio newsman, back in the late fifties when we were both at WKMH radio. After I went to WXYZ Frank left 'KMH and the next time I heard from him was years later when he called me at the school.

"Lee, I'm in the advertising business now". He said.

"Got to make a presentation to a new advertising client Monday and need one of your crazy ideas".

And that's how I started in the advertising business. Doing creative commercial campaigns for Frank Imburg so he could go out and get new advertising clients. The way he talked, he was building a terrific business and needed a Creative Director and partner.

After the school was sold and I was let go at WHFI and still unable to leave Detroit to go chasing dreams, I agreed to go in with Frank and see if I could make it in advertising.

I went to his "office".

His office was a desk.

One desk and one chair. His chair.

Both in a small part of another sub-leased office complex in the Harvard Office Building on 8 Mile Road in Southfield, Michigan ("8 Mile" there it is again). There was a single black phone. When it rang it was a bell. A bell!

"Frank where's your staff. How many people work for you"? Frank flashed a sheepish smile and said: "You're looking at him".

So I brought a typewriter and a chair from home and we started.

Frank had one advertising client in New York State. An automobile dealer that barely paid him enough to pay the rent. In other words, there was no advertising business. But, he was a good guy and a respectable salesman and we started prospecting for business.

I reached back to the advertisers I met while I was on the radio. One of them was a Chevrolet Dealer. Dexter Chevrolet in Detroit. Guess where in Detroit? You got it. EIGHT MILE ROAD! Ha!

Back when I was with WJBK I put in some time broadcasting from the Dexter Chevrolet showroom while I was sitting in for Don McLeod. So now I called the owner, Joe Slatkin and told him what I was doing.

"Lee, we've never had an advertising agency. Nobody ever brought us a good idea. I'm not opposed though so call my General Manager, Bob Finder. Whatever you guys come up with, something or nothing is OK with me. Good luck Lee".

Bob Finder, the General Manager of Dexter Chevrolet was a soft-spoken automobile sales genius. He started out as a used car salesman on Livernois Avenue in Motown when it had more used car lots than practically anywhere in America.

"Listened to you for years Lee. Joe told me you'd be calling".

Out of 40 Chevrolet Dealers in the Detroit zone, Dexter Chevrolet was 20th and Mr. Slatkin didn't like it! This was all new to me, but it started sounding as if car dealers were like radio stations.

Somebody was number one and the rest were not.

In 1972, the number one Chevrolet Dealer was Merollis Chevrolet. The same dealership I had broadcast from in that Fred Wolf trailer on WXYZ. The same place where Fred Weiss sealed his fate when he didn't know the mike was on.

Mr. Finder wasn't really doing any advertising, but was willing to listen and give me a chance if I could get back to him with a solid idea. Back at the "office" I decided to buy a couple of questions on an upcoming Market Opinion Research survey. The first question asked one thousand people to give us the names of five Chevrolet Dealers. The next asked for their locations.

Over 80 percent could only recall the names of two dealers and more than 90 percent of those could only give the location of one. Forty Chevrolet dealerships and the public could only remember two! After a while that sunk in and raised more questions. The biggest was:

What happened to the millions of dollars in advertising the Chevy Dealers had spent over the years?

And, why didn't anyone know their names?

Radio and television stations have microphones and cameras and even they have to constantly pound their name (call letters) and locations (Dial position or channel) into the public mind.

What was wrong with Dealer Advertising? And how could I create something that would make the listeners remember Dexter Chevrolet and the location without boring them to death or chasing them away from the commercial?

Before I had hours to do a radio show. Now, in the world of advertising I had 30 seconds on television and 60 seconds on radio and that's all. I considered the commercials to be little radio shows. Besides, no one likes commercials. They're only a rude interruption to the reason we listen to the radio or watch TV in the first place and we push buttons and use remotes to run from them.

As usual, I had an idea and grabbed the Yellow Pages. I learned that on the entire length of 8 Mile Road (There it is again) there was no other Chevrolet Dealership.

I went back to a radio program, then off the air called "Duffy's Tavern". It was a half hour comedy program that took place every week inside Duffy's Tavern. Sort of the first "Cheers", but on the radio. Each week it started out with the sound of a telephone ringing and a man answering:

"Hello, Duffy's Tavern where the elite meet to eat.

Archie the manager speaking, Duffy ain't here. Oh, hello Duffy......"

The listener would never hear Duffy's voice, but what he said to "the manager" would set the scene for the entire half hour.
And that was my idea. I decided to build the Dexter Chevrolet commercials in the image of Duffy's Tavern.

The commercials for Merollis Chevrolet, the number one Chevy Dealer, which had been running for years, were called:

"THE GREAT GREAT GUY", a commercial campaign so successful that dealerships were using it in scores of other cities all over the country. Same commercials. Just change the names. Here's an example:

Music (Singing):	Merollis, oh what a great great guy He'll save you money on that Chevy buy On eight and a half mile and Gratiot Ave....
Ernie: (spoken)	Mr. Merollis, there's a man out there in the showroom who wants to buy that new Chevy Impala.
Merollis:	Ernie, that's terrific

Ernie:	But Mr. Merollis there's a problem. He forgot his checkbook.
Merollis:	That's OK Ernie….we'll take cash.
Music: (Singing)	Merollis, What A Great Great Guuuyyyyyy.

Merollis had hundreds of these commercials. All humorous and the whole town knew them. Interestingly enough the Manager of Production for the company that produced them was BOB BAKER, my ex program director at WXYZ. Small world.

I wrote a short piece of music, had it recorded in the basement of a musician I knew, went back to Bob Finder at Dexter, told him about the survey results, that no one knew the name of the dealership or its location. He believed me.

Fact is that 60 percent of the radio listeners don't know what station they're listening to or the name of the person on air. How could they possibly retain the name of a car dealer? So, I explained:

"When buyers come into the market for a Chevy, the first thing they think is":

"Where can I go and see it and where are they located?"

"At that precise moment," I went on, "If the prospect draws a blank, all your advertising money spent from the beginning of time is wasted….down the drain".

Bob Finder bought into my reasoning.

"So, how do we start getting the public to remember our name, location, and some kind bargain image"? He said.

"First", I explained your have to get their attention and in your commercials we're going to do it with the most urgent sound in the world."

"What's that?"

"The sound of a telephone. When a telephone rings everything stops. Meetings, conversations, everything."

It was time to play him my "Duffy's Tavern" commercial idea. The first idea I ever produced outside of radio. Here's what it was:

SOUND: Telephone Rings

BOB MGR: Hello, Dexter Chevrolet, the Only Chevy Dealer On Eight Mile Road, Bob the manager speaking, Dexter ain't here. Oh, Hello Dexter. Right, goodbye Dexter.

VOICE 2: (In Background) Well...What'd He Want?

BOB MGR: Dexter Says cut the prices on all new Chevy's and he's going Hunting.

VOICE 2: Dexter's going hunting? What for?

BOB MGR: Yeah something about hunting for a GREAT GUY with real high prices.

MUSIC: (singing) THE ONLY CHEVY DEALER ON EIGHT MILE ROAD. DEXTER CHEVROLET.

Bob Finder broke into a very wide and revealing smile.

I played another:

SOUND: Telephone Rings.

BOB MGR: Hello, Dexter Chevrolet, the only Chevy dealer on Eight Mile Road. Bob the manager speaking Dexter ain't here. Oh, Hello Dexter. Right, Goodbye Dexter.

VOICE 2: (In Background) What He Want....?

BOB MGR: He says give even GREATER DEALS on all Chevy Impalas and send all the other Chevy Dealers a banana.

VOICE 2: Why send 'em a banana?

BOB MGR: Those other dealers need a banana. With Dexter's l   o   w prices those other dealers no longer have A PEAL

VOICE 2: Ohhhhh....that's bad...

MUSIC:	(Singing) The Only Chevy Dealer On Eight Mile Road. Dexter Chevrolet.
ANNCR:	(Thirty seconds of selling information then music to end)

By this time Mr. Finder was rolling in laughter.

"Lee", he said. "Those are so bad………that they're good."

SOUND:	Telephone Rings.
BOB MGR:	Hello, Dexter Chevrolet, the only Chevy dealer on Eight Mile Road. The dealer with super service, custom body repair, and hundreds of late model, low mileage used cars. Bob the manager speaking Dexter ain't here. Oh, Hello Dexter. Right, Goodbye Dexter.
VOICE 2:	(In Background) What He Want….?
BOB MGR:	He says do not sell that used Corvette over there. The one with the policeman leaning on it.
VOICE 2:	How come…………..?
BOB MGR:	Because, it is against the law…………..
VOICE 2:	Bob……that's enough
MUSIC:	(Singing) The Only Chevy Dealer On Eight Mile Road.

Ha approved the concept! We bought commercial time on WDEE, the country music station at the time, in two days my first commercial campaign was on the air, and the rest is history.

Bob Finder knew what to do with new prospects coming in the door of the dealership. Within a few months, everyone knew the Dexter name and location and six months after The Only Dealer campaign started, Merollis was no longer on top.

Dexter was number one and stayed that way until Bob

Finder's death of a brain tumor almost 15 years later. He was one of only a handful of dealer General Managers who understood the power of what happens when the public remembers your commercials; you stay consistent, and never deviate.

And now I was back on the air. Only now my shows were 60 seconds long. Commercials. And I did all the voices.

After about two years of this Frank Imburg decided he was going to break up the partnership and go on his own. One morning there was a note on my desk that said he had gone to the Oakland County Clerk's office and dissolved the company. I didn't object. We finally got together, settled our differences and went our separate ways. We couldn't continue in business, but we were friends.

Frank moved to California and for a while went into the advertising business there. 15 years later he came down with diabetes. Didn't treat it and went blind. Then, his wife left him. I called. We talked about old times. He seemed optimistic, but I knew he wasn't. His said wife of nearly forever abandoned him.

Two weeks later he died of diabetes.

And a broken heart.

I was about to be visited by the same potential demon.

Chapter 71
SUSPICION

IN 1981, I HIRED A NEW APPRENTICE/RECEPTIONIST. It was her job to learn the business and hopefully advance to the position of media buyer. A media buyer is knowledgeable about all the media; radio, television, print, outdoor display, and more. The buyer/planner knows the value of each, exactly what to recommend to the advertiser (our Dealer or client) and how to put proposals together that will sell the client and be accepted by the media. That's a simple explanation, but will do for now.

Mickey Shorr was a client and demanded attention when he called or needed to get on the air. I needed another media buyer, but couldn't afford to hire anyone who was already top flight in the business so I decided to find someone new and teach the ropes.
That's when I hired Marlene (not her real name).

She was young, very bright, and caught on fast to all the office procedures and got along well with Mickey.

At the time I was working with The William B. Tanner Company in Memphis, Tennessee, a music and commercial production company. I frequently wrote our commercial music and traveled to Memphis to produce it.. In Memphis I could buy it one time, own it, and not have to pay residual payments to singers and musicians. Memphis and the Tanner Company were professional and inexpensive. I went there often, 6 or 7 times a year.

Tanner was also a media company with a large (and I mean large) media-buying department. A dozen or more seasoned buyers with established methods and systems of dealing with Radio and Television stations, and newspapers. I needed help and asked them to spend a few days training Marlene in some of the fine points of the media buying and planning procedure. They agreed.

Before I went I was spending too much time at the office and frankly too much time in the lounge and restaurant in the same building with friends and office staff. It was getting to be an everyday after work habit. My wife, became suspicious that something was going on between Marlene and me other than media buying.

I flew to Memphis. Marlene flew to Memphis. We stayed in the same hotel. One afternoon a man in the elevator struck up a conversation with me.

"Here for business…. pleasure?", he said.

Strange, I thought. He was standing five people away from me talking from the other side of the elevator. I don't remember what I said to him, but I remembered the incident and wondered.

I will not go into the activities of the two or three days in Memphis except to say that I was not totally innocent. Yes, Marlene was there and so was I. But the obvious did not happen. It was close, and I admit that I was tempted, and thinking back on it, really stupid; but it did not happen.

Marlene spent two days with the Tanner Media Department and I was recording. We had dinner and spent some time together, but the worst did not happen.

I flew home.

When I got off the plane and started toward baggage claim, Sharon suddenly stepped out from the cover of an airport restaurant near the gate.

"Where's Marlene?!!!", she said.

I told her I didn't know. And I didn't.

Sharon had hired a private detective to watch me in Memphis, (obviously the man in the elevator) and accused me of having sex with Marlene.

She was furious and visibly hurt.

She had already filed for divorce.

I admitted that Marlene was there in Memphis, that I was tempted, but just couldn't do what she suspected.

The man in the elevator may have embellished somewhat and told her some things that weren't quite accurate. Let's just say that he surmised. Drew conclusions and they were wrong.

I was wrong. I never should have gone there. Never should have been there at the same time as Marlene. I never should have allowed anything to even appear as if there was involvement; there or here. But, I did. Sharon was serious. I did my best to convince her that there was nothing really there. That it was just a silly, stupid, case of bad judgment. We went to a counselor, someone from church who knew us both. That was a mistake. Pete, (the counselor) just listened and then made another appointment for next week. Seventy-Five Dollars a meeting. Finally, Sharon dropped the proceedings, we stopped going to counseling, and once again went on with our lives. I thought all would be ok. It never was. She never forgot what she thought was true. We were never close again.

Choices.

Life changing choices.

The years went on.

Chapter 72
ADVERTISING

I NOW REALIZED THAT IF I STAYED ONLY A LOCAL BUSINESS I would soon run out of ideas and the company would die. So, I got in my little car, went to Indiana, and saw a half dozen Car Dealers. When I came back I had 4 new advertising accounts. Each one was about to use the same campaigns as my Detroit Dealers. Only the names were changed. This was Syndication. Multiplication of the same campaigns. And the financial part was terrific. I was making more money than I had ever seen or could have seen by staying on the radio.

After Dexter, there were scores of other campaigns:

DON'T MAKE THE ONE HUNDRED DOLLAR MISTAKE

THE LOW PRICE GENIUS

THE FAMILY – With children singing

THE TROY MOTOR MALL

THE KIDS.

HONDA

Eventually over 300 different campaigns in all. Radio, Television, Billboards, Direct Mail, Infomercials, all media.

Convincing automobile dealers and retailers that the basic principals of advertising are all that matters was the most difficult task in all my years in the advertising agency business. Most believe that they have to spend themselves into oblivion buying full page newspaper ads (or would if they could afford it) that only get some results, are only good for today's business because the paper is thrown away by tomorrow, and are never remembered by anyone.

Most believe that they are advertising experts and that all you have to do is buy time and space, let the radio or TV station come up with the commercial, or the newspaper create the ad and the public will react and rush to their door. Or, they even believe the broadcast stations when they are told that:

"You'd be Great doing the commercials yourself." Ever see a car dealer doing his own commercial that you didn't run from....?

Nothing could be more off target.

Here's an example of what I mean.

You contact the radio station and buy a sixty second commercial.

AND.....I contact the same station and buy a sixty second spot.

When you run your spot, you read a script or something with commercial content.

When I run MY spot, I leave it blank. Sixty seconds of silence. Nothing.

Which one of us will get results? Of course the answer is obvious. You get the action, and I got nothing. You were creative enough to at least say something and I wasn't.

The fact is that the media is only a delivery system for the adverting message. The message is what counts. The creative.
CREATIVE IS EVERYTHING!!

I have created hundreds of advertising campaigns, but only two automobile dealers really listened, believed, followed and stuck with the game plan. Many tried my approaches for a while, were not patient enough to stay the course for more than a year or two without "trying something new", or made such radical changes to the basic campaign that it stopped working for them.

That's what radio stations do. Panic, change the format, take wild guesses, go with personal preferences instead of proven ways. And fail.

One of the dealers was Bob Finder, my late friend and General Manager of Dexter Chevrolet:
"THE ONLY CHEVY DEALER ON EIGHT MILE ROAD" in Detroit.
That campaign that has now been in 51 different cities and known nationally as:
"THE ONLY DEALER"
The other was the most recognizable and successful advertising campaign in the last twenty years in the Detroit market. I stumbled on it by accident. Here's how it happened.

In 1982 I had an appointment to see a dealer in the Detroit area. My meeting with the owner was interesting and informative and I told him that I would like to come back when I had an idea that I felt would work for his dealership. He agreed and I went left.

Four weeks went by.

Nothing. I had no ideas. Painful as it was I decided to call the owner and tell him that I was getting nowhere. There were no cell phones in the early 80s, so I stopped at a pay phone and called information for the number.

"The number of BIRMINGHAM CHRYSLER PLYMOUTH please", I said.

After a long pause the operator said:

"Sorry Sir, I don't show a Chrysler Plymouth Dealer in

Birmingham. I did find it though, but not in BIRMINGHAM." And then she said:

"BIRMINGHAM'S IN TROY"!!!!!

I didn't wait for the number, hung up the phone, got back in the car, and raced to the dealership.

Richard Mealey, the owner was in his office and I barged right in.

"Mr. Mealey", I said. "Listen to this."

"BIRMINGHAM'S IN TROY"

He didn't miss a beat and asked:

"How long before you can make something out of that?"

"See you tomorrow." I said and left.

Years before, Birmingham Chrysler was in the affluent suburb of Birmingham, Michigan, but moved to The Troy Motor Mall, a new motor mall complex a few miles away in the adjacent suburb of Troy, Michigan, where now more than a dozen or so dealerships are located.

So, Birmingham Chrysler Plymouth was no longer in Birmingham and thus:

"BIRMINGHAM'S IN TROY".

Back at my recording studios it took only about an hour to come up with the first commercial. Here it is. Just the way Richard Mealey heard it in 1982. Just the way the script was recorded and broadcast for nearly 4 months until the entire market not only knew the dealership's name, but their location as well. And oh yes, it starts out with that most urgent sound again. The sound of a telephone. Notice how many times the dealership name is mentioned. And the location.

And also, if there's anyone who's never heard these commercials, let me explain that the operator's voice is a calm, controlled, male voice. The other is a pleasant, high voice that sounds a little like Lou Costello of Abbott and Costello.

Both voices were always me...Ha!

SOUND:	Telephone
OPERATOR:	Thank you for calling Birmingham Chrysler Plymouth.
LITTLE GUY:	Oh I'm glad I got the right number; it's my last 20 cents. Are you sure this is really Birmingham Chrysler Plymouth?
OPERATOR:	Yes Sir, this is Birmingham Chrysler Plymouth.
LITTLE GUY:	Oh, that's good. Listen I drove over seven hundred miles day and night to get to Birmingham Chrysler Plymouth.
OPERATOR:	To see the new K CARS?
LITTLE GUY:	Just to see the new K CARS and I'm tired, hungry, almost out of gas. I gotta get to Birmingham Chrysler Plymouth.
OPERATOR:	You've come a long way. Where you calling from Sir?
LITTLE GUY:	Right here in Birmingham.
OPERATOR:	Sir, where'd you drive from?
LITTLE GUY:	Right here in Birmingham!
OPERATOR:	Seven hundred miles???
LITTLE GUY:	All in Birmingham. I can't find Birmingham Chrysler Plymouth anywhere in Birmingham.
OPERATOR:	Sir, Birmingham Chrysler Plymouth is not in Birmingham.
LITTLE GUY:	I was, HUH?
OPERATOR:	Birmingham Chrysler Plymouth is on Maple Road in Troy.
LITTLE GUY:	Well, it's too late now I gotta get back to work.

OPERATOR:	Where do you work Sir?
LITTLE GUY:	The Troy Post Office. You know where that is The Troy Post Office?
OPERATOR:	Where's that Sir....?
LITTLE GUY:	(irritated) RIGHT HERE IN BIRMINGHAM!!!!!!!
MUSIC:	(Singing) We're the Chrysler Plymouth Dealer on Maple Road Birmingham....Chrysler Plymouth in Troy. B I R M I N G H A M' S I N T R O Y!!!

After four months of running the same commercial this was the next one.

SOUND:	Telephone
LITTLE GUY:	Hello, Troy Post Office
OPERATOR:	Sir, this is Birmingham Chrysler Plymouth calling.
LITTLE GUY:	Huh...?
OPERATOR:	We have that new brochure you wanted on the new Chryslers.
LITTLE GUY:	Wait a minute. Is this some kind of running joke? I don't think there IS a Birmingham Chrysler Plymouth. I looked everywhere in Birmingham. Side streets, Front streets, Even inside the other stores. I can't find Birmingham Chrysler Plymouth anywhere in Birmingham.
OPERATOR:	Sir, Birmingham Chrysler Plymouth is not in Birmingham. Birmingham Chrysler Plymouth in on Maple Road in Troy.

LITTLE GUY:	Troy, that was my wife's home town. She was very famous.
OPERATOR:	What is her name Sir….
LITTLE GUY:	HELEN!
OPERATOR:	HELEN…….?
LITTLE GUY:	Yeah….HELEN OF BIRMINGHAM YOU GET IT…?!
OPERATOR:	Yes I get it Sir…
MUSIC:	(Singing) We're the Chrysler Plymouth Dealer on Maple Road. Birmingham Chrysler Plymouth in Troy. B I R M I N G H A M' S I N T R O Y!!!

That second commercial was blasted on radio stations for another two months and then a third one and a new character. A truck driver with a deep, gruff, raspy voice:

SOUND:	Telephone
OPERATOR:	Thank you for calling Birmingham Chrysler Plymouth.
TRUCK DRIVER:	Yeah, is this Birmingham Chrysler Plymouth?
OPERATOR:	Yes Sir this is Birmingham Chrysler Plymouth…?
TRUCK DRIVER:	Yeah well, listen I been spendin' most of the day tryin' to find Birmingham Chrysler Plymouth. I looked everywhere in Birmingham. I'm in Birmingham now.
OPERATOR:	Sir………..!
TRUCK DRIVER:	I can't find Birmingham Chrysler anywhere in Birmingham!
OPERATOR:	Sir, Birmingham Chrysler Plymouth is not in Birmingham. Birmingham Chrysler Plymouth

	is on Maple Road in Troy.
TRUCK DRIVER:	Yeah, well…I got a load of new Chrysler's and Plymouths for delivery at BIRMINGHAM CHRYSLER PLYMOUTH.
OPERATOR:	Bring 'em right over. Maple Road In Troy.
TRUCK DRIVER:	Yeah well…I think I'll hold on to these Chryslers and Plymouths. Open up my own dealership right here in BIRMINGHAM and you know what I'm gonna call it..?
OPERATOR:	What Sir….?!
TRUCK DRIVER:	TROY CHRYSLER PLYMOUTH, ya get it Sonny?
OPERATOR;	Yeah, I get it Sir…………..
MUSIC:	(Singing) We're the Chrysler Plymouth Dealer on Maple Road Birmingham….Chrysler Plymouth in Troy. B I R M I N G H A M' S I N T R O Y!!!

And finally after about eight months the most famous of all the Birmingham commercials was introduced:

SOUND:	Telephone
OPERATOR:	Thank you for calling Birmingham Chrysler Plymouth.
LITTLE GUY:	I finally got the answer
OPERATOR:	Sir…?
LITTLE GUY:	I FOUND BIRMINGHAM CHRYSLER PLYMOUTH.
OPERATOR:	Sir………..!
LITTLE GUY:	Anyone could have all those low prices if they keep hiding from us. I knew you were in BIRMINGHAM the whole time.

OPERATOR: Sir, you know very well Birmingham Chrysler Plymouth is on Maple Road in Troy.

LITTLE GUY: (laughing) Ha! What a joke! Listen you see that real big box down on the floor, right by your desk?

OPERATOR: (away from the mike) No Sir, I don't……

LITTLE GUY: I addressed the box. Sealed it. And mailed it to Birmingham Chrysler Plymouth in BIRMINGHAM. It was soooo easy.

OPERATOR: Oh THAT box…………

LITTLE GUY: (Laughing) Ha Ha Ha…Yeah that box!!

OPERATOR: Sir, we've been ordered by Birmingham litter control to haul away a big box laying on the curb in front of our old dealership in Birmingham know anything about that…?

LITTLE GUY: I…uh…..

OPERATOR: You wife's name wouldn't be Helen would it?

LITTLE GUY: Well uh……….

OPERATOR: You wouldn't know anything about a truck driver over in Birmingham with a big load of Chryslers and Plymouths..!?

LITTLE GUY: Truck driver…..?

OPERATOR: Where're you calling from Sir…

LITTLE GUY: (loud rustling of papers….long pause) INSIDE THE BOX………..

MUSIC: (Singing) We're the Chrysler Plymouth Dealer on Maple Road
Birmingham……Chrysler Plymouth in Troy.
B I R M I N G H A M'S I N T R O Y!!!

And Mr. Mealey stuck with it. Over the next twenty years there were nearly 300 of those. All with the same characters. All based on something back in radio program history that worked.

The Birmingham campaign was like Abbott and Costello's humor all over again. We won over 20 national awards for Best Automobile Dealer Campaign, Best Humor in a commercial, and most importantly it worked. That campaign has now been in more than 20 cities. No one stuck with it though. Not like Richard Mealey at Birmingham Chrysler. He had the foresight and the willingness to think outside the box (no pun intended) and go with something that had never been done before.

If you're ever driving around Motown watch for a Chrysler or Jeep license plate from his dealership. " Birmingham's In Troy." Or go there sometime.

Maple Road between Coolidge and Crooks in Troy, Michigan.

Look on the back wall of the new dealership. There, permanently displayed is the phrase:

"BIRMINGHAM'S IN TROY"

There were scores more like this……….

And thanks to my mom who made me practice that piano I wrote hundreds of Musical Images (otherwise known as commercial jingles).

Over the next 25 or so years I stayed in the Advertising business, traveled to nearly every state and saw over a thousand Auto Dealerships. I learned their business.

I taught them how to advertise; what to say in their commercials. How to say it. What medium to use. Radio, TV, newspaper. How much to pay for the advertising and how to budget for it. I did it all for them.

It was very profitable. I built audio recording studios, television editing suites, and even added commercial art design facilities.

I sent out direct mail to car dealers all over America. When they responded I called, made appointments, and traveled. California to Maine. Fargo to Florida. I traveled to 36 different states and Canada in pursuit of auto dealer accounts.

Not long after I started all of this a dealer asked me if I would address his Twenty Group. A dealer Twenty Group is a group of twenty automobile dealers of the same brand (Chevy Dealers for instance) who meet two or three times a year in some exotic place to trade information and ideas. They usually meet in the mornings and play golf or have some other leisure activity in the afternoons and evenings. They invite speakers to their meetings. Experts in various fields like Service Department Operations, Sales, Leasing, and sometimes Advertising and Marketing.

I was asked to address a Twenty Group of Chevrolet dealers at their meeting at Frenchman's Reef in St Thomas, the Virgin Islands. I went. I presented two morning long seminars on Marketing and Advertising. I used my creative material as examples, shared media secrets, and generally tried to help them with every phase of their advertising. The dealers had specific questions relating to their own cities. When it was over 12 of the dealers invited me to call them when I got back to my office and then visit their dealerships.

I traveled to all of them. Out of the 12 I ended up with 5 new advertising accounts. Three of them bought The Only Dealer. The same campaign I had created for Dexter Chevrolet.

Syndication.

Multiplication.

And the campaigns worked.

After that I was invited to more "Twenty Groups". At one of them, during one of the question and answer sessions a man asked:

"Lee, have you ever spoken at the national convention?"

He was referring to the annual National Automobile Dealers

Association convention attended by thousands of dealers. To speak at that convention would be the pinnacle of opportunities.

"Lee, I'm a representative of N.A.D.A. You'll get a letter."

Two weeks later I was invited to present six 45-minute seminars at the National Automobile Dealers Association convention at the Moscony Convention Center in San Francisco.

I went there. I met everyone in the car business. Heard everyone speak. Listened to their presentations. And gave my own. There were about 2,000 Auto Dealers and their General Managers at each session. It was like I was on the air again. On stage again. I played my radio commercials, showed them television spots, went among the audience with a cordless mike, answered their questions. Told them jokes. Even about my now retired "Fine Toned Horn". I had a terrific time and so did they. I made a lot of friends, and after each session scores of dealers gave me their business cards and asked me to call and visit them in their respective cities.

As a result I was now on a national stage. Automobile publications were calling for quotes, ideas, and wrote articles about the ex DJ now in the car advertising business.

In every state there is a State Auto Dealers Association. I was asked to speak at those too. It was a great ride and for a while I made myself believe that I liked it.

There were other accounts. Clothiers, Shows, Expos, Retailers of all kinds, Industrial accounts.

After not being able to get the Michigan Legislature to pass a law that would clean up the state, the Michigan United Conservation Clubs went out and got four hundred thousand signatures on petitions and put the issue on the ballot. Using what I knew about advertising I helped pass their proposed "Bottle Bill" in Michigan that banned throw away bottles and containers of carbonated beverages, the detachable ring-pull tabs on cans, and that placed a deposit on them.

It was a gigantic battle, but we won. Now people returned the containers for the deposit. If you're ever in Michigan, look at the landscape. No bottles and cans in the parks, on the road, parking lots, or anywhere. It cleaned up the state and I am very proud of that win. There were other political campaigns. Issues and candidates.

I have created more than 300 different advertising campaigns for automobile dealers in America, personally recorded over 15,000 commercials and written more than a thousand commercial music jingles. It was all a challenge and very profitable.

Opportunity was everywhere. But, like Mickey Shorr and his "Tape Shacks" that made him a wealthy man, I was earning a living and supporting my family, but in the back of my mind I knew the years were escaping and I was not doing what I thought God intended for me...

It wasn't radio or television.

So, in the 1990s I started playing around with creating new programs....

Chapter 73
THE AMERICANS

PART OF HAVING THE AD AGENCY MEANT THAT I HAD TO have recording studios. So, there I was almost daily in the studio recording commercials, music, sound tracks for television or whatever.

In 1991 one of my advertising clients was The Shrine Circus at the Michigan State Fair Coliseum. It was my assignment to produce the pageantry for Shrine Night , a night when all the Shriners come to the circus wearing their funny hats and medals.

The first gulf war was just over and America's feeling of patriotism was at what seemed to be an all time high. Along with the traditional Grand Entrance of the Shriners, the music, elephants, other animals, and circus performers, I was able to get about thirty US Army people all dressed in the Desert Storm uniforms to be part of the entourage.

Also I called on Byron MacGregor, one of the Detroit's most outstanding and recognizable radio journalists to appear and perform.

As I recall in June of 1973 when he was the big voice of "CKLW 20-20 News", Byron read an editorial on the air written and originally aired by a storied Canadian commentator, Gordon Sinclair

– One of the best known voices ever in Canada on Toronto's CFRB-AM. It made such impact on the air that Byron recorded the words in his booming voice over a special rendition of "America The Beautiful" played in the studio by members of the Detroit Symphony.

With music playing in the background, Byron read performed his recording of The Americans live before 9,000 mesmerized people in the coliseum.

Here is the Text of Byron's famous recording:

"This Canadian thinks it is time to speak up for the Americans as the most generous and possibly the least appreciated people on all the earth. Germany, Japan and, to a lesser extent, Britain and Italy were lifted out of the debris of war by the Americans who poured in billions of dollars and forgave other billions in debts.

None of these countries is today paying even the interest on its remaining debts to the United States. When France was in danger of collapsing in 1956, it was the Americans who propped it up, and their reward was to be insulted and swindled on the streets of Paris. I was there. I saw it.

When earthquakes hit distant cities, it is the United States that hurries in to help. This spring, 59 American communities were flattened by tornadoes. Nobody helped. The Marshall Plan and the Truman Policy pumped billions of dollars into discouraged countries. Now newspapers in those countries are writing about the decadent, war mongering Americans.

I'd like to see just one of those countries that is gloating over the erosion of the United States dollar build its own airplane. Does any other country in the world have a plane to equal the Boeing Jumbo Jet, the Lockheed Tri-Star, or the

Douglas DC10?

If so, why don't they fly them? Why do all the International lines except Russia fly American Planes? Why does no other land on earth even consider putting a man or woman on the moon? You talk about Japanese technocracy, and you get radios. You talk about German technocracy, and you get automobiles. You talk about American technocracy, and you find men on the moon - not once, but several times - and safely home again.

You talk about scandals, and the Americans put theirs right in the store window for everybody to look at. Even their draft-dodgers are not pursued and hounded. They are here on our streets, and most of them, unless they are breaking Canadian laws, are getting American dollars from ma and pa at home to spend here.

When the railways of France, Germany and India were breaking down through age, it was the Americans who rebuilt them. When the Pennsylvania Railroad and the New York Central went broke, nobody loaned them an old caboose. Both are still broke.

I can name you 5000 times when the Americans raced to the help of other people in trouble. Can you name me even one time when someone else raced to the Americans in trouble? I don't think there was outside help even during the San Francisco earthquake.

Our neighbors have faced it alone, and I'm one Canadian who is damned tired of hearing them get kicked around. They will come out of this thing with their flag high. And when they do, they are entitled to thumb their nose at the lands that are gloating over their present troubles. I hope Canada is not one of those." Stand proud, America! Wear it proudly!!

When Byron finished there was a long silence. A hush of emotion for the words and for our country. Then, the entire throng burst into wild applause. What a Shrine Night it was!

When it was over I told Byron that I had always wanted to write a radio program specifically for the fourth of July. I believe that there are generations in America who celebrate the holiday, but don't really know what the Fourth Of July means or really why it is a holiday. I asked Byron:

"If I can write the program, will you help me narrate it"?

He said yes and I went to work.

It was March already and if we were to get something on the air for the Fourth of July there was no time to waste.

I went to Florida with a laptop and started to write. The script was finished in eight days and two days later we were in production. Dozens of Detroit celebrities helped with the project. Well known voices and not so well known.

Erik Smith, a long time friend and news anchor at ABC TV Channel seven in Detroit, Tommy McIntyre news hound and investigative reporter, and other voices.

Production and final mixing took 8 days. The program was three hours in length. I invited the entire cast to my studios to hear the finished show.

Music ranged from James Brown to the Boston Pops and everything in between. Byron was at his very best. I was proud of the effort.

Now what?

We had a show, but no place to broadcast it.

Tommy McIntyre had a friend and he arranged a dinner meeting. His friend was Bob Lutz, President of Chrysler Corporation at the time. We met at a restaurant in West Bloomfield, a suburb of Detroit. Getting to see and talk with the president of

Chrysler was not possible for someone like me. Not without Tommy, that is.

The restaurant was The Machus Red Fox, the same one where years earlier Jimmy Hoffa was last seen alive.

It was an early dinner. The three of us talked about Bob and his recent crash of a helicopter nearly killing him. He was a terrific conversationalist and spoke jokingly about the incident. When we were finished with dinner Bob said:

"I've got to run. Early flight tomorrow".

I said: "My studio is on your way home and there's no one there. Tommy and I want to show you something in confidence and ask your advice. Can you stop there for a few minutes"?

Bob agreed, we paid the tab and left.

I was the last one to arrive at the studio. When I drove into the parking lot there was Tommy McIntyre and Bob Lutz, President of the Chrysler Corporation standing out front smoking the longest cigars I had ever seen. That's how they met. They belonged to the same cigar club.

Once inside we spun through the program for Bob. He laughed where he should have laughed and cried where he should have cried. It is a very emotional and red white and blue program.

We told Bob we had no place to run the show because we needed sponsors and asked his advice. He responded by saying:

"I can't buy it guys. I'm just the president of the company but tomorrow morning you'll get a call from someone who can. I like it a lot".

And that's the way it happened. Next morning there was a call from the Chrysler VP of marketing and the very next morning he and others were in my studio listening.

"How many stations could you get to run this by the fourth?", one asked.

"About 200", I said, not knowing where that came from. So

far we didn't even have one.

Then came the big question:

"How much?", the marketing guy asked. And I blurted out a substantial six figure number.

"Sounds reasonable to me", he said. "Can you come to my office at Chrysler tomorrow morning? We'll firm it up".

We did. And they did.

Stations all over the America jumped at the program. I hired phone sales people to call stations and actually give them the program as long as they would run the Chrysler commercials. We had 380 stations that first year. The second year, 560 stations, and the third year over 1,000 radio stations and the armed forces radio network in 80 countries ran our salute to freedom.

The show was called:

THE AMERICANS – PRESENTING THE FOURTH OF JULY

In 1992 I submitted the program for a Peabody Award.

Well, I had hopes anyway.

Chapter 74
BACK IN THE 60s - AGAIN

IN THE EARLY 1990S, AFTER PRODUCING The Americans – Presenting the Fourth of July and running it on thousands of stations around the world, I had another idea.

What if we could go back in time? I mean really go back in time and listen to the past as if it were taking place right now? Not an old recording full of static and scratchy music, but high quality sound the way it is today?

With that thought in my head I made a trip to the main branch of Detroit Public Library here in Motown and buried myself in the newspapers and magazines from the 60s. After a day of reading those publications it almost seemed like I was there again, back in the 60s. Names, places, events, and the people I knew. There they were, their names in print. They were alive, well and young again just the way I remembered them.

I decided to select three specific dates in the 60s, produce three pilot programs and call them:

"BACK IN THE 60S AGAIN"

Each two hour program would be a specific and different date in the sixties. A time capsule. "The Lee Alan Shows" would be presented exactly as they were then, before ABC radio buried its head in the sand and let other Motown/Detroit stations send them packing. The music and personality of radio would be exactly as it was. Music, craziness, the fun, the exhilaration, the voices of my colleagues as they were…then..making it all something to collect and really remember.

Each program would have the news events, movies, and entertainment reported in the present tense just as it was by the same news people who were there…then. Yes, and even the commercials. I reasoned that today we listen to Oldies not only for the music; but the memories they trigger. Some place we were. Someone we knew. Oldies bring pictures back to our minds that we might never remember.

So, I did the research of the era, found the pieces of the puzzle that are our past, and carefully put them back together.

Even producing the three pilot programs required hundreds of hours of research in microfilm for news, entertainment events, and listening to scores of tapes recorded in the sixties. Some from my personal collection and some from friends like Bob Green, one of the sixties' finest radio personalities on WKNR-KEENER. It was more work, more fun, and more exciting that I ever expected. I became consumed with it. Sometimes after days of research, the memories rushed back to me. There were some sleepless nights. Everything I was reading in the research was in the present tense and the quality of the old tapes was surprisingly good, so much so that at times it all seemed real. Current. As if everything was actually happening again.

This was also a very painful experience. The voices of many of my colleagues, artists and friends have been stilled forever. But there they were. I was reading about them in newsprint and hearing them alive and well again on tape. I loved them and I miss them.

When the first three programs were finished I called the general managers of five radio stations in Motown/Detroit. They all wanted to run the shows as a complete series. I chose 102.7, KISS-FM.

After a full run of almost two years the program switched to CLKW-FM where Dave Shafer was program director and was trying to revive the Big 8 of the 60s and 70s. The shows were wildly successful and ran there until the station was sold to a Canadian company, which once again killed the Big 8. I wasn't on the air live, but I *was* on the air and it felt good again.

What follows here is a segment from the Classic CKLW Web page.

THE LEGEND" - CKLW RETURNS IN THE '90'S

For a period of time in the early 1990's, CKLW-FM 93.9 in Windsor recreated the original "Big 8" format. Dave Shafer was the operations manager during this period, and Charlie O'Brien was the program director. Together they recreated the classic "Big 8" format, playing the oldies from the original "Big 8" era with all the classic jingles and sounds. Later on, "The Legend" name was added to the format, when Lee Alan came on board.

As Charlie O'Brien tells the story: "Lee was on the air in Detroit in the 60's at WXYZ in its Top 40 heyday. He was 'Lee Alan on The Horn' and would blow this big horn thingy on air as schtick. Pretty wild shows back then and he was successful at it. He got into his own biz teaching a radio course then started a radio/video production company at which he became very successful." Lee specialized in auto company accounts, and voiced many of his spots. He had also been producing a show called "Back In the 60's again", which was running on WKSG-FM "Kiss-FM" until they dropped oldies. At that time CKLW-FM picked up the show. When Lee came to CKLW-FM he offered his marketing expertise (much of it to be bartered for running his radio show) and he came up with "The Legend" name, which was added to the already-running oldies format.

Actually, the first attempt at an oldies format on 93.9 was back in 1984. Charlie O'Brien explained as follows (in a message posted to the discussion forum in January, 2001):

"The first time 93.9 went oldies in 1984 Dave Shafer was the Program Director. The Drake/Chenault tape automation system provided the music. I came back to work there as mid-day jock. About a year later I was Dave's Music Director and started the job of adding the 'local' flavor to the national songs. I spent a lot of time in the dusty 45 room going through the left over lists of songs. Bless the person who saved Rosalie's filing system - most of the file cards and 45's were still organized by year from 1964 through 1980. The lists of golden oldies that The Big 8 played from 1956 to 1963 were also still filed. Then dubbing the 45's to cart was a pretty big job. We didn't have a lot of manpower.

"Later, Sandy Davis was the Program Director who took More 94 to air - I was the music director and mid-day jock. Sandy wanted a very tight sound (read short list) on the station. Sound like WOMC?

"After he left, Dave Shafer (who had stayed through all that time as the AM800 PD) let me make over 93.9 and we started the Legend. That was a big thrill re-making the Big 8 piece by piece. Grant Hudson was around in the Newsroom [and that] really helped the 'sound', as did Big Jim Edward's voicing of the station ID's. Lee Alan's Back in The 60's show helped the sound of Motown come through.

"We were severely under funded in promotion (and pretty much everything else) but the station really cooked on air from the jocks to the music to the jingles - it was a mini-Big 8.

"It was a real thrill."

For Me Too...

Chapter 75
CRIMESTOPPERS

FROM THE FIRST TIME I MET HIM SOMETIME IN 1998 I was impressed with Michael J. Bouchard. His personal manner, his obvious genuine interest in people, and sincerity are immediately apparent. His storied career includes, among other lists of accomplishments are in law enforcement as a policeman, member of the Michigan State House of Representatives, Michigan State Senator and Sheriff of Oakland County, Michigan, one of the largest and most affluent counties in America.

In January of 1999, Michael Bouchard then a Michigan State Senator and Majority Floor Leader accepted the appointment as successor to John F. Nichols, Oakland County Sheriff who passed away suddenly. In November of 2000, Sheriff Bouchard was returned to Office with the largest number of votes for any contested candidate in Oakland County. .

When appointed, Sheriff Bouchard carried through on a promise he'd made to start a chapter of CrimeStoppers in Oakland County.

CrimeStoppers, an international organization, was originated in New Mexico in 1976 by Detective Greg MacAleese who was faced with a tragic and baffling case of senseless, cold-blooded murder of a student only two weeks away from marrying his high school sweetheart while working in a gas station. The student was brutally shot in the abdomen from a distance of ten feet with a .12-gauge shotgun.

Detective MacAleese decided to do something about it. The general manager of KOAT-TV in Albuquerque agreed to reenact the crime on a newscast. Next morning there was a call. An eyewitness! The killers were caught and subsequently convicted. The detective convinced the Albuquerque Police Department that they needed this kind of program on a regular basis. Crime Stoppers was a reality.

Today there are over a thousand Crime Stoppers chapters in 18 countries and U.S territories offering cash rewards and anonymity. As a result over 425,000 crimes have been solved. Hundreds of thousands of tips, thousands of criminals behind bars and billions have been recovered in stolen property and narcotics.

Sheriff Michael J. Bouchard with a board of directors in place; a tipster phone line active, and an unrelenting statewide effort to let no crime go unsolved was poised to begin. I was asked to be a member of the board and attended the first meeting where I suggested that we produce a daily radio series.

After acquiring sponsorship to pay for the production, more then 50 radio stations covering every inch of Michigan came on board to broadcast the program entitled:

"CRIME STOPPERS – AT LARGE AND WANTED IN MICHIGAN."

The program, three minutes in length, was broadcast at the same time each day, five times a week per station. Listeners heard five different, actual, recent cases, or cold cases of unsolved criminal events dramatically reenacted with actors, narrators, music and sound effects.

In each episode, Sheriff Bouchard was introduced, and set

the scene for the unsolved event, which was then dramatized. At the end the Sheriff summarized the crime, provided additional details, and gave the CRIME STOPPERS HOTLINE. Listeners had the ability to make an anonymous call and be eligible for up to a $1,000 reward. The program was like "America's Most Wanted", but a radio version.

Producing it was time consuming and complicated.

A staff of newsmen was hired to gather details of unsolved crimes from the FBI and police organizations statewide; then it was my responsibility to take the raw information and write scripts for announcers, actors, and Sheriff Bouchard with dramatic music, and sound effects.

Once a month when the scripts were finished, Sheriff Bouchard would come to my studios and record his parts. Announcers and actors recorded theirs at a different time. After all the spoken lines were recorded everything had to be assembled on tape with music and sound effects, mixed, duplicated on CDs and then sent to more than 50 stations for broadcast.

There were hundreds of scripts and programs, all factual, all depicting actual events. As a result criminals were caught and brought to justice.

A few months into the series I remembered a case from nearly thirty years earlier. In fact, I knew one of the people involved. Possibly the murderer himself. A case yet unsolved. So I decided this one was mine to research, write, produce, and follow through to the end.

You may remember from an earlier chapter that in the early seventies I was working in a small office in the Harvard Plaza Office Building on eight-mile road in Motown trying to make a go of a new advertising agency with my partner at the time, Frank Imburg. In the office next to us was a quiet little man who seemed to be in some type of marketing business. Everyone called him "Joe". I never knew his full name. I saw him almost every morning around the office and sometimes coming and going during the day. Rumor had it that his secretary was his mother.

When Frank and I split the partnership he stayed in that office and I opened my new company in a nearby building. One morning I had a call from Frank.

"They found Joe this morning. Dead in his office. Police are crawling all over this place" That's all he said. Later I learned all about Joe. Who he was, why he was there, and what everyone thought he had done.

Thirty years later I wrote the chilling eleven part radio series for Crimestoppers about Michigan's worst mass murder that everyone concluded Joe was responsible for.

Here is the synopsis I wrote that led to the actual written scripts that were, dramatized, and broadcast:

Michigan's Worst Mass Murder
A Special Crime Stoppers Report
With
Oakland County Sheriff
Michael J. Bouchard

A quiet summer evening in Good Hart, a northern Michigan town nestled in the hardwood forest overlooking Lake Michigan. A town so peaceful, quiet, and small that unless you knew it was there you could miss it altogether.

Expensive cottages hidden along a road following the craggy shoreline. This is where it happened.

Where, on June 25th, 1968, at about 9PM, the serenity of summer was suddenly interrupted by a loud, crashing rage filled with gunshots, panic, and fear. Then in less than three minutes, the sleepy village was thrust into the national spotlight and changed forever.

Where, 42-year-old advertising executive, Richard Robison, his wife, and all four children were literally assassinated.

Where moments before the murders, Richard Robison was relaxing in an easy chair with his 12 year old son Randy beside him. His wife, 40-year-old Shirley was sitting nearby. At a table in the same room, 17-year-old son Gary and 19-year-old Richard Jr. were playing double solitaire and the youngest; 8 year old Suzan was occupied on the living room floor.

Outside in the woods a figure peers through a window near the front door raises a 22-caliber rifle and fires. Three shots break the silence of summer.

Richard Robison is hit twice in the chest. Son Gary is struck in the back. The killer, now inside the cabin shoots again. This time hitting Shirley Robison, 12 year old Randy, and as she was running away, 8 year old Suzan.

The older boys scramble for a bedroom; possibly to retrieve a hidden rifle. But they too are gunned down.

The killer clubs the little girl with a hammer and then methodically shoots each of the others once in the head with a 25-caliber handgun. The Robisons are all dead.

The assassin then locks the doors, covers the bullet holes in the window with cardboard, draws the curtains, leaves the heater running, and vanishes.

The bodies are not discovered for 27 days. When police enter the cottage wearing gas masks, they find a scene no horror film could ever depict. The heat was still on in the cabin. Shirley Robison's body, nude from the waist down, was covered by a blanket. Mr. Robison was piled over a heating vent with 8-year-old Suzan and 12-year-old Randy. The bodies of Richard Robison Jr., 19 a sophomore at Eastern Michigan University and Gary Robison 17, a senior at Southfield-Lathrop High School were in the bedroom.

The murder guns were never found. Fingerprints on the hammer used by the killer on 8-year-old Suzan were destroyed when a sheriff's deputy held it high in the air in his hand for photographers to see.

BACKGROUND:

RICHARD ROBISON WAS THE OWNER OF R.C. ROBISON AND ASSOCIATES, a high profile Southfield advertising and Publishing firm. Although Robison appeared to have no enemies, after the murders investigators learned that his agency had been losing money and to replace it somehow they swindled something close to $50,000 from its largest client, Delta Faucet.

Police discovered that IMPRESSARIO, a magazine published by Robison's firm, was running unpaid full-page ads to make it look more successful.

On the morning of the murders Robison's business partner, Joe Scolaro engaged in heated phone conversations with Robison. Money was missing from the agency account. After the phone call, at about 10:30 that morning, Scolaro left the office for the day. Although police considered him to be a prime suspect he was never charged.

An engraving on the back of a St Christopher medal worn by Richard Robison read:

"Richard - -To my chosen son and heir- - God Bless You." It was signed, Roebert. From letters police learned of an organization called Superior Table that refers to the mysterious Roebert as chairman presiding over 5 other investors:

Mr, Thomas, Mr. Richard, Mr. Joseph, Mr. Peters, and Mr. Martin. The letters, written by Mr. Robison said The Superior Table was a world wide organization dedicated to complete peace and unity among all countries of the Earth.

Police could never confirm the existence of Roebert or the others mentioned in the letters or learn anything about the mysterious organization.

19 year old Richard Robison Jr. was a student at Eastern Michigan University and a member of a college fraternity when he became acquainted with John Norman Collins, another student who would soon become known as a cold blooded killer. In 1969 John Norman Collins, suspected of many co-ed killings, was convicted of the brutal sex murder of Karen Sue Bienamen and sentenced to life in prison with no chance of parole.

A police report filed on August 8, 1969 places Collins near the Robison's cottage on July 11, 1968 at approximately 9PM. Because Richard Robison Jr. knew Collins, and because he was reported seen near the cottage, Crime Stoppers requested an interview with Collins who is incarcerated in the maximum security prison at Marquette. Collins did not reply.

MONNIE BLISS WAS THE CARETAKER OF THE ROBISON COTTAGE in Good Hart. He was also the builder of the cabin and many others in the same area. Two days before the Robisons were murdered, Bliss' son, Norman was killed in a strange motorcycle incident on a nearby back road. Mr. Robison, saying he could not make it to the funeral, left 20 dollars for flowers with Mrs. Bliss. 29 days later Monnie Bliss told police he discovered the bodies of the Robisons after noticing a foul odor coming from the cottage. Bliss became a suspect.

ORGANIZED CRIME WAS SUSPECTED. Because of business and money problems in his advertising agency, sources reported to police that Robison had borrowed from organized crime. They said that he was supposed to have been paying them $12,000 a month, but wasn't.

The partner, the caretaker of the cottage, a convicted murderer, organized crime, a neighbor of the Robisons in Lathrop Village and others. All are suspects and yet, no firm conclusions.

Five years later on March 8, 1973 a note on the door of suite 112 at the Harvard Plaza office building in Southfield read:

"Mother-don't come in".

Inside, seated in a high back chair, was Joe Scolaro, dead of what investigators said was a self-inflicted gunshot.

A typewritten note read:

"Mother, where do I start? I'm a liar-cheat-phony,
but I am not a killer. I did not kill the Robisons.
Joe."

Crime Stoppers believed that someone in Michigan knew the answers and after more than thirty years, and the Crime Stoppers guarantee of anonymity, someone may have been willing to come forward.

The Robison family is buried together in a cemetery in Birmingham, Michigan.

Who killed the Robisons and why?

In spite of one of the most extensive police investigations in Michigan History, this case remains unsolved.

Joe Scolaro was the "JOE" whose office was next to ours. We saw him nearly every day for a year and a half. He was hounded for months in the newspapers and continuously accused of the murders.

I saw him, spoke with him, and occasionally had coffee with him. Was he the murderer? No one knows for sure. That's why I wrote and broadcast the Crimestoppers series and dramatized the case, hoping someone would come forward.

What do I believe?

I believe that Joe Scolaro, the quiet man who occupied the office next to Frank and me in 1972 was responsible for the worst murder in Michigan history.

I believe that Joe Scolaro murdered the Robisons.

A far cry from the Rock D.J. of the sixties....Yes?

Chapter 76

CASINO - THE FINAL DEATH

So there I was in April of 2003, nearly 40 years later, standing alone in the open field that once was Walled Lake Casino. Now just an empty thirteen-acre plot of grass and trees on the shores of Walled Lake. No clue to it's past. Nothing to signify that for almost 50 years hundreds of thousands came here, played here, sang here, laughed and loved here, met wives and husbands here, made music here. There's no historic plaque here, not one word telling what this was. It's just a quiet, lonely, mute witness to other days.

I remembered Wallace's words.

"I been here a while", he said.

"Are you Lee Alan? I listened to you on the radio all the time back then," he said.

"It was great out here in those days. I remember when Chuck Berry was here, Stevie Wonder, Fabian. Couldn't get in the place.

You could hear the music for miles. And the roller coaster in the park over there. Way up in the air so high I swear some nights you couldn't see the top of it. But you could hear it. Click, click, click", he said. "When the clicking stopped we knew in only another second the screamin' would start.

Clicks on the way up, screams on the way down. Always the same".

That coaster was the first thing everybody saw when they came into town.

I asked him:

"What if we could recreate those days, do it again just for a weekend or two, rebuild the Amusement Park and bring all those entertainers back to the site of that old Dance hall, the same ones and maybe some from today's music. Would people come and pay a little something to see it again?"

He just squinted, looked at me, smiled that big grinning smile, made all those wrinkles again and said: "Yeah, they would."

So, in late May of 2003, I tried. I went to the city manager of Walled Lake, the Walled Lake Downtown Development Authority, and the Walled Lake Mayor and City Council. They loved the idea. The Walled Lake City Council officially approved the concept pending details to come.

June 24, 2003

Dear Lee Alan,

On behalf of the City of Walled Lake I would like to thank you for your inspiring presentation (unanimously approved by council June 17th) on bringing back the Legend (Walled Lake Casino & Amusement Park) that once lived in Walled Lake for the past 75 years for our 50th Anniversary coming next year. I look forward to working with you and your staff on the details over the coming months and for an overwhelming success for the city.

Sincerely Yours (City Manager of Walled Lake)

Although the Casino was on the shores of the lake it was actually in the city of Novi. I went to the City Manager of Novi, and to Novi's CEO. They told me they were enthusiastic, but asked me not to introduce the idea, "even conceptually" until their Music & Motor Fest was over in late July. Here is the email I received from them after that first meeting.

6/5/2003:

Lee, (name) and I both enjoyed our meeting yesterday. You really bring back the memories of the 60's and the Walled Lake Casino days with a passion and enthusiasm that is both exciting and contagious. I had a similar reaction last night listening to your CD. We agree with your assessment that the potential for a community event, and all the possible spin offs from such an activity is almost unlimited

We are very supportive of this concept, and please feel free to share this fact with the people that you are discussing these ideas with as you move through the early planning process. While there is a lot of work to do, and there will certainly be challenges and obstacles to overcome, we think that a schedule for holding an event next year, perhaps late summer, would be realistic.

As we mentioned yesterday, we are sensitive to not introducing this idea, even conceptually, until the Music & Motor Fest (July 24 - 27) has been held. At that point we may wish provide some background information, or share some of the Walled Lake Casino history, with our City Council members as a prelude to discussing specific events. However we decide to proceed, we are looking forward to seeing you again, and continuing our dialogue. Best wishes, (name) Novi CEO – (Note: A copy of the actual email is on file.)

It wasn't until 4 months later that I received permission to address the Novi City Council and ask to use the old property as the site for the festival. They gave me exactly 10 minutes to explain, asked no questions, and then tabled it for another two weeks. After checking with the CEO's office to see how much detail I needed to provide the council I delivered a packet of outline information for each council member in advance of the second session.

On the afternoon of the meeting I called the CEO to see if he wanted more than what I had already submitted. He told me no; but there was a petition circulated and signed by some of the homeowners surrounding the property.

The Music & Motor Fest had learned of our plans!

The petition objected to my proposal.

Too much traffic they said.

Too much noise.

People would park in front of their houses.

Their children would be in danger.

Their lawns would be trampled.

I should take note here that a plan had already been devised to prevent all that. Their homes were not in the path to the event and further, we planned to allow no cars within miles. We intended to get permission from the nearby Twelve Oaks Mall to shuttle everyone convention style by bus from there directly to the site of the show.

Not a good idea they said.

When I arrived at the Novi council chambers it was standing room only. They were all there. All the petition signers. One after another they went to the podium and spoke against the event and me.

Most had written statements.

The final speaker was the man in charge of the "Music & Motor Fest", the same one the City Manager and CEO cautioned against introducing the idea to "even conceptually" until it was over. The speaker's comments were a scathing attack on any event other than his and he sided with the petitioners.

The worst was yet to come.

When I was finally called to speak I couldn't. One after another the council members climbed on a soapbox and made eloquent speeches against our Walled Lake / Novi Music Festival. Each one scolded me for not bringing details to the meeting and most of all I was chastised for NOT TALKING WITH THE 50S FESTIVAL …FIRST!!!

One member even got after me for calling the media before talking with the Council.

I didn't call the media. Two newspapers were in council chambers during the meeting two weeks before and printed prominent stories of my proposal. There was even a Detroit News Editorial criticizing the council and applauding the Festival idea.

Finally, I had the chance to speak. When the Mayor asked me why I didn't talk with the 50s Festival I told him, the council, and the television audience (yes, the entire session was broadcast) that I was specifically told not to introduce the idea until after the 50s festival was over!!!!

"Who told you that"? said the Mayor. And then something like: "And who told you not to bring more detail to the meeting?"

"The City CEO and the City Manager", I replied.

They were both there, in the room, nervously sitting at the end of the council table. Both protested and denied saying anything of the kind and said I was not telling the truth. The council believed them.

Read the above email again. You be the judge.

Then came the worst blow.

A council member who, only a few days before, told me in person that he was totally in favor of the project spoke up against the project." I think the words were "this would be a disservice to the people of Novi".

Ambushed by them all, I left the chamber, embarrassed with my tail between my legs.

I understood though.

Elections were only a few weeks off and they weren't talking to me at all. They were speechmaking to the voters in the room and in the TV audience. A number of council members were running for new terms and two of them were running against each other for Mayor of Novi. So, in the council chamber with proceedings being televised, and residents railing at them with speeches and petitions, politics ruled.

(Note: The minutes of this meeting and a video of it all are public and available in Novi)

Newspaper Coverage:
Wednesday, October 15, 2003
GIVE OLD TIME ROCK 'N' ROLL FESTIVAL A HOME IN NOVI

Concerns over proposed 1950s festival are misplaced; the public can decide if event is worth attending.

A proposed festival based on the 1950s is in jeopardy in Novi, and the city officials should rethink their initial concerns.

The festival is planned by Metro Detroit's famed 1960s disc jockey Lee Alan. He wants to revive a taste of the 1950s on the site of the defunct Walled Lake Casino.

Some Novi officials fret over crowds and traffic. But traffic is manageable and crowds are the very things that turn acreage into public events. You can't have a festival without a crowd.

Others say Alan's proposed gathering in June would detract from the Oakland County city's later Music and Motor Fest. But Novi's council is on shaky ground trying to arbitrate the esthetic and economic merits of festivals. A final decision is pending.

Overall, public officials have a crummy record of sizing up festivals. Up and down Woodward Avenue in 1994, they looked askance when Ferndale Plumber Nelson House first proposed the Woodward Dream Cruise, which is now a world-class auto event.

For the record, Novi is the same suburb that recently obstructed a housing development south of 13 Mile Road. The developer went to court and won a $72 million settlement for the city's attempt at micromanagement.

Barring any unforeseen permit issues, let the rock 'n' roll festival happen. The public will decide if it's worth the effort

With plans to hold the actual event somewhere else I went ahead anyway. The first step was to hold a Kickoff to raise money for the festival. To pay for the Walled Lake Music festival we needed to come up with more than a million dollars over the next six months.

MUSIC FESTIVAL PLANNED FOR WALLED LAKE
November 14, 2003
FREE PRESS POP MUSIC WRITER

In its heyday Walled Lake Casino was one of Detroit's premier spots – home to Stevie Wonder's first gig, the place where Mitch Ryder earned his stripes and a regular stop for countless national acts.

Now the lakefront site near 13 Mile and Novi Road, which has sat vacant since the hall burned on Christmas night in 1965, is about to get a blast of new life. If all goes as planned, the Walled Lake Music Festival will take over the grounds in early July for four days of classic cars and rock 'n' roll nostalgia.

Spearheading the festival is former WXYZ-AM disc jockey Lee Alan, who made his name with live broadcasts from the venue in the early '60s. Oakland County Executive L. Brooks Patterson heads the event's board of advisors.

The festival effort kicks off with a Nov. 29 fund-raising gala at Walled Lake Northern High School featuring Chuck Berry, the rock pioneer whose shows once packed Walled Lake. Tickets are $100.

Alan is confident a Walled Lake revival will spark sentimental memories for countless Detroiters who enjoyed the old concert hall. "People have told me, 'If we could go back to Walled Lake, we'd stop everything else to be there,' " he says.

The Kick off entitled: "The Walled Lake Casino Rockin' Reunion" was held at Walled lake Northern high school on November 29, 2003.

The star of the show was 77 year old Chuck Berry, who else?
Tickets were $100.
There were about 900 seats.

Prior to the show four hundred Walled Lake businesses were invited to a news conference where they were to be asked to buy (or sell) two tickets each.

The Walled Lake Downtown Business authority and their members were asked to help sell tickets.

I attended endless meetings, spoke to the Walled Lake Chamber of Commerce, The Rotary Club, The Walled Lake Historical Society, and made personal appearances for two Walled Lake City events. All for the purpose of filling the Kickoff auditorium so an office could be funded to work for the next few months raising a million plus dollars to pay for The Walled Lake Music Festival on the Fourth of July 2004.

Here are the results:

Out of 400 businesses, two attended the news conference. TWO!

One of them bought two tickets. TWO TICKETS!

The Chamber Of Commerce did nothing.

NOTHING!

The Walled Lake Downtown Development Authority, took some tickets, sold none and never returned the rest.

I asked a small local car club comprised of 38 members to sell at least two tickets each or buy two tickets each. Only two tickets each.

They sold one ticket at half price and gave me $50.

They bought none!

NONE!

One of their members worked hard to supply us with a set for the stage.

He was the only one who really worked on the project.

A high ranking official of Walled Lake was given ten tickets to sell. He sold and paid for none, but attended the show!

The Walled Lake Consolidated Schools promised to help promote the show and inform the students that they could get in for $40. No students came. Did they even know about it ?

I arranged with the school sound technician, who knew everyone at the school, for about 20 or 30 students to come to the show dressed in 60s clothes and to be dancing in the aisles as the audience filed into the auditorium. In return the kids would be admitted free to see the show.

No students showed up. Late on the afternoon of the show we had no dancers.

The tech told me that school officials instructed the students to stay away and not participate.

There is a lighted, moving marquee sign in front of the school that was to have displayed " Chuck Berry Live – November 29 – 7PM." It was never done. Up until an hour before the event the sign said nothing about it. Finally we were able to get a janitor to turn it on.

Tommy "C" and his great band opened the show and other than Chuck himself they put on the best performance of the evening. A different band that played with Chuck performed poorly and was badly out of tune with him for the entire performance.

The performance of another band that closed the show was marred by a member of the car club who was swearing and yelling for all to hear because I had to put Chuck on before them. The band was weak, typically local sounding, and should never have been on the show.

Although Chuck Berry's performance was outstanding he was hampered because the band did not do a sound check before the show to make sure everything was good and in tune. Chuck himself was terrific though, and gracious. After the show he allowed pictures with everyone and signed endless autographs.

Before the final song I went to the front of the stage and reminded the audience that this was a fundraiser. I told them that we needed money to pay the bills and to provide for the next six months of work getting ready for the Music Festival.

I said:

"For those of you in the audience who received free tickets or who came in without a ticket, please stop at the round booth on your way out this evening and either pay for your ticket or make a donation."

I designated The Fallen Heroes Fund spearheaded by Oakland County Sheriff Michael J. Bouchard (Police and Firefighters who have died in the line of duty) as a charity for the July 4th Music Festival.

"Please", I said, "for those who paid for tickets we thank you. For those who didn't, please stop at the round booth".

Incidentally, the entire show was recorded. I have it all on videotape. The out of tune band, the car club member yelling and swearing on stage, my plea to the audience. I have all of it in embarrassing living color.

None of the volunteers, businesses, or the car club members (except one) sold tickets; but they came to see the show.

Fewer than 350 people were in the audience.

About half came in without paying anything.

When the show ended and after my plea to " stop on the way out and just pay for your own ticket or donate something at the round booth", no one did.

No one donated anything.

Nothing.

Not one cent!

The Downtown Development Authority members and their guests quickly dismantled their *free exhibit* and made a wide circle to the exit door avoiding the round booth.

Council members in attendance, other city officials, a state congressman who promised to send his check in the mail, and even the car club members who dismantled their *free booth* followed the same route.

The room emptied so fast it could have been a fire drill.

All left without paying or donating anything.

No one stopped at the round booth.

No one!

On the other hand, knowing that this was a fundraiser, Chuck Berry's talent agency waived half their fee.

Tommy C and his band played free of charge. They wanted to see the Music Festival happen.

Allied Printing, Inc. in Ferndale, Michigan gladly donated the printing of all tickets and posters.

Red Robin Restaurants, who were denied any access to the kitchen by school officials, cheerfully made the best of it, provided free food and made a donation as well. There were a few anonymous donors whose money paid for Chuck Berry.

The others refused to donate.

Months of work, meetings, appearances and presentations, prospecting and pleading for sponsor money, planning and negotiating. All wasted.

I emailed the Walled Lake city official and asked him to pay for the ten tickets. He refused. And none of the other Walled Lake officials ever came forward to pay for their tickets either.

No one!

The congressman's check never came!

The car club picked up on all the false gossip and spread it to anyone who'd listen.

None of my team who worked for months was paid anything.

All volunteers.

Not even expenses.

The show lost major money. No one in Walled Lake or Novi has ever stepped up, recognized the effort we tried to make and offered to help with the loss.

So, the balance owed to those who refused to donate their service is being paid out of my own pocket. Simply put, I am personally paying for each ticket for those who slipped through the door that night; saw a free show and left. I am still paying for the loss.

Days before the event I was advised to cancel it.

"Just cancel and avoid a probable loss," they said.

I couldn't.

I promised a show with Chuck Berry and I couldn't cancel.

Walled Lake Casino and its heritage are now finished. For good!

The bands have permanently lost a possible annual venue that could have been re-created through revival of a legendary tradition older than nearly anyone now alive in Walled Lake.

The businesses in Walled Lake that refused to buy even one ticket or pay for the ones they used that could have insured future economic growth may never realize the benefits that come with major tourism events. A tradition that may have attracted new business, new people, and new opportunity is now lost.

Those thirteen acres on the lake in Novi will eventually be sold to a developer or someone with millions to pay the city for the land.

When that happens those same objecting petitioners will come to the council chambers again. This time because big money is involved they will be ignored. Turned away.

Soon, no one will know or remember what happened for so many years here on the shores of Walled Lake.
No one will care.
No one cares now.
And because so many people came and left in a flash without paying for their tickets that night in November of 2003 . . .

The music has finally died.
Old Wallace was wrong.
They didn't come….
There was no Walled Lake Music Festival the following summer.
And now …
Walled Lake Casino is dead forever!

EPILOGUE

I didn't fill this book with the hundreds of small and minute details that radio buffs might prefer. That was never intended. It is my memory alone. A small part of a much larger window in time. When I started writing I actually thought I would probably get part way through it and then stop. It was meant to be more of a personal catharsis than anything. It was a terrible time in my life when I needed something. Maybe writing this was it, I thought. Then, as one page filled and another began, and in an effort to immerse myself in memories and personal examination I realized that I had lived through a special time, a moment in radio history that needed to be preserved, even if only from my small perspective. So, the pages turned.

So many wonderful careers seem to be entwined with personal tragedy. Mine is no exception. Wrong turns. Personal choices that led down roads to nowhere and pain for me and for others.

Personal, hurtful, and tragic.

Things people do to people.

Choices.

I had dreams.

Big dreams. I wanted to follow them.

I was good at what I did.

God gives each of us certain gifts. I wanted to make the best use of the ones He gave me. To develop them further. To learn more and in a higher arena.

I wanted to see how far those dreams would take me. New York, Chicago, L.A., wherever. It takes dreams to make anything happen. You have to have dreams. You need them. The bigger they are, the more you can expect, the more you can do, the farther you'll go.

I had dreams.

Radio.

A shot at network television.

Doing voice work in the movies.

Producing movies and television.

Directing.

Others from Detroit did it. Who said I couldn't make it?

I wanted to at least try, not wonder for the rest of my life if I could have made it.

Wondering.

Questioning.

Instead, for the better part of 30 years I was professionally dormant.

On the wrong road.

I was personally dishonest with myself.

Pretending that I was doing what I wanted. I wasn't.

Was I wasting the best years of my life?

First starting a Broadcasting School.

Then, as an advertising agency, creating advertising campaigns for car dealers. Except for a few, they were basically unappreciative, fickle, not thinking of steady growth; only today's business and couldn't stick with a plan for long term success.

Car dealers who thought that dumping hundreds of thousands

of dollars into cheap looking classified newspaper ads that get results only today, if at all, was the way to the public mind.

Some were smart enough to listen. Most were not.

Richard Mealey of Birmingham Chrysler Jeep in Troy, Michigan listened. Because of it, he has the nucleus of an advertising campaign that will last him forever.

"Birmingham's In Troy".

The late Bob Finder, General Manager of the former Dexter Chevrolet listened and was responsible for adopting an ad campaign that propelled his dealership to number one from 20th in his selling zone.

"The Only Chevy Dealer On Eight Mile Road".

There were hundreds of car dealers in my career. Those are the only two that adopted a theme and stuck with it. The rest took the campaigns, but didn't hold on to them. Their money and my time were wasted.

In spite of total distaste for my profession, in 2001, I was about to realize financial success beyond my wildest expectations when everything totally collapsed.

I will not bore you with the details except to say that after years of difficulty and a cold, distant relationship in my second marriage I came home on the 25th of July to find an empty house. There, on the fifteen thousand-dollar granite Kitchen Island was a lone object. A note from my wife of 35 years saying that she had left and "needed to think …and please don't try to call".

In fact she had already thought. And planned.

She had confided in a number of female friends and at least one relative, even asking one for the name of an attorney. She called him, hired him days before that dreadful night, and filed a complaint of divorce in Oakland County, Michigan Circuit Court. After the filing and before she left she acted the part of a devoted wife. We shopped together for birthday presents, lunch at a small middle eastern restaurant, a movie, even a family birthday party at the lake where my grand daughter's birthday was the focus with presents, swimming, laughing, and picnicking took place. All the time she and some others in my family were aware that the divorce had been filed.

Three days later she waited until I went to work, and quickly left.

She was gone.

No warning.

No discussion.

It was a number of days before I knew where she was, only to learn that she had driven with my youngest daughter to California to the home of my niece who never had discussed any of this with me either.

A few days after she left she called and left a voice mail on my business phone for all to hear at my office that she had filed for divorce. She had been divorced before and twice before this had filed for divorce in our marriage.

Although we had had no substantive relationship for years, I was shocked and taken totally by surprise. I will now say openly that after a few days of searching for her I took another wrong fork in the road. I turned to the bottle.

I thank God it was only for a few days, but in the privacy of my home I did. My older son actually had to come over and remove bottles I had strategically placed for safekeeping. While in that state of chaos I called my children. One son helped. One daughter was critical of me and to this day has not spoken to me again. The other son was aloof. The younger daughter was in California with her mother.

At the time all this happened we were living in a ten thousand square foot home in an exclusive suburb of Detroit, owned a condo on the beach in Florida, and a 36 foot Tiara Sport Fisherman.

Our business was on the way to a record year with three large clients and numbers of small ones.

For over three months I was unable to function as a person, let alone as a creative leader in my company. Clients were ignored, commercials were incomplete, and deadlines went unmet. Then the unthinkable happened. Terrorists flew two planes into the World Trade Center. It was 911. All business stopped. Advertising was non existent. My business went from record setting to nothing in less than 45 days.

What was it that the late Gilda Radner used to say?

"It's always something"!!

Bills were left unpaid to us and consequently we were unable to pay our own bills.

I sought counseling and found it. Harry Broomfield a PHD and wonderful Christian Councilor in Troy, Michigan who, over a period of time, literally saved my life.

The boat was gone, the house was sold, so was the beloved family condo in Florida where so many family reunions and good times had happened. In a matter of a couple of months, all was gone or going. I was living alone in an apartment and the divorce was final a few months later.

I place no blame for any of it. I will not discuss my private personal feelings here. I know a great deal more about all this, but I have only stated what happened and how it affected everything. In retrospect, it should have happened many years before.

I should have been the one to leave.

Should have followed my dreams.

God has given us a wonderful thing.

Its called time. Time and rebirth.

Time has healed the wounds.

Like my late friend and colleague, Mickey Shorr, and probably like hundreds of others, I spent a lifetime in a business I abhorred just to earn money and support my family.

I loved radio. I loved being in front of a microphone with you or someone on the other side of the speaker.

I felt a special bond between us.

I blasted the music as loud as it would play in the studios and in my earphones. I was IN the shows; not on them.

I had thousands of ideas, wrote hundreds of scripts, compositions, and promotions. I had more fun than anyone who ever listened.

I loved all of it.

I wanted to keep doing it.

I wanted to act.

I wanted to sing.

I am a piano player. I wanted to play.

I can do hundreds of voices.

Casey Kasem came from Detroit. We went to the same high school, he many years before me. We worked at the same stations here in Motown. He went to California, worked for the studios that do cartoons, he did their voices, appeared in network television shows, had radio shows that ran on hundreds of stations.

I yearned to do all those things.

When I think about the 60s and 70s I knew all the names from Detroit; from Motown that we still listen to.

We grew up together.

We performed together.

We loved each other.

Stevie, Diana, Mary Wilson, Florence Ballard, dear sweet Marvin Gaye, The Temptations, Jackie Wilson, Junior Walker, Mary Wells, Hank Ballard, Smoky Robinson, Rare Earth, Jamie Coe, Jack Scott, The Funk Brothers – more of them - all of them.

I didn't want to stop knowing them. I wanted to stay and perform, be with them, and always be a part of it.

I knew I couldn't leave Detroit so sometime in the late seventies I asked Dick Kernan, my friend from the WXYZ and Walled Lake Casino days to make a call for me. Dick was then the Vice President of the Specs Howard School of Broadcast Arts. I asked him to call Henry Baskin, a fine attorney and more importantly, a very influential agent in Motown. Maybe if Henry knew I wanted back in he could quietly look around.

Dick made the call.

A few weeks later Dick told me he had heard from Baskin.

Dick said Henry told him there was no way. "Lee Alan is old news". I have never met Henry Baskin and didn't hear him actually say that, but that's what I was told.

Unfortunately I took it as fact and never tried again. Until now.

After those halcyon years I was not finished. I was still young and in my prime, but like Mickey Shorr and others, I couldn't get hired in Detroit.

Can't now.

Radio had changed.

Younger program managers either felt threatened or didn't want anyone older than they were. The only opportunity was elsewhere. I never went. Except for sending a couple of taped auditions, I never tried.

When Patti, my first wife and I divorced, it was my choice.

My daughter Dawne lived with her in the Detroit area.

I stayed in Detroit because I couldn't leave my daughter.

I was remarried.

Dawne was with us nearly every weekend and most summers on vacations.

I couldn't just go chasing dreams and leave her without a father.

She couldn't have gone with us to any out of state permanent location.

Dawne needed a father who at least lived in the same city,
That's the main reason I stayed.
That's why I started a broadcast school.
That's why I spent years in the advertising business.
That's why I put my dreams away.
Dawne never knew. She never asked.
But she had a father and a family who loved her.
Finally - -
People used to ask me if I missed it.
If I missed being on the air.
I always said no.
Always said I had a fear of waking up someday and being a 50-year old disc jockey with no ratings and not knowing how to do anything else.
That was my stock answer.
That was a lie.
I was lying to them and to myself.
I yearned to be back.
Every minute of those years I ached to be back on the air.
If an offer had come from a Detroit station I would have closed the ad agency.
I jumped at every chance to be interviewed, to be quoted in the newspapers, to fill in for someone on the air for a day or so or to make a guest appearance on television.
In the 70s, my friend and ex employee Tom Moser, General Manager of WDRQ asked me to come back and do a New Year's Eve Party. I did it.
In the 80s Ed Christian, my friend and then general manager of WNIC in Detroit and now CEO of Saga Communications, Inc., also asked me to come back on the air for one night and do a five hour New Year's Eve radio show. I accepted. I prepared for weeks.

For the first time in my career I was nervous. I was scared, really.

When the time came I drove to the station alone, walked into the studio and then, surrounded by friends and family, sat down at the mike. The nervousness disappeared. I was home. Music was playing, earphones blasting, people were calling, laughing, remembering and saying things I really wanted to hear but then again didn't. Things like:

"We love you Lee Alan". They said the word "love".

"We missed you".

"We grew up with you and want you back".

"How can we get you back on the radio permanently"?

"What's the name of that song by Frank Sinatra you always played when you signed off"?

"Where's your horn"? Ha!

I knew everyone was listening.

My mom and dad were listening, the two greatest fans I ever had.

They were listening.

At times I was overcome. I had never heard people calling someone on the air telling saying they loved them.

Loved them?

There were tears to hide.

Feelings to mask.

Things not to say.

Not just a few times I choked up, couldn't talk anymore and had to start some music.

Ed Christian asked me back again and again in the 80s to do the New Year's Eve parties. Jim Harper, a popular radio personality with WNIC was always cordial and seemed excited to have these New Year's specials on the air.

Last year (2003) a call was placed to the new station where Jim was on the air to see if they would carry my New Year's Eve party just like in the 80s.

I was refused.

Not long ago I saw a movie entitled "The Rookie". It was the true story of the life of Jimmy Morris, a Texas school teacher and baseball coach who, as a young man loved baseball, played baseball, dreamed of making it to the major leagues as a pitcher. After hurting his arm Morris could only throw the ball 80 miles an hour. His dreams dashed, he had to quit baseball and pursue another profession. His life was productive, but the nagging question always plagued him.

Years later, at too old an age for anyone to think of it, Jimmy Morris was challenged to try again. To everyone's' surprise, especially Morris's he was throwing the baseball 99 miles an hour.

99 miles per hour!

After some time in the minors he actually made it to the big show.

His family and friends were there, smiling and cheering him on for his debut.

His father, was there too.

His dream was finally a reality.

After I started this book, and before I reached this point in it, I decided to take advantage of an opportunity to actually return to the air. For four hours a day in Detroit and with a repeat at night it turned into a total of eight hours a day. On the air again in Motown and on the Internet around the world. The reaction from listeners has been the same.

They call.

They email.

They use those words. Love – missed you – please stay and so on.

Like Jim Morris I spent most of my life doing something else and now I am a rookie.

A rookie again.

Perhaps the worlds oldest. But guess what? I am throwing 99 miles an hour and loving each and every second of it.

No major networks are clamoring to sign me to a big contract.

No major Detroit stations have lined up to snatch me away. None will.

These days, the stations are all controlled by large corporations that own many stations in the same city.

Those words: "Love" – "Lifelong Friend" – "Please come back" don't mean much to a board of directors.

They mean a lot to people who listen to the radio though.

And they mean a lot to me.

So, for a while at least, I am back on the air.

And I now realize my years were not wasted at all.

Dawne had a father.

My daughter Sara and my two sons Bill and Lee grew up, were provided for, had a father who loved them supported them and gave them all the education they wanted.

Starting The Lee Alan School of Broadcast Arts, later purchased from me by Specs Howard when ABC radio refused to renew the contract of the Martin & Howard morning radio show, was the reason that tens of thousands of lives have been changed and directed toward radio and television.

Like the movie: "It's A Wonderful Life" I have often wondered where those lives would be if there had been no Broadcast School and if God had not allowed me to do what small things I have done.

Surely there has been a reason and a purpose for all of this.

And personally?

You'll be glad to know that as I write this sentence I have

only two and a half hours before I will stand at the altar and be married to Nancy, the love of my life and the inspiration for this outpouring of my soul.

So, if you're near a radio in Motown, or if have a computer and can get on the internet I'll be there….somewhere

TURN YOUR RADIO ON…
To be continued…

MY FRIENDS & COLLEAGUES NOW IN HEAVEN

CHARLES D. (CHUCK) FRITZ
Purchased WXYZ AM and other stations. Died of Cancer in 1998.

CHARLEY PARK
Long time Chief Announcer at WJR who offered me a job when he chose WJBK and rock radio instead.

DEL SHANNON
The great singer and my close personal friend who helped me get the first Beatles interview. A victim of depression and Prozak. Or was he?

DICK OSGOOD
One of the world's first electronic theater critics, actor, newsman, newspaper columnist, first face on Channel 7 in Detroit, and author of "WYXIE WONDERLAND" an unauthorized 50-Year Diary of WXYZ Detroit. Died of complications of a stroke February 29, 2000 at the age of 98. Friend and kind Man.

DON LARGE
Creator of the Don Large Make Way for Youth chorus on WJR Radio, CBS in Detroit, my first radio experience at the age of 14.

DON McCLEOD
Afternoon Drive Time radio personality at WJBK in Detroit who had a great influence on me while growing up, and after joining that station.

DON ZEE
WXYZ Radio. "Daddy Zee". Leader of The Zee Zombies. The all night show that followed me on WXYZ for many years and later on CKLW and WHFI amoung others. Don was the best all night radio personality I have ever heard. Died from a gun accident in Texas in August, 1984

ED HARDY
My friend and News Director of many radio stations including WXYZ and WABC in New York. Later years worked for the Governor of Oklahoma. Ed gave me the original "Letter From Michael".

ERNIE (Frantic Ernie) DURHAM
My lifelong friend and benefactor without whom I never would have started in radio and followed the path I did. A wonderful man who, like Mickey Shorr was thrown away by the radio industry at the end of his life. He belongs in The Hall Of Fame.

FERN ROBINSON
Head of the Music Department at Cooley High in Detroit who gave me my very first public speaking part in a Christmas Concert. Little did she know what effect that choice would have.

FLORENCE BALLARD
Original member of The Supremes. Possibly the best voice, but it was never really heard. Flo was unceremoniously ejected from the group. She died of a broken heart.

FRED WOLF
One of the two best Morning Drive Time radio personalities ever in Detroit. Professional bowler. One of my benefactors and a wonder-

ful friend. Suffered a stroke in 1978 and lost his speaking ability. Died in 2002.

H. DOUGLAS KOLE
Director ABC Television, Soupy Sales shows, and college friend from Wayne State University who gave me the auditions for WXYZ –TV announcing job after I was fired from radio.

HARRY BURT KEELER
My Iowa Grandfather. Juvenille Probation Officer in Clinton, Iowa. The most influential man in my life. A good, simple, jovial man who loved his wife, his family, and life itself. He taught me laughter.

HY LEVINSON
Leader in Detroit Broadcasting. Owner of WCAR, my first commercial radio station where Mrs Levinson called me on the Red Phone.

DON LARGE
Creator of the Don Large Make Way for Youth chorus on WJR Radio, CBS I Detroit, my first radio experience at the age of 14.

J.P. McCARTHY
One of the two best Morning Drive Time personalities ever in Detroit.

JIM CHRISTI
The WXYZ sales rep who arranged for the remote broadcasts at Walled Lake Casino. Without him this story would have been very different.

JOEL SEBASTIAN
My television partner on Club 1270 with a golden voice. Joel died of bone cancer in Chicago in 1986. He was only 53 years old.

JOHN F. PIVAL
The last person to be President of WXYZ Channel 7, Detroit. Forced out of his position by Charles D. Fritz and others at ABC. Mr. Pival was my benefactor. Not long after he left the station, while fishing on the dock of his home on Marco Island, Florida, he apparently slipped, fell off the dock, became entangled in a rope and drowned. His wife, Ginny found him moments later.

LEON McNEW
WXYZ-TV News Anchor in the 60s. My friend and supporter during tough times.

MARC AVERY
Morning Radio Personality in Detroit during the 60s and 70s. Died in 2004.

PAUL WINTER
WXYZ Radio Personality and the voice I admired most while growing up in Detroit. Gentleman, and true scholar.

TOM CLAY
One of the finest, yet most controversial radio personalities ever. The best production technician I ever heard for live radio. Tom died of cancer on November 24, 1995.

WHERE ARE THEY NOW......

ANN HUTCHISON SAWALHA
Ann lives with her husband Sami in Amaan, Jordan where they are in the hotel business. She is a wife, mother, grandmother, and life-long friend.

BOB GREEN
Bob, former WKNR personality, and radio expert has been living in Houston, Texas for many years and operating Bob Green Productions a leading audio-video production company.

CHUCK SNEAD
Director of television show Club 1270. Whereabouts unknown.

CLARK REID
Former air personality on WJBK and executive with Jam Handy productions. Retired and living in the Detroit Area.

CURLEY DIMITRO
The music promotion man who delivered the original Lee Alan Fine Toned Horn to me. Whereabouts unknown.

DANNY TAYLOR
One of the great voices in radio. Danny Taylor is not his real name and thus, whereabouts remain unknown.

DAVE PRINGLE PRINCE
Somewhere in Michigan.

DICK KERNEN

Began his broadcast career as a mail courier for WXYZ-AM/FM/TV in 1956. Was producer at Walled Lake Casino, and program director at WRIF-FM. In 1972, Dick began working at Specs Howard School of Broadcast Arts after Specs bought it from me. Today he is Vice President there and a member of the Michigan Broadcast Hall of Fame.

DICK RAKOVAN

The DOT record promotion man and later broadcast executive who called me in Cincinnati to tell me I was going to WXYZ. Unknown.

JOEY REYNOLDS

Joey is now living in New York and doing the all night show on WOR there. His book, "Let A Smile Be Your Umbrella..But Don't Get A Mouthful of Rain", is terrific. Joey proved that I was right about his intellect, his talent, and genius. He remains the best I ever heard.

PAT MURPHY

Real name Len Wolenson. Last seen about 1985 doing all night movie hosting in Las Vegas television.

RUSS KNIGHT

Replaced Lee Alan on WXYZ in 1964, but after ratings decline returned to his home station, KLIF in Dallas. Now retired and in the Texas Rock N Roll Hall of Fame.